Is the Visual World a Grand Illusion?

edited by

Alva Noë

IMPRINT ACADEMIC

Published in the UK by Imprint Academic
PO Box 1, Thorverton EX5 5YX, UK

Published in the USA by Imprint Academic
Philosophy Documentation Center, PO Box 7147, Charlottesville, VA 22906-7147, USA

ISBN 0907845 23 1

British Library Cataloguing in Publication data
A catalogue record for this book is available from the British Library
Library of Congress Card Number 2002102390

ISSN: 1355 8250 (*Journal of Consciousness Studies*, **9**, No. 5–6, 2002)

JCS is indexed and abstracted in
Social Sciences Citation Index[R], *ISI Alerting Services* (includes *Research Alert*[R]),
Current Contents[R]: *Social and Behavioral Sciences, Arts and Humanities Citation Index*[R],
Current Contents[R]: *Arts & Humanities Citation Index*[R], *Social Scisearch*[R], *PsycINFO*[R]
and *The Philosopher's Index*.

Journal of Consciousness Studies

controversies in science & the humanities

Vol. 9, No. 5–6, 2002

SPECIAL ISSUE: 'IS THE VISUAL WORLD A GRAND ILLUSION?'

Edited by Alva Noë

TABLE OF CONTENTS

iv Contributors

v Editor's Preface

1 Is the Visual World a Grand Illusion? — *Alva Noë*

13 How Could I Be Wrong? How Wrong Could I Bc? — *Daniel C. Dennett*

17 There Is No Stream of Consciousness — *Susan Blackmore*

29 The Grand Illusion and Petit Illusions:
Interactions of Perception and Sensory Coding — *Bruce Bridgeman*

35 How Well Do We Know Our Own Conscious Experience?
The Case of Visual Imagery — *Eric Schwitzgebel*

54 Our Perception of the World Has To Be an Illusion — *Dana H. Ballard*

72 Visual Worlds: Construction Or Reconstruction? — *Temre N. Davies, Donald D. Hoffman & Antonio M. Rodriguez*

88 The Tinkerbell Effect: Motion Perception and Illusion — *Frank H. Durgin*

102 Is the Visual World a Grand Illusion? A Response — *Arien Mack*

111 Change Blindness Blindness As Visual Metacognition — *Daniel T. Levin*

131 Is Visual Experience Rich Or Poor? — *Charles Siewert*

141 The Grand Grand Illusion Illusion — *Jonathan Cohen*

158 Two Dogmas of Consciousness — *Mark Rowlands*

181 Is Seeing All It Seems? Action, Reason and the Grand Illusion — *Andy Clark*

CONTRIBUTORS

Dana H. Ballard, Department of Computer Science, University of Rochester, Rochester, NY 14627, USA. *dana@cs.rochester.edu*

Susan Blackmore, c/o Imprint Academic, PO Box 1, Thorverton, Devon, UK. *sjb_ac@hotmail.com*

Bruce Bridgeman, Department of Psychology, University of California at Santa Cruz, Santa Cruz, CA 95064, USA. *bruceb@cats.ucsc.edu*

Andy Clark, Cognitive Sciences Program, Indiana University, Bloomington, IA 4705, USA. *andy@indiana.edu*

Jonathan Cohen, Department of Philosophy, University of California at San Diego, 9500 Gilman Drive, La Jolla, CA 92093-0119, USA. *joncohen@aardvaak.ucsd.edu*

Temre N. Davies, Department of Cognitive Sciences, University of California at Irvine, Irvine, CA 92697, USA. *daviest@uci.edu*

Daniel C. Dennett, Center for Cognitive Studies, Tufts University, 520 Boston Avenue, Medford, MA 02155-5555, USA. *daniel.dennett@tufts.edu*

Frank H. Durgin, Department of Psychology, Swarthmore College, 500 College Avenue, Swarthmore, PA 19081, USA. *fdurgin1@swarthmore.edu*

Donald D. Hoffman, Department of Cognitive Sciences, University of California at Irvine, Irvine, CA 92697, USA. *dhoffman@orion.oac.uci.edu*

Daniel Levin, Dept of Psychology, PO Box 5190, Kent State University, Kent, OH 44242-0001, USA. *dlevin@kent.edu*

Arien Mack, Psychology Department, New School for Social Research, 65 Fifth Avenue, New York City, NY 10003, USA. *mackarie@newschool.edu*

Alva Noë, Department of Philosophy, University of California at Santa Cruz, Santa Cruz, CA 95064, USA. *anoe@cats.ucsc.edu*

Antonio M. Rodriguez, Department of Cognitive Sciences, University of California at Irvine, Irvine, CA 92697, USA. *tonyr@uci.edu*

Mark Rowlands, Department of Philosophy, University College Cork, Cork, Ireland. *mrowlands@philosophy.ucc.ie*

Eric Schwitzgebel, Department of Philosophy, University of California at Riverside, Riverside, CA 92521- 0201, USA. *eschwitz@citrus.ucr.edu*

Charles Siewert, Department of Philosophy, University of Miami, PO Box 248054, Coral Gables, FL 33124, USA. *csiewert@miami.edu*

Editor's Preface

The study of perceptual consciousness must begin with an adequate phenomenology of perceptual experience. The aim of this book is to bring together new writings by philosophers and cognitive scientists that respond to the need for a better phenomenology of perceptual experience.

No writer in recent years has done more to demonstrate the importance of careful reflection on the character of experience than Francisco J. Varela. This book is dedicated to his memory.

The question which forms the title — Is the visual world a grand illusion? — is provoked by recent work in psychology on change blindness, inattentional blindness, and related phenomena. Research in this area calls into question whether we really enjoy perceptual experiences which represent the environment in rich detail. If we do not enjoy experiences of this sort, then we need to rethink the idea that perception is a process aiming at the production of such experiences. Most of the papers collected here take their start from this empirical research. All attend to its broader theoretical and philosophical implications.

Change blindness was more or less predicted by Daniel Dennett in his 1991 book *Consciousness Explained* (see, for example, pp. 467–8). His philosophical work forms the natural backdrop against which to try to understand its significance as well as that of the title question. My own interest in these questions began while a postdoc at his Center for Cognitive Studies at Tufts University. As far as I know, he is the first philosopher to recognize the importance of the then brand-new change blindness literature. The debate would not unfold as it has if not for his work.

The first use of the phrase 'the grand illusion' in reference to this domain was, as far as I know, in a paper published in 2000 by Evan Thompson, Luiz Pessoa and myself ('Beyond the grand illusion: What change blindness really teaches us about vision', *Visual Cognition*, **7**, 1/2/3, pp. 93–106). I find it hard to believe we really were the first, however, to use this term in the way we did. Certainly when David Chalmers organized a session with the same title as this book at the 2000 Tucson Conference 'Towards a Science of Consciousness', he was able to do so with no particular thought of our paper. The term seemed to be in wide use already. In any case, it was this conference session that led Anthony Freeman, the managing editor of the *Journal of Consciousness Studies*, and myself to conceive the idea of this volume. I would like, therefore, to express my gratitude not only to Anthony Freeman and David Chalmers, but also to Luiz Pessoa and Evan Thompson.

Alva Noë

Alva Noë

Is the Visual World a Grand Illusion?

In this paper I explore a brand of scepticism about perceptual experience that takes its start from recent work in psychology and philosophy of mind on change blindness and related phenomena. I argue that the new scepticism rests on a problematic phenomenology of perceptual experience. I then consider a strengthened version of the sceptical challenge that seems to be immune to this criticism. This strengthened sceptical challenge formulates what I call the problem of perceptual presence. I show how this problem can be addressed by drawing on an enactive or sensorimotor approach to perceptual consciousness. Our experience of environmental detail consists in our access to that detail thanks to our possession of practical knowledge of the way in which what we do and sensory stimulation depend on each other.

Traditional scepticism about perceptual experience questions whether we can know that things are as we experience them as being. This paper targets a new form of scepticism about experience that takes its start from recent work in perceptual psychology and philosophy of mind. The new scepticism questions whether we even have the perceptual experience we think we have. According to the new scepticism, we have radically false beliefs about what our perceptual experience is like. Perceptual consciousness is a kind of false consciousness; a sort of confabulation. The visual world is a grand illusion.

The new scepticism raises important questions for philosophy, psychology, and consciousness studies. What is the character of our perceptual experience? And who does the sceptic mean by 'we' anyway? Ordinary perceivers? Ordinary perceivers in unusual reflective contexts? Or psychologists and philosophers? These are surprisingly difficult questions. I argue, in what follows, that the new scepticism, and perhaps also the new perceptual psychology it has spawned, rests on a misguided and overly simplistic account of perceptual phenomenology.

I

According to a conception of visual experience that has been widely held by perceptual theorists, you open your eyes and — *presto!* — you enjoy a richly detailed picture-like experience of the world, one that represents the world in sharp focus, uniform detail and high resolution from the centre out to the periphery. Let us call this the snapshot conception of experience.

Empirical investigation of the nature of vision takes its start from the snapshot conception. The puzzle visual theory faces is that of understanding how it is we come to enjoy such richly detailed snapshot-like visual experiences when our actual direct contact with the world in the form of information on the retina is so limited. The limitations are familiar: there are two retinal images, not one, and they are distorted, tiny, and upside-down (Gregory, 1966/1997, p.1). In addition, the resolving power of the eye is limited and nonuniform; outside the high-resolution foveal region, the retina is nearly colour-blind and its powers of discrimination are severely limited. On top of this, the eye is in nearly constant motion, saccading from point to point in the visual field three or four times a second. As a result of saccadic suppression, the data made available to the retina takes the form of a succession of alternating snapshots and grey-outs.

How, on the basis of this fragmented and discontinuous information, are we able to enjoy the impression of seamless consciousness of an environment that is detailed, continuous, complex and high-resolution? This is *the* problem faced by visual theory.

The orthodox strategy is to suppose that the brain integrates information available in successive fixations into a stable, detailed model or representation. This stable representation then serves as the substrate of the actual experience. According to this orthodox approach, vision just is the process whereby the patchy and fragmentary bits of information on the retina are transformed into the detailed stable representations underlying actual perceptual experience. This is what David Marr had in mind, I think, when he wrote that 'Vision is the process of discovering from images what is present in the world, and where it is' (Marr, 1982, p. 3).

II

Recent work in perceptual psychology challenges this traditional framing of the problem for visual theory by questioning whether we really enjoy the sort of richly detailed, snapshot-like visual experiences we think we do. If we do not enjoy such experiences, then we are not faced with the problem of how the brain gives rise to them. Indeed, from the standpoint of what I am calling the new scepticism, the central problem of visual theory is not: how do we see so much on the basis of so little? It is, rather, why does it seem to us as if we see so much when in fact we see so little?

The point is beautifully epitomized by Dennett, who is the *éminence grise*, and strongest proponent, of the new scepticism. Edelman had written 'One of the most striking things about consciousness is its continuity' (1989, p. 119). Dennett writes in response:

> This is utterly wrong. One of the most striking features about consciousness is its discontinuity — as revealed in the blind spot, and saccadic gaps, to take the simplest examples. The discontinuity of consciousness is striking because of the *apparent* continuity of consciousness (1991, p. 356).

This remark is wonderful because it makes very clear that the worry is about the nature of experience or consciousness itself. We are misled as to the true nature of consciousness, Dennett is saying. Consciousness is really discontinuous. It appears to us to be continuous. A paradoxical way to put the point would be: it turns out that we are mistaken in our assessment of how things seem to us be.

III

How does the argument for the new scepticism about experience go? What is the argument that experiences are not what they seem to be? The *locus classicus* is Dennett's discussion of filling in at the blind spot (Dennett, 1991, pp. 344–56).[1]

There is a blind spot in each eye in the sense that there is a place on each retina where there are no photoreceptors. We don't usually notice the blind spot. What falls on the blind spot of one eye doesn't fall on the blind spot of the other, and the eyes are in nearly constant motion anyway, so what falls on the blind spot now doesn't fall on the blind spot a moment later. But you don't experience a hole in your visual field even when you stare with one eye at a white wall (say). It takes special care to demonstrate the existence of the blind spot. Shut your right eye and fixate the star below. If you move the page to the right distance from your face (about 8–12 inches), you will be unable to see the black disc on the left. The black disc disappears because it falls in your blind spot.

Demonstrations like this are frequently cited as evidence that the brain *fills in* the gap in our internal representation of the visual field (e.g., Palmer, 1999, p. 617). How else can you explain the phenomenon? Dennett noticed that the fact that we do not experience a gap in the visual field corresponding to the blind spot does not entail that the brain fills in the gap. This discounts other possibilities, such as that the brain simply ignores the blind spot. If the brain ignores the absence of information from the part of the field corresponding to the blind spot, then it doesn't represent that information as absent. But then there is nothing to be filled in. Even if the brain *does* represent the absence of information, it isn't obvious that it must fill the missing information in. After all, if the brain knows what it needs to fill in, then for whose benefit is the operation of filling in performed?

---

[1] See Pessoa *et al.* (1998) and Thompson *et al.* (1999) for a more detailed critical assessment of Dennett's account of filling in.

The brain's job is finding out, Dennett asserts, not filling in. In the absence of direct evidence of the process of filling in itself, and not merely of the putative effects of filling in — namely, a gap-free experience — we aren't entitled to suppose that filling in occurs.

What does this have to do with the new scepticism? Dennett seems to have believed that there is no such good evidence of processes of filling in.[2] Let's grant him this assumption. The interesting bit is what he takes to follow from this. If there is no filling in at the blind spot, then, he reasons, there must be a gap in our experience of the visual world; a gap which, however, we fail to notice. This, presumably, is an example of the discontinuity of experience despite its apparent continuity. We take our experience to be gap-free when it is not. We are the victims of an illusion of visual consciousness.

IV

But does this sceptical reasoning go through? It is certainly right that you don't notice a gap in the visual field corresponding to the blind spot even under monocular viewing conditions. In general, if you shut your eye and stare at the wall, you have a visual experience as of a gap-free expanse of the wall. That is, it looks to you as if there is an unbroken expanse of wall. But this is not to say that it seems to you as if, as it were in a single fixation, you experience *the whole of the wall's surface*. If you reflect on what it is like for you to look at the wall, you will notice that it seems to you as if the whole wall is there at once, but not as if every part of the wall's surface is represented in your consciousness at once. Rather, you experience the wall as present and you experience yourself as having access to the wall by looking here, or there, attending here, or there. It is no part of ordinary phenomenology that we experience the whole wall, every bit of it, in consciousness all at once.[3]

The sceptical argument seems to turn on attributing to us, as lay perceivers, something like the snapshot conception of experience. According to this conception, visual experiences are like snapshots that represent the scene in high-resolution focus and sharp detail. Dennett then points out, convincingly, that our experience is not like a snapshot — there's a blind spot, bad parafoveal vision, etc. — and he concludes that we are victims of an illusion about the character of our own consciousness.

But the mistake in question — the snapshot conception of experience — is not one to which perceivers themselves are committed. Perhaps it is an idea about perception that psychologists or philosophers find natural. Perhaps it is way of describing experience that many ordinary perceivers would be inclined to assent

---

[2] Pessoa *et al.* (1998) argued that, Dennett's claims to the contrary notwithstanding, there is in fact evidence of the process of filling in itself. However, we also argued that, once Dennett's critical observations are taken on board, filling in loses much of its theoretical importance. I won't revisit these issues here. It's worth mentioning, however, that recent work in the lab of Shinsuke Shimojo at Cal Tech seems to provide strong evidence of filling in. In particular, Shimojo and his colleagues show that amodally filled-in figures generate afterimages (Shimojo *et al.*, 2001).

[3] See Thompson *et al.* (1999) and Noë (forthcoming) for further development of this line of criticism.

to if they were asked appropriately leading questions. But this is compatible with its being the case that we do not really take our experience to be this way.

V

A second important source for the new scepticism is recent work on change blindness and inattentional blindness in the psychology of scene perception.[4]

To set the stage, consider the following familiar sort of gag. I say to you as you tuck into your lunch: 'Hey? Isn't that Mick Jagger over there?' You turn around to look. When you do, I snatch one of your french fries. When you turn back, you're none the wiser. You don't remember the exact number or layout of fries on your plate and you weren't paying attention when the fry was snatched. Your attention was directed elsewhere.

It turns out — this is the central finding of work on change blindness conducted by O'Regan, Rensink, Simons, Levin, and others[5] — that this sort of failure to notice change is a pervasive feature of our visual lives. Usually, when changes occur before us, we notice them because our attention is grabbed by the flickers of movement associated with the change. But if we are prevented from noticing the flicker of movement when the change occurs, say because at the same time flickers occur elsewhere, we may fail to notice the change (O'Regan et al., 1996; 1999). What is striking — and this will become important later on — is the fact that we will frequently fail to notice changes even when the changes are fully open to view. Even when we are looking right at the change when it occurs, something we can test with eye trackers, we may fail to see the change (O'Regan et al., 2000).

The fact of change blindness is widely thought to have several important consequences. First, perception is, in an important sense, attention-dependent. You only see that to which you attend. If something occurs outside the scope of attention, even if it's perfectly visible, you won't see it. In one study, perceivers are asked to watch a video tape of a basketball game and they are asked to count the number of times one team takes possession of the ball (Neisser, 1976; Simons & Chabris, 1999). During the film clip, which lasts a few minutes, a person in a gorilla suit strolls onto the centre of the court, turns and faces the audience and does a little jig. The gorilla then slowly walks off the court. The remarkable fact is that perceivers (including this author) *do not* notice the gorilla. This is an example of inattentional blindness.[6] Second, perception is gist-dependent. Some changes, for example, in the features that affect the gist of the scene, are more likely to be noticed (Simons & Levin, 1997). Third, it seems that the brain does

---

[4] For recent reviews of the change blindness literature, see O'Regan (forthcoming); Simons (2000); Simons & Levin (1997). For a discussion of philosophical implications, see Noë et al. (2000); Noë & O'Regan (2000); and O'Regan & Noë (2001a). See Mack & Rock (1998) for a thorough treatment of inattentional blindness.

[5] O'Regan et al. (1996; 1999); Rensink et al. (1997; 2000); Simons & Levin (1998).

[6] The term is due to Mack and Rock (1998). A detailed study of the phenomenon is contained in their book. For further discussion in connection with the themes of this paper, see Noë & O'Regan (2000).

not build up detailed internal models of the scene; that is, it doesn't perform the integration of information across successive fixations, contrary to the assumption of traditional orthodoxy (Blackmore *et al.*, 1995; Rensink *et al.*, 1997; O'Regan *et al.*, 1999; Rensink *et al.*, 2000; Noë *et al.*, 2000). Or if it does, we have little easy access to this detail. If we did, then presumably we'd keep track of change better than we do.

VI

Many of the investigators on change blindness believe that this work supports the grand illusion hypothesis. For example, Susan Blackmore and her colleagues (1995, p. 1075), write:

> we believe that we see a complete, dynamic picture of a stable, uniformly detailed, and colourful world, but [o]ur stable visual world may be constructed out of a brief retinal image and a very sketchy, higher-level representation along with a pop-out mechanism to redirect attention. The richness of our visual world is, to this extent, an illusion.

In a similar vein, O'Regan (1992, p. 484) writes:

> despite the poor quality of the visual apparatus, we have the subjective impression of great richness and 'presence' of the visual world. But this richness and presence are actually an illusion. . .[7]

The problem with this reasoning is the same as we saw above in connection with Dennett's discussion of the blind spot. It just is not the case that we, normal perceivers, believe we see a complete, dynamic picture of a stable, uniformly detailed and colourful world. Of course it *does* seem to us as if we have perceptual access to a world that is richly detailed, complete and gap-free. And we do! We take ourselves to be confronted with and embedded in a high-resolution environment. We take ourselves to have access to that detail, not all at once, but thanks to movements of our eyes and head and shifts of attention.[8]

Consider a question posed by Rensink *et al.* (2000, p. 28): 'Why do we feel that somewhere in our brain is a complete, coherent representation of the entire scene?' But this question rests on a false presupposition. It does not seem to us as if somewhere in our brain there is a complete, coherent representation of the scene. Perceptual experience is directed to the world, not to the brain.

VII

If I am right that perceivers are not committed to the idea that they have detailed pictures in the head when they see (the snapshot conception), then how can we explain the fact that perceivers are surprised by the results of change blindness? Does not the surprise itself register our commitment to the problematic, snapshot

---

[7] O'Regan no longer defends the grand illusion hypothesis. See, for example, O'Regan & Noë (2001a).

[8] For more on this line of criticism, see Noë *et al.* (2000); Noë & O'Regan (2000); and O'Regan & Noë (2001a).

conception of experience? This objection has been raised by Dennett (Dennett, 2001; see also Dennett, this volume):

> why do normal perceivers express such surprise when their attention is drawn to [the relevant facts about their perceptual limitations]. Surprise is a wonderful dependent variable, and should be used more often in experiments; it is easy to measure and is a telling betrayal of the subject's *having expected something else*. These expectations are, indeed, an overshooting of the proper expectations of a normally embedded perceiver–agent; people shouldn't have these expectations, but they do. People are shocked, incredulous, dismayed; they often laugh and shriek when I demonstrate the effects to them for the first time. These behavioral responses are themselves data in good standing, and in need of an explanation.

This is an important objection, but one that is easy to answer. The astonishment people experience when confronted with the facts of change blindness and inattentional blindness does indeed demonstrate that their beliefs are upset by these demonstrations. But one need not attribute to them (to us) a commitment to the snapshot conception. The surprise is explained simply by supposing that we tend to think we are better at noticing changes than in fact we are, or that we are much less vulnerable to the effects of distracted attention than we in fact are. This is a plausible explanation of the surprise we feel when confronted with the results, and one that does not foist on us the ideology of the snapshot conception.

Surprise requires explanation, but so does the lack of surprise. Notice that we are not surprised or in any way taken aback by our need to move eyes and head to get better glimpses of what is around us. We peer, squint, lean forward, adjust lighting, put on glasses, and we do so automatically. The fact that we are not surprised by our lack of immediate possession of detailed information about the environment shows that we don't take ourselves to have all that information in consciousness all at once. If we were committed to the snapshot conception, wouldn't we be surprised by the need continuously to redirect our attention to the environment to inform ourselves about what is there?

Finally, it is worth noting that artists, magicians, stage designers and cinematographers — people who live by the maxim that the hand is quicker than the eye — would not be surprised by the change blindness results. Why should they be? Our perceptual access to the world is robust, but fallible and vulnerable. How could one really think otherwise?[9]

VIII

Let us summarize what we have found so far. First, the new scepticism is right about some things. For example, it is right that experience does not conform to the snapshot conception. And so it is right that visual science should not concern itself with how the brain produces experiences thought of like that. But the new scepticism seems to rest on a substantially false characterization of what

---

[9] An artist friend of mine, working on a portrait series, asked me to sit for him. I was struck by the frenzy of his looking-activity. The rendering proceeded by means of an uninterrupted pattern of looking back and forth from me to the canvas and then back again. The detail wasn't in his memory, or in his internal representations. It was to be found in his subject (in me).

perceptual experience actually seems to us — that is, to lay perceivers — to be like. In particular, it attributes to us something like the snapshot conception. The scepticism can be resisted if we recognize that we are not committed to the snap-shot conception. We don't take ourselves to experience all environmental detail in consciousness all at once. Rather, we take ourselves to be situated in an environment to have access to environmental detail as needed by turns of the eyes and head, and repositioning of the body.

IX

But we are not done yet. We must not be too quick in dismissing the grand illusion hypothesis. One of the results of change blindness is that we only see, we only experience, that to which we attend. But surely it is a basic fact of our phenomenology that we enjoy a perceptual awareness of at least some unattended features of the scene. So, for example, I may look at you, attending only to you. But I also have a sense of the presence of the wall behind you, of its colour, of its distance from you. It certainly seems this way. If we are not to fall back into the grip of the sceptic's worry, we must explain how it is we can enjoy perceptual experience of unattended features of a scene. Let us call this the problem of perceptual presence.

The problem of perceptual presence forces us to confront the grand illusion puzzle again. But this version of the sceptical worry is stronger, for it does not rely on the misattribution to us of the phenomenologically inadequate snapshot conception of experience. All that it requires is that we acknowledge that we are perceptually aware, sometimes, of unattended detail. And who could deny that?

We can sharpen the worry. One of the main upshots of work on change blindness is that the brain does not produce a detailed world model corresponding to perceived detail. The sceptical problem then becomes: how can we enjoy experiences of the world as richly detailed when we lack internal representations of all that detail?

X

To begin to see our way clear to a solution of the problem of perceptual presence, consider as an example a perceptual experience such as that you might enjoy if you were to hold a bottle in your hands with eyes closed. You have a sense of the presence of a whole bottle, even though you only make contact with the bottle at a few isolated points. Can we explain how your experience in this way outstrips what is actually given, or must we concede that your sense of the bottle as a whole is a kind of confabulation?

Or consider a different case: there is a cat sitting motionless on the far side of a picket fence. You have a sense of the presence of a cat even though, strictly speaking, you only see those parts of the cat that show through the fence. How is it that we can in this way enjoy a perceptual experience as of the whole cat?

One way we might try to explain this is by observing that you draw on your knowledge of what bottles are, or what cats are. You bring to bear your conceptual skills. This is doubtless right. But it does not, I think, do justice to the phenomenology of the experience. For crucially, your sense of the presence of the bottle is a sense of its *perceptual* presence. That is, you do not merely *think* or *infer* that there is a bottle present, in the way, say, that you think or infer that there is a room next door. The presence of the bottle is not inferred or surmised. It is *experienced*. And so with the cat: you see it there, you experience it, even though you only see parts of it.[10]

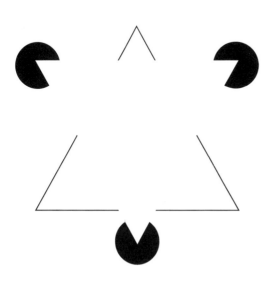

This is an example of what psychologists call *amodal perception*. As an illustration, consider the famous Kanisza figure (left). Most perceivers take themselves to experience two triangles, one of which is above, and so partly blocks from view, the other. In addition, the topmost triangle partially covers the three black disks. The hidden portions of the disks and the lower triangle are said to be *amodally* perceived as complete. Here you experience as perceptually present something which is, in fact, hidden from view.

Amodal perception is an important phenomenon. It is involved in our perception of solidity, as, for example, when you experience a tomato as three-dimensional and round, even though you only see its facing side, or when you experience a chair as whole and intact, even though it is partially blocked from view by the table.

Amodal perception is paradoxical in that it is perceiving what is, strictly speaking, out of view. I would like to suggest that we approach the problem of perceptual presence as, in essence, a problem about amodal perception. The proposal — this is a step toward the solution of the problem of perceptual presence — is that the detail of the world is present to consciousness, but in the way that amodally perceived features of scenes or objects are amodally present. They are perceived without being really perceived. The question whether the visual world is a grand illusion then transposes itself into the question whether amodal perception should be thought of as illusory.

XI

Traditional orthodoxy speaks to the problem of perceptual presence by supposing that we build up an internal model corresponding to the experienced detail. But this sort of approach faces obstacles. As we have noticed, work on change blindness seems to suggest that we may not in fact actually produce such detailed internal models.

---

[10] See Thompson *et al.* (1999) for more on this distinction.

But consider a more basic point: why should the brain go to the trouble of producing a model of the bottle when the bottle is right there in your hands and can
serve as a repository of information about itself? All the information about the
bottle you need is available to you in the world — you need only move your hands
to gather it. And so for the cat. Why represent the cat in all its detail when all
the information you need is available, when you need it, by eye and head
movements?[11]

I think that what makes the orthodox move seem so attractive is that theorists
tend to rely on a snapshot conception of experience according to which we take
ourselves in experience to represent the cat or the bottle in consciousness in all its
detail. But this distorts the phenomenology. It does not seem to me as if every
part of the cat is visible to me now, even though it does seem to me now as if I perceive a whole cat and as if the unperceived parts of the cat's body are present.
After all, I can *see* that the cat is partly hidden behind the fence! This is just the
thing with amodal perception: one experiences the presence of that which one
perceives to be out of view.

XII

The solution to the problem of perceptual presence is achieved in two steps.[12]
First, we need to reflect more carefully on the phenomenology. When we do so, it
becomes clear that our sense of the presence of the cat as a whole now does not
consist in our representation, now, of the whole of the cat in consciousness. It
consists rather in the fact that we *now* have access to the whole of the cat. Second,
the basis of this access is our possession of sensorimotor skills (O'Regan & Noë,
2001a). In particular, its basis is those skills — practical knowledge of the ways
what we do gives rise to sensory stimulation — whose possession is constitutive
of sensory perception. My relation to the cat behind the fence is mediated by such
facts as, when I blink, I lose sight of it altogether, but when I move a few inches to
the right, a part of its shoulder that was previously hidden comes into view. My
sense of the perceptual presence, now, of that which is now hidden behind a slat
in the fence consists in my expectation that by movements of the body I can produce the right sort of new cat stimulation.

In general, our sense of the perceptual presence of the detailed world does not
consist in our representation of all the detail in consciousness now. Rather, it consists in our access now to all of the detail, and to our knowledge that we have this
access. This knowledge takes the form of our comfortable mastery of the rules of
sensorimotor dependence that mediate our relation to our immediate environment. My sense of the presence of the whole cat behind the fence consists precisely in my knowledge, my implicit understanding, that by a movement of the

---

[11] O'Regan (1992) makes this point. There is no need to represent the detail of the environment in memory because we can let the world serve as its own 'outside memory'. Brooks (1991) makes a very similar point: the world, he proposes, can serve as its own best model.

[12] The solution to the problem of perceptual presence is developed in a series of papers I have written
with Kevin O'Regan: O'Regan & Noë (2001a,b); Noë & O'Regan (2000). See also Noë (2001;
forthcoming).

eye or the head or the body I can bring bits of the cat into view that are now hidden. This is one of the central claims of the enactive or sensorimotor approach to perception (O'Regan & Noë, 2001a; Noë, forthcoming).[13]

XIII

Note: my sense of the presence of the hallway next door is not in this way mediated by patterns of sensorimotor dependence (O'Regan & Noë, 2001a). I can jump up and down, turn around, turn the lights on and off, blink, and so on, and it makes no difference whatsoever to my sense of the presence of the room next door. My relationship to the room next door — however strongly I believe or know or assume that it is present — is not a perceptual relation. My relation to the cat, however, or to the bottle, is. It is my implicit understanding of this that gives me the feeling and that justifies me in the feeling that the cat and the bottle are present to me.[14]

XIV

The enactive approach to perception — with its emphasis on the centrality of our possession of sensorimotor skills — provides the basis, then, for a satisfying reply to the sceptic, but only provided that we adopt a more plausible phenomenology of perceptual experience. On this more plausible account, it is not the case that we take ourselves to represent the whole scene in consciousness all at once. The enactive, sensorimotor account explains how it can be that we enjoy an experience of worldly detail which is not represented in our brains. The detail is present — the perceptual world is present — in the sense that we have a special kind of access to the detail, an access controlled by patterns of sensorimotor dependence with which we are familiar. The visual world is not a grand illusion.

Acknowledgements
The ideas in this paper grow out of my collaborations with Evan Thompson and Kevin O'Regan. I wish to make explicit my debt to them. Thanks also to audiences at UC Riverside, UC Irvine, Cal Tech, Brooklyn College, and Cal Arts, where I have presented this material. Thanks to Jeff Barrett, Sue Blackmore, Dave Chalmers, Tori McGeer, Dominic Murphy, Philip Pettit, Kyle Sanford and Eric Schwitzgebel for helpful conversation. Finally, I would like gratefully to acknowledge the support of a University of California President's Fellowship in the Humanities and faculty research funds of the University of California, Santa Cruz.

[13] I borrow the term 'enactive' from Varela *et al.* (1991).

[14] Of course, there are sensorimotor dependencies mediating my relation to the room next door as well. Indeed, no sharp line can be drawn between that which is amodally perceived as present and that which is merely thought of as inferred. This is a strength of the view I am defending here. It suggests a way in which thought is grounded in the sort of sensorimotor knowledge that is, on just about any view, shared by humans and other animals.

References

Blackmore, S.J., Brelstaff, G., Nelson, K., Troscianko, T. (1995), 'Is the richness of our visual world an illusion? Transsaccadic memory for complex scenes', *Perception,* **24**, pp. 1075–81.

Brooks, R.A. (1991), 'Intelligence without reason', *Proceedings of the 1991 International Joint Conference on Artificial Intelligence,* pp. 569–95.

Dennett, D.C. (1991), *Consciousness Explained* (Boston, MA: Little, Brown & Co.).

Edelman, G. (1989), *The Remembered Present: A Biological Theory of Consciousness* (New York: Basic Books).

Gregory, R.L. (1966/1997), *The Intelligent Eye: The Psychology of Seeing,* Fifth edition (Princeton, NJ: Princeton University Press).

Mack, A., Rock, I. (1998), *Inattentional Blindness* (Cambridge, MA: The MIT Press).

Marr, D. (1982), *Vision* (New York: WH Freeman).

Neisser, U. (1976), *Cognition and Reality: Principles and Implications of Cognitive Psychology* (San Francisco, CA: W.H. Freeman).

Noë, A. (2001), 'Experience and the active mind', *Synthese,* **129** (1), pp. 41–60.

Noë, A. (forthcoming), *Action in Perception* (Cambridge MA: The MIT Press).

Noë, A. and O'Regan, J.K. (2000), 'Perception, attention and the grand illusion', *Psyche,* **6** (15) URL: http://psyche.cs.monash.edu.au/v6/psyche-6-15-noe.html.

Noë, A., Pessoa, L., Thompson, E. (2000), 'Beyond the grand illusion: what change blindness really teaches us about vision', *Visual Cognition,* **7**, (1/2/3), pp. 93–106.

O'Regan, J.K. (1992), 'Solving the "real" mysteries of visual perception: the world as an outside memory', *Canadian Journal of Psychology,* **46**, pp. 461–88.

O'Regan, J.K. (forthcoming), 'Change blindness', *Encyclopedia of Cognitive Science* (London: Macmillan, Nature Publishing Group).

O'Regan, J.K., Deubel, H., Clark, J.J., Rensink, R.A. (2000), 'Picture changes during blinks: looking without seeing and seeing without looking', *Visual Cognition,* **7**, pp. 191–212.

O'Regan, J.K. and Noë, A. (2001a), 'A sensorimotor account of vision and visual consciousness', *Behavioral and Brain Sciences,* **24** (5).

O'Regan, J.K. and Noë, A. (2001b), 'What it is like to see: A sensorimotor theory of perceptual experience', *Synthese,* **129** (1), pp. 79–103.

O'Regan, J.K., Rensink, J.A., Clark, J J. (1996), '"Mud splashes" render picture changes invisible', *Invest. Ophthalmol. Vis. Sci.,* **37**, p. S213.

O'Regan, J.K., Rensink, R.A., Clark, J J. (1999), 'Change-blindness as a result of "mudsplashes"', *Nature,* **398**, p. 34.

Palmer, S.E. (1999), *Vision Science: Photons to Phenomenology* (Cambridge, MA: MIT Press).

Pessoa, L., Thompson, E., Noë, A. (1998), 'Finding out about filling in: a guide to perceptual completion for visual science and the philosophy of perception', *Behavioral and Brain Sciences,* **21** (6), pp. 723–802.

Rensink, R.A., O'Regan, J.K., Clark, J.J. (1997), 'To see or not to see: The need for attention to perceive changes in scenes', *Psychological Science,* **8** (5), pp. 368–73.

Rensink, R.A., O'Regan, J.K., Clark, J.J. (2000), 'On the failure to detect changes in scenes across brief interruptions', *Visual Cognition.*

Shimojo, S., Kamitani, Y., Nishida, S. (2001), 'Afterimage of perceptually filled-in surface', *Science,* **293**, p. 1677.

Simons, D.J. (2000), 'Current approaches to change blindness', *Visual Cognition,* **7** (1/2/3), pp. 1–15.

Simons, D.J. and Chabris, C.F. (1999), 'Gorillas in our midst: sustained inattentional blindness for dynamic events', *Perception,* **28** (9), pp. 1059–74.

Simons, D.J. and Levin, D.T. (1997), 'Change blindness', *Trends in Cognitive Sciences,* **1** (7), pp. 261–7.

Simons, D.J. and Levin, D.T. (1998), 'Failure to detect changes to people in a real-world interaction', *Psychonomic Bulletin and Review,* **5**, pp. 644–9.

Thompson, E., Noë, A., Pessoa, L. (1999), 'Perceptual completion: a case study in phenomenology and cognitive science', in *Naturalizing Phenomenology: Issues in Contemporary Phenomenology and Cognitive Science,* ed. J. Pettitot, F.J. Varela, Pachoud and J-M. Roy (Stanford, CA: Stanford University Press).

Varela, F.J., Thompson, E., Rosch, E. (1991), *The Embodied Mind* (Cambridge, MA: MIT Press).

Daniel C. Dennett

How Could I Be Wrong?
How Wrong Could I Be?

One of the striking, even amusing, spectacles to be enjoyed at the many work-shops and conferences on consciousness these days is the breathtaking overcon-fidence with which laypeople hold forth about the nature of consciousness — their own in particular, but everybody's by extrapolation. Everybody's an expert on consciousness, it seems, and it doesn't take any knowledge of experimental findings to secure the home truths these people enunciate with such conviction.

One of my goals over the years has been to shatter that complacency, and secure the scientific study of consciousness on a proper footing. *There is no prop-osition about one's own or anybody else's conscious experience that is immune to error, unlikely as that error might be.* I have come to suspect that refusal to accept this really quite bland denial of what would be miraculous if true lies behind most if not all the elaboration of fantastical doctrines about consciousness recently defended. This refusal fuels the arguments about the conceivability of zombies, the importance of a 'first-person' science of consciousness, 'intrinsic intentionality' and various other hastily erected roadblocks to progress in the sci-ence of consciousness.

You can't have infallibility about your own consciousness. Period. But you can get close — close enough to explain why it seems so powerfully as if you do. First of all, the intentional stance (Dennett, 1971; 1987) guarantees that any entity that is voluminously and reliably predictable as an intentional system will have a set of beliefs (including the most intimate beliefs about its personal expe-riences) that are mainly true. So each of us can be confident that *in general* what we believe about our conscious experiences will have an interpretation accord-ing to which we are, in the main, right. How wrong could I be? Not that wrong. Not about most things. There *has* to be a way of nudging the interpretation of your manifold beliefs about your experience so that it comes out largely innocent of error — though this might not be an interpretation you yourself would be inclined to endorse. This is not a metaphysical gift, a proof that we live in the best of all possible worlds. It is something that automatically falls out of the method-ology: when adopting the intentional stance, one casts about for a maximally

Journal of Consciousness Studies, **9**, No. 5–6, 2002, pp. 13–16

charitable (truth-rendering) interpretation, and there is bound to be one if the entity in question is hale and hearty in its way.

But it does not follow from this happy fact that there is a path or method we can follow to isolate some privileged set of guaranteed-true beliefs. No matter how certain you are that p, it may turn out that p is one of those relatively rare errors of yours, an illusion, even if not a grand illusion. But we can get closer, too. Once you have an intentional system with a capacity for communicating in a natural language, it offers itself as a candidate for the rather special role of self-describer, not infallible but *incorrigible* in a limited way: it may be wrong, but there may be no way to correct it. There may be no truth-preserving interpretation of all of its expressed *opinions* (Dennett, 1978; 1991) about its mental life, but those expressed opinions may be the best source we *could* have about what it is like to be it. A version of this idea was made (in-)famous by Richard Rorty back in his earlier incarnation as an analytic philosopher, and has been defended by me more recently (Dennett, 2000). There I argue that if, for instance, Cog, the humanoid robot being developed by Rodney Brooks and his colleagues at MIT, were ever to master English, its own declarations about its subjectivity would systematically tend to trump the 'third-person' opinions of its makers, even though they would be armed, in the limit, with perfect information about the micro-mechanical implementation of that subjectivity. This, too, falls out of the methodology of the intentional stance, which is the only way (I claim) to attribute content to the states of anything.

The price we pay for this near-infallibility is that our heterophenomenological worlds may have to be immersed in a bath of metaphor in order to come out mainly true. That is, our sincere avowals may have to be rather drastically reconstrued in order to come out literally true. For instance, when we sincerely tell our interrogators about the mental images we're manipulating, we may not *think* we're talking about convolutions of data-structures in our brain — we may well *think* we're talking about immaterial ectoplasmic composites, or intrinsic qualia, or quantum-perturbations in our micro-tubules! — but if the interrogators rudely override these ideological glosses and disclaimers of ours and forcibly re-interpret our propositions as actually being *about* such data-structure convolution, these propositions will turn out to be, in the main, almost all true, and moreover deeply informative about the ways we solve problems, think about the world, and fuel our subjective opinions in general. (In this regard, there is nothing special about the brain and its processes; if you tell the doctor that you have a certain sort of travelling pain in your gut, your doctor may well decide that you're actually talking about your appendix — whatever you may think you're talking about — and act accordingly.)

Since we are such reflective and reflexive creatures, we can participate in the adjustment of the attributions of our own beliefs, and a familiar philosophical 'move' turns out to be just such reflective self-re-adjustment, but not a useful one. Suppose you say you know just what beer tastes like to you now, and you are quite sure you remember what beer tasted like to you the first time you tasted it, and you can compare, you say, the way it tastes now to the way it tasted then.

Suppose you declare the taste to be the same. You are then asked: Does anything at all follow from this subjective similarity in the way of further, objectively detectable similarities? For instance, does this taste today have the same higher-order effects on you as it used to have? Does it make you as happy or as depressed, or does it enhance or diminish your capacity to discriminate colours, or retrieve synonyms or remember the names of your childhood friends or. . . . .? Or have your other, surrounding dispositions and habits changed so much in the interim that it is not to be expected that the very same taste (the same *quale,* one may venture to say, pretending to know what one is talking about) would have any of the same effects at this later date? You may very well express ignorance about all such implications. *All you know*, you declare, is that this beer now *tastes just like* that first beer did (at least in some ineffable, intrinsic regard) *whether or not* it has any of the same further effects or functions. But by explicitly jettison-ing all such implications from your proposition, you manage to guarantee that it has been reduced to a vacuity. You have jealously guarded your infallibility by seeing to it that you've adjusted the content of your claim all the way down to zero. You can't be wrong, because there's nothing left to be right or wrong about.

   This move is always available, but it availeth nought. It makes no difference, by the way, whether you said the beer tastes the same or different; the same point goes through if you insist it tastes different now. Once your declaration is stripped of all powers of implication, it is an empty assertion, a mere demonstra-tion that *this* is how you fancy talking at this moment. Another version of this self-vacating move can be seen, somewhat more starkly, in a reaction some folks opt for when they have it demonstrated to them that their colour vision doesn't extend to the far peripheries of their visual fields: They declare that on the con-trary, their colour *vision* in the sense of colour *experience* does indeed extend to the outer limits of their phenomenal fields; they just disavow any implications about what this colour experience they enjoy might enable them to do — for example, identify by name the colours of the objects there to be experienced! They are right, of course, that it *does not follow* from the proposition that one is having colour experiences that one can identify the colours thus experienced, or do better than chance in answering same-different questions, or use colour differ-ences to detect shapes (as in a colour-blindness test) to take the most obvious fur-ther effects. But if *nothing* follows from the claim that their peripheral field is experienced as coloured, their purported disagreement with the researchers' claim that their peripheral field lacks colour altogether evaporates.

   O'Regan and Noë (2001) argue that my heterophenomenology makes the mis-take of convicting naive subjects of succumbing to a grand illusion.

> But is it true that normal perceivers think of their visual fields this way [as in sharp detail and uniform focus from the centre out to the periphery]? Do normal perceivers really make this error? We think not . . . normal perceivers do not have ideological commitments concerning the resolution of the visual field. Rather, they take the world to be solid, dense, detailed and present and they take themselves to be embedded in and thus to have access to the world.

My response to this was:

Then why do normal perceivers express such surprise when their attention is drawn to facts about the low resolution (and loss of colour vision, etc) of their visual peripheries? Surprise is a wonderful dependent variable, and should be used more often in experiments; it is easy to measure and is a telling betrayal of the subject's *having expected something else*. These expectations are, indeed, an overshooting of the proper expectations of a normally embedded perceiver–agent; people shouldn't have these expectations, but they do. People are shocked, incredulous, dismayed; they often laugh and shriek when I demonstrate the effects to them for the first time (Dennett, 2001).

O'Regan and Noë (see also Noë *et al.*, 2000; Noë, 2001; and Noë and O'Regan, 2000) are right that it need not seem to people that they have a detailed picture of the world in their heads. But typically it does. It also need not seem to them that they are not 'zombies' but typically it does. People *like* to have 'ideological commitments'. They are inveterate amateur theorisers about what is going on in their heads, and they can be mighty wrong when they set out on these paths.

For instance, quite a few theorisers are very, very sure that they have something that they sometimes call original intentionality. They are prepared to agree that interpretive adjustments can enhance the reliability of the so-called reports of the so-called content of the so-called mental states of a robot like Cog, because those internal states have only *derived* intentionality, but they are of the heartfelt opinion that we human beings, in contrast, have the real stuff: we are endowed with genuine mental states that have content quite independently of any such charitable scheme of interpretation. That's how it seems to them, but they are wrong.

How could they be wrong? They could be wrong about this because they could be wrong about anything — because they are not gods. How wrong could they be? Until we excuse them for their excesses and re-interpret their extravagant claims in the light of good third-person science, they can be utterly, bizarrely wrong. Once they relinquish their ill-considered grip on the myth of first-person authority and recognize that their limited incorrigibility depends on the liberal application of a principle of charity by third-person observers who know more than they do about what is going on in their own heads, they can become invaluable, irreplaceable informants in the investigation of human consciousness.

References

Dennett, D.C. (1971), 'Intentional systems', *J.Phil*, **68**, pp. 87–106.
Dennett, D.C. (1978), 'How to change your mind' in *Brainstorms* (Cambridge, MA: MIT Press).
Dennett, D.C. (1987), *The Intentional Stance* (Cambridge, MA: MIT Press).
Dennett, D.C. (1991), *Consciousness Explained* (Boston: Little, Brown, and London: Allen Lane, 1992).
Dennett, D.C. (2000), 'The case for Rorts', in *Rorty and his Critics*, ed. Robert Brandom (Oxford: Blackwells).
Dennett, D.C. (2001), 'Surprise, surprise', commentary on O'Regan and Noë, 2001, *BBS*, **24** (5).
Noë, A., Pessoa, L. and Thompson, E. (2000), 'Beyond the grand illusion: what change blindness really teaches us about vision', *Visual Cognition*, **7**, pp. 93–106.
Noë, A. (2001), 'Experience and the active mind', *Synthese*, **129**, pp. 41–60.
Noë, A. and O'Regan, J.K. (2000), 'Perception, attention and the grand illusion', *Psyche*, **6** (15), URL: http://psyche.cs.monash.edu.au/v6/psyche-6-15-noe.html
O'Regan, J.K. and Noë, A. (2001), 'A sensorimotor theory of vision and visual consciousness', *Behavioral and Brain Sciences*, **24** (5).

Susan Blackmore

There Is No Stream of Consciousness

What is all this? What is all this stuff around me; this stream of experiences that I seem to be having all the time?[1]

Throughout history there have been people who say it is all illusion. I think they may be right. But if they are right what could this mean? If you just say 'It's all an illusion' this gets you nowhere — except that a whole lot of other questions appear. Why should we all be victims of an illusion instead of seeing things the way they really are? What sort of illusion is it anyway? Why is it like that and not some other way? Is it possible to see through the illusion? And if so what happens next.

These are difficult questions, but if the stream of consciousness is an illusion, we should be trying to answer them rather than more conventional questions about consciousness. I shall explore these questions though I cannot claim that I will answer them. In doing so I shall rely on two methods. First, there are the methods of science, based on theorising and hypothesis testing — on doing experiments to find out how the world works. Second, there is disciplined observation — watching experience as it happens to find out how it really seems. This sounds odd. You might say that your own experience is infallible — that if you say it is like this for you then no one can prove you wrong. I only suggest you look a bit more carefully. Perhaps then it won't seem quite the way you thought it did before. I suggest that both these methods are helpful for penetrating the illusion — if illusion it is.

We must be clear what is meant by the word 'illusion'. An illusion is not something that does not exist, such as a phantom or phlogiston. Rather, it is something that it is not what it appears to be, such as a visual illusion or a mirage. When I say that consciousness is an illusion I do not mean that consciousness does not exist. I mean that consciousness is not what it appears to be. If it seems to be a continuous stream of rich and detailed experiences, happening one after the other to a conscious person, this is the illusion.

What's the Problem?

For a drastic solution like 'it's all an illusion' even to be worth considering, there has to be a serious problem. There is. Essentially, it is the ancient mind–body

---

[1] This paper is based on a conference presentation at 'Towards a Science of Consciousness 2001' in Skövde, Sweden, 7–11 August, 2001. The oral style of the original has largely been retained.

Journal of Consciousness Studies, **9**, No. 5–6, 2002, pp. 17–28

problem, which recurs in different guises in different times. Victorian thinkers referred to the gulf between mind and brain as the 'great chasm' or the 'fathomless abyss'. Advances in neuroscience and artificial intelligence have changed the focus of the problem to what Chalmers (1995) calls the 'hard problem'; that is, to explain how subjective experience arises from the objective activity of brain cells.

Many people say that the hard problem does not exist, or that it is a pseudoproblem. I think they fall into two categories — those few who have seen the depths of the problem and come up with some insight into it, and those who just skate over the abyss. The latter group might heed Nagel's advice when he says 'Certain forms of perplexity — for example, about freedom, knowledge, and the meaning of life — seem to me to embody more insight than any of the supposed solutions to those problems' (Nagel, 1986, p. 4).

This perplexity can easily be found. For example, pick up any object — a cup of tea or a pen will do — and just look, smell, and feel its texture. Do you believe there is a real *objective* cup there with actual tea in it, made of atoms and molecules? Aren't you also having a private *subjective* experience of the cup and the taste of the tea — the 'what it is like' for you? What is this experience made of? It seems to be something completely different from actual tea and molecules. When the objective world out there and our subjective experiences of it seem to be such different kinds of thing, how can one be caused by, or arise from, or even depend upon, the other?

The intractability and longevity of these problems suggests to me that we are making a fundamental mistake in the way we think about consciousness — perhaps right at the very beginning. So where is the beginning? For William James, whose 1890 *Principles of Psychology* is deservedly a classic, the beginning is our undeniable experience of the 'stream of consciousness'; that unbroken, ever-changing flow of ideas, perceptions, feelings and emotions that make up our lives. In a famous passage he says 'Consciousness . . . does not appear to itself chopped up in bits . . . it flows. A "river" or a "stream" are the metaphors by which it is most naturally described. In talking of it hereafter, let us call it the stream of thought, of consciousness, or of subjective life' (James, 1890, i, p. 239). He referred to the stream of consciousness as '. . . the ultimate fact for psychology' (James, 1890, i, p. 360).

James took introspection as his starting method, and the stream of consciousness as its object. 'Introspective Observation is what we have to rely on first and foremost and always. The word introspection need hardly be defined (it means, of course, the looking into our own minds and reporting what we there discover). Everyone agrees that we there discover states of consciousness. . . . I regard this belief as the most fundamental of all the postulates of Psychology, and shall discard all curious inquiries about its certainty as too metaphysical for the scope of this book.' (1890, i, p. 185.)

He quotes at length from Mr. Shadworth Hodgson, who says:

> What I find when I look at my consciousness at all is that what I cannot divest myself of, or not have in consciousness, if I have any consciousness at all, is a sequence of

different feelings. I may shut my eyes and keep perfectly still, and try not to contribute anything of my own will; but whether I think or do not think, whether I perceive external things or not, I always have a succession of different feelings. . . . Not to have the succession of different feelings is not to be conscious at all (quoted in James, 1890, i, p. 230).

James adds 'Such a description as this can awaken no possible protest from any one'. I am going to protest. I shall challenge two aspects of the traditional stream; first that it has rich and detailed contents, and second that there is one continuous sequence or succession of contents.

Before we go any further it is worth considering how it seems to you. I say this because sometimes people propose novel solutions to difficult problems only to find that everyone else says 'Oh I knew that all along'. Many people say that it feels something like this. *I feel as though I am somewhere inside my head looking out. I can see and hear and feel and think. The impressions come along in an endless stream; pictures, sounds, feelings, mental images and thoughts appear in my consciousness and then disappear again. This is my 'stream of consciousness' and I am the continuous conscious self who experiences it.*

If this is how it seems to you then you probably also believe that at any given time there have to be contents of your conscious stream — some things that are 'in' your consciousness and others that are not. So, if you ask the question 'what am I conscious of now?' or 'what was I conscious of at time t?' then there has to be an answer.

For many years now I have been getting my students to ask themselves as many times as possible every day 'Am I conscious now?'. Typically, they find the task unexpectedly hard to do, and hard to remember to do. But when they do it, they find some very odd effects. First, they often report that they always seem to be conscious when they ask the question, but become less and less sure about whether they were conscious a moment before. With more practice they say that asking the question itself makes them more conscious, and that they can extend this consciousness from a few seconds to perhaps a minute or two. What does this say about consciousness the rest of the time?

Just this starting exercise (we go on to various elaborations of it as the course progresses) begins to change many students' assumptions about their own experience. In particular they become less sure that there are always contents in their stream of consciousness. How does it seem to you? It is worth deciding at the outset because this is what I am going to deny. I suggest that there is no stream of consciousness. And there is no definite answer to the question 'What am I conscious of now?'. Being conscious is just not like that.

I shall try to explain why, using examples from two senses; vision and hearing.

The Stream of Vision

When we open our eyes and look around it seems as though we are experiencing a rich and ever-changing picture of the world; what I shall call our 'stream of vision'. Probably many of us go further and develop some sort of theory about what is going on — something like this perhaps.

'When we look around the world, unconscious processes in the brain build up a more and more detailed representation of what is out there. Each glance provides a bit more information to add to the picture. This rich mental representation is what we see at any time. As long as we are looking around there is a continuous stream of such pictures. This is our visual experience.'

There are at least two threads of theory here. The first is the idea that there is a unified stream of conscious visual impressions to be explained, what Damasio (1999) calls 'the movie-in-the-brain'. The second is the idea that seeing means having internal mental pictures — that the world is represented in our heads. People have thought this way at least for several centuries, perhaps since Leonardo da Vinci first described the eye as a camera obscura and Kepler explained the optics of the eye (Lindberg, 1976). Descartes' famous sketches showed how images of the outside world appear in the non-material mind and James, like his Victorian contemporaries, simply assumed that seeing involves creating mental representations. Similarly, conventional cognitive psychology has treated vision as a process of constructing representations.

Perhaps these assumptions seem unremarkable, but they land us in difficulty as soon as we appreciate that much of vision is unconscious. We seem forced to distinguish between conscious and unconscious processing; between representations that are 'in' the stream of consciousness and those that are 'outside' it. Processes seem to start out unconscious and then 'enter consciousness' or 'become conscious'. But if all of them are representations built by the activity of neurons, what is the difference? What makes some into conscious representations and others not?

Almost every theory of consciousness we have confronts this problem and most try to solve it. For example, global workspace (GW) theories (for example, Baars, 1988) explicitly have a functional space, the workspace, which is a serial working memory in which the conscious processing occurs. According to Baars, information in the GW is made available (or displayed, or broadcast) to an unconscious audience in the rest of the brain. The 'difference' is that processing in the GW is conscious and that outside of it is not.

There are many varieties of GWT. In Dennett's (2001) 'fame in the brain' metaphor, as in his previous multiple drafts theory (Dennett, 1991 and see below), becoming conscious means contributing to some output or result (fame is the aftermath, not something additional to it). But in many versions of GWT being conscious is equated with being available, or on display, to the rest of the system (for example, Baars, 1988; Dehaene and Naccache, 2001). The question remains; the experiences in the stream of consciousness are those that are available to the rest of the system but why does this availability turn previously unconscious physical processes into subjective experiences?

As several authors have pointed out there seems to be a consensus emerging in favour of GWTs. I believe the consensus is wrong. GWTs are doomed because they try to explain something that does not exist — a stream of conscious experiences emerging from the unconscious processes in the brain.

The same problem pervades the whole enterprise of searching for the neural correlates of consciousness. For example, Kanwisher (2001) suggests that the neural correlates of the contents of visual awareness are represented in the ventral pathway — assuming, as do many others, that visual awareness has contents and that those contents are representations. Crick asks 'What is the "neural correlate" of visual awareness? Where are these "awareness neurons"; are they in a few places or all over the brain and do they behave in any special way?' One might think that these are rhetorical questions but he goes on '. . . this knowledge may help us to locate the awareness neurons we are looking for' (Crick, 1994, p. 204). Clearly he, like others, is searching for the neural correlates of that stream of conscious visual experiences. He admits that '. . . so far we can locate no single region in which the neural activity corresponds exactly to the vivid picture of the world we see in front of our eyes' (Crick, 1994, p. 159). Nevertheless, he obviously assumes that there is such a 'vivid picture'. What if there is not? In this case he, and others, are hunting for something that can never be found.

I suggest that there is no stream of vivid pictures that appear in consciousness. There is no movie-in-the-brain. There is no stream of vision. And if we think there is we are victims of the grand illusion.

Change blindness is the most obvious evidence against the stream of vision. In 1991 Dennett reported unpublished experiments by Grimes who used a laser tracker to detect people's eye movements and then change the picture they were looking at just when they moved their eyes. The changes were so large and obvious that under normal circumstances they could hardly be missed, but when made during saccades, the changes went unnoticed. In fact expensive eye trackers are not necessary. I suggested moving the whole picture instead, and this produced the same effects (Blackmore *et al.*, 1995). Other, even simpler, methods have since been developed, and change blindness observed with brief blank flashes between pictures, with image flicker, during cuts in movies or during blinks (Simons, 2000).

That the findings are genuinely surprising is confirmed in experiments in which people were asked to predict whether they or others would notice the changes. A large metacognitive error was found — that is, people grossly overestimated their own and others' ability to detect change (Levin *et al.*, 2000). James long ago noted something similar; that we fail to notice that we overlook things.

> It is true that we may sometimes be tempted to exclaim, when once a lot of hitherto unnoticed details of the object lie before us, 'How could we ever have been ignorant of these things and yet have felt the object, or drawn the conclusion, as if it were a *continuum*, a *plenum*? There would have been *gaps* but we felt no gaps (James, 1890, p. 488).

Change blindness is not confined to artificial laboratory conditions. Simons and Levin (1998) produced a comparable effect in the real world with some clever choreography. In one study an experimenter approached a pedestrian on the campus of Cornell University to ask for directions. While they talked, two men rudely carried a door between them. The first experimenter grabbed the back of the door and the person who had been carrying it let go and took over the conversation. Only half of the pedestrians noticed the substitution. Again, when people are asked whether they think they would detect such a change they are convinced that they would — but they are wrong. Change blindness could also have serious consequences in ordinary life. For example, O'Regan *et al.*, (1999) showed that dangerous mistakes can be made by drivers or pilots when change blindness is induced by mud splashes on the windscreen.

Further experiments have shown that attention is required to notice a change. For example, there is the related phenomenon of 'inattentional blindness' (Mack and Rock, 1998) in which people attending to one item of a display fail to detect the appearance of unexpected new items, even when these are clearly visible or in the centre of the visual field. However, though attention is necessary to detect change, it is not sufficient. Levin and Simons (1997) created short movies in which various objects were changed, some in arbitrary locations and others in the centre of attention. In one case the sole actor in the movie went to answer the phone. There was a cut in which the camera angle changed and a different person picked up the phone. Only a third of the observers detected the change.

What do these results mean? They certainly suggest that from one saccade to the next we do not store very much information; for if we did we would surely notice the change. So the 'stream of vision' theory I described at the start has to be false. The richness of our visual world is an illusion (Blackmore *et al.*, 1995). Yet obviously something is retained otherwise there could be no sense of continuity and we would not even notice if the entire scene changed. Theorists vary in how much, and what sort of, information they claim is retained.

Perhaps the simplest interpretation is given by Simons and Levin (1998). During each visual fixation we experience a rich and detailed visual world. This picture is only detailed in the centre, but it is nevertheless a rich visual experience. From that we extract the meaning or gist of the scene. Then when we move our eyes the detailed picture is thrown away and a new one substituted, but if the gist remains the same our perceptual system assumes the details are the same and so we do not notice changes. This, they argue, makes sense in the rapidly changing and complex world we live in. We get a phenomenal experience of continuity without too much confusion.

Slightly more radical is Rensink's (2000) view. He suggests that observers never form a complete representation of the world around them — not even during fixations. Rather, perception involves 'virtual representation'; representations of objects are formed one at a time as needed, and they do not accumulate. The impression of more is given because a new object can always be made 'just in time'. In this way an illusion of richness and continuity is created.

Finally, O'Regan (1992) goes even further in demolishing the ordinary view of seeing. He suggests that there is no need for internal representations at all because the world can be used as an external memory, or as its own best model — we can always look again. This interpretation fits with moves towards embodied cognition (for example, Varela *et al.*, 1991) and towards animate vision in artificial intelligence (Clark, 1997) in which mind, body and world work together, and sensing is intertwined with acting. It is also related to the sensorimotor theory of perception proposed by O'Regan and Noë (2001). On this view seeing is a way of acting; of exploring the environment. Conscious visual experiences are generated not by building representations but by mastering sensorimotor contingencies. What remains between saccades is not a picture of the world, but the information needed for further exploration. A study by Karn and Hayhoe (2000) confirms that spatial information required to control eye movements is retained across saccades. This kind of theory is dramatically different from existing theories of perception. It entails no representation of the world at all.

It is not yet clear which of these interpretations, if any, is correct but there is no doubt about the basic phenomenon and its main implication. Theories that try to explain the contents of the stream of vision are misguided. There is no stable, rich visual representation in our minds that could be the contents of the stream of consciousness.

Yet it seems there is, doesn't it? Well, does it? We return here to the problem of the supposed infallibility of our own private experiences. Each of us can glibly say 'Well, I know what my experience is like and it is a stream of visual pictures of the world, and nothing you say can take away my experience'. What then do we make of the experiments that suggest that anyone who says this is simply wrong?

I suggest that we all need to look again — and look very hard, with persistence and practice. Experimental scientists tend to eschew personal practice of this kind. Yet we should encourage it for two reasons. First, we cannot avoid bringing implicit theories to bear on how we view our own experiences and what we say about them. So perhaps we should do this explicitly. As we study theories of consciousness, we can try out the proposals against the way it seems to us. As we do so our own experience changes — I would say deepens. As an example, take theories about change blindness. Many people find the evidence surprising because they are sure that they have rich visual pictures in their mind whenever they are looking at something. If you ask 'What am I conscious of now?' again and again, this certainty begins to fall apart, and the change blindness evidence seems less surprising. This must surely help us to become better critics. At the very least it will help us to avoid dismissing theories of consciousness because of false assumptions we make about our own experiences.

The second reason is that this kind of practice can give rise to completely new hypotheses about consciousness. And this in turn can lead to testable predictions and new experiments. If these are derived from a deeper understanding of one's own awareness then they are more likely to be productive than those based on the mistake of believing in the stream of consciousness.

Note that what I am proposing here is first-person practice — first-person discipline — first-person methods of inquiry. But the results of all this practice will be words and actions; saying things to oneself and others. This endeavour only becomes science when it is put to use in this way and it is then, of course, third-person science.

How does one do it? There have been many methods developed for taking 'the view from within' (Varela and Shear, 1999) but I am suggesting something quite simple here. Having learned about the results of the change blindness research we should look hard and persistently at our own visual experiences. Right now is there a rich picture here in my experience? If there seems to be, something must be wrong, so what is wrong? Look again, and again. After many years of doing this kind of practice, every day, it no longer seems to me that there is a stream of vision, as I described at the start. The research has changed not only my intellectual understanding of vision but the very experience of seeing itself.

The Stream of Sounds

Listening to what is going on it might seem as though there is a stream of sounds to match the stream of pictures. Suppose we are listening to a conversation, then turn our attention to the music in the background, and then to the conversation again. We may say that at first the conversation was in the conscious stream while the music remained unconscious, then they reversed and so on. If asked 'what sounds were in your stream of consciousness at a particular time?' you might be sure that there definitely was an answer, even if you can't exactly remember what it was. This follows from the idea that there is a stream of consciousness, and sounds must either be in it or not.

Some simple, everyday experiences cast doubt on this natural view. To take a much-used favourite, imagine you are reading and just as you turn the page you become aware that the clock is striking. You hadn't noticed it before, but now you feel as though you were aware of it all along. You can even remember that it has struck four times already and you can now go on counting. What has happened here? Were the first three 'dongs' really outside the stream (unconscious) and have now been pulled out of memory and put in the stream? If so, what was happening when the first one struck, while you were still reading? Was the sound out of the stream at the time, but after you turned the page it just felt as though it had been in there all along — with the contents of the previous page — even though it wasn't really? Or have you gone back in time and changed the contents of the stream retrospectively? Or what? You might think up some other elaborations to make sense of it but I don't think any will be very simple or convincing (in the same spirit, Dennett [1991] contrasts Orwellian with Stalinesque revisions). The trouble all comes about because of the idea that there is a stream of consciousness and things are either in or out of it.

There are many other examples one could use to show the same thing. For example, in a noisy room full of people talking you may suddenly switch your attention because someone has said 'Guess who I saw with Anya the other day — it was Bernard'. You prick up your ears — surely not — you think. At this point you seem to have been aware of the whole sentence as it was spoken. But were you really? The fact is that you would never have noticed it at all if she had concluded the sentence with a name that meant nothing to you.

Even simpler than this is the problem with all speech. You need to accumulate a lot of serial information before the meaning of a sentence becomes unambiguous. What was in the stream of consciousness while all this was happening? Was it just meaningless words? Gobbledegook? Did it switch from gobbledegook to words half way through? It doesn't feel like that. It feels as though you listened and heard a meaningful sentence as it went along, but this is impossible.

Or take just one word, or listen to a blackbird trill its song. Only once the trill is complete, the word finished, can you know what it was that you heard. What was in the stream of consciousness before this point? Would it help to go even smaller? to try to break the stream down into its constituent bits? Perhaps there is a stream of raw feels, or indivisible bits of conscious stuff out of which the larger chunks are made. The introspectionists assumed this must be the case and tried — in vain — to find the units. James did a thorough job of disposing of such ideas in 1890, concluding 'No one ever had a simple sensation by itself' (James, 1890, i, p. 224) and there have been many objections since. There is no easy way to answer these questions about what really was in the stream of consciousness at a given time. Perhaps the idea of a stream of consciousness is itself the problem.

Of course we should have known all this. Dennett (1991) pointed out much the same using the colour phi phenomenon and the cutaneous rabbit. To produce colour phi a red light is flashed in one place and then a green light flashed a short distance away. Even on the first trial, observers do not see two distinct lights flashing, but one moving light that changes from red to green somewhere in the middle. But how could they have known what colour the light was going to turn into? If we think in terms of the stream of consciousness we are forced to wonder what was in the stream when the light seemed to be in the middle — before the second light came on.

There's something backwards about all this. As though consciousness is somehow trailing along behind or making things up after the fact. Libet's well-known experiments showed that about half a second of continuous cortical activity is required for consciousness, so consciousness cannot be instant. But we should not conclude that there is a stream of consciousness that runs along half a second behind the real world; this still wouldn't solve the chiming clock problem. Instead, I suggest that the problem lies with the whole idea of the stream.

Dennett (1991) formulated this in terms of the Cartesian Theatre — that non-existent place where consciousness happens — where everything comes together and I watch the private show (my stream of experiences) in my own theatre of the mind. He referred to those who believe in the existence of the Cartesian Theatre as Cartesian materialists. Most contemporary consciousness researchers deny being Cartesian materialists. Typically, they say that they do not believe that 'everything comes together' at a point in the brain, or even a particular area in the brain. For example, in most GWTs the activity of the GW is widely distributed in the brain. In Edelman and Tononi's (2000) theory neural activity in a widely distributed dynamic core underlies conscious experience.

However, many of these same theorists use phrases that imply a show in the non-existent theatre; such phrases as 'the information in consciousness', 'items enter consciousness', 'representations become conscious', or 'the contents of consciousness'. But consciousness is not a container — whether distributed or not. And, if there is no answer to the question 'what is in my consciousness now?', such phrases imply assumptions about something that does not exist. Of course, it is difficult to write clearly about consciousness, and people may write this way when they do not really mean to imply a show in a Cartesian Theatre. Nevertheless, we should beware these phrases. If there is an answer to the question 'what is in my consciousness now?', then it makes sense to speak of things 'entering consciousness' and so on. If there is no answer it does not.

How can there not be an answer? How can there not be a stream of consciousness or a show in the theatre of the mind? Baars claims that 'all of our unified models of mental functioning today are theater metaphors; it is essentially all we have' (1997, p. 7) but it is not. It is possible to think about consciousness in other ways — I would say not just possible but necessary.

Dennett's own suggestion is the theory of multiple drafts. Put simply, it is this. At any time there are multiple constructions of various sorts going on in the brain — multiple parallel descriptions of what's going on. None of these is 'in' consciousness while others are 'out' of it. Rather, whenever a probe is put in — for example, a question asked or a behaviour precipitated — a narrative is created. The rest of the time there are lots of contenders in various stages of revision in different parts of the brain, and no final version. As he puts it (Dennett, 1991), 'there are no fixed facts about the stream of consciousness independent of particular probes' (p. 138). 'Just what we are conscious of within any particular time duration is not defined independently of the probes we use to precipitate a narrative about that period. Since these narratives are under continual revision, there is no single narrative that counts as the canonical version, . . . the events that happened in the stream of consciousness of the subject' (p. 136).

I would put it slightly differently. I want to replace our familiar idea of a stream of consciousness with that of illusory backwards streams. At any time in the brain a whole lot of different things are going on. None of these is either 'in' or 'out' of consciousness, so we don't need to explain the 'difference' between conscious and unconscious processing. Every so often something happens to create what seems to have been a stream. For example, we ask 'Am I conscious now?'. At this point a retrospective story is concocted about what was in the stream of consciousness a moment before, together with a self who was apparently experiencing it. Of course, there was neither a conscious self nor a stream, but it now seems as though there was. This process goes on all the time with new stories being concocted whenever required. At any time that we bother to look, or ask ourselves about it, it seems as though there is a stream of consciousness going on. When we don't bother to ask, or to look, it doesn't, but then we don't notice so it doesn't matter. This way the grand illusion is concocted.

There are some odd implications of this view. First, as far as neuroscience is concerned we should not expect always to find one global workspace, or other unified correlate of the contents of consciousness. With particular sorts of probes there may, for a time, be such a global unification but at other times there may be several integrated patterns going on simultaneously, any of which might end up being retrospectively counted as contents of a stream of consciousness. Second, the backwards streams may overlap with impunity. Information from one ongoing process may end up in one stream, while information from another parallel process ends up in a different stream precipitated a bit later but referring to things that were going on simultaneously. There is no requirement for there really to be only one conscious stream at a time — even though it ends up seeming that way.

This is particularly helpful for thinking about the stream of sounds because sounds only make sense when information is integrated over appreciable lengths of time. As an example, imagine you are sitting in the garden and can hear a passing car, a bird singing, and some children shouting in the distance, and that you switch attention rapidly between them. If there were one stream of consciousness then each time attention switched you would have to wait while enough information came into the stream to identify the sound — to hear it as a passing car. In fact, attention can switch much faster than this. A new backwards stream can be created very quickly and the information it uses may overlap with that used in another stream a moment later, and another, and so on. So at time t was the bird song really in your stream of consciousness or was it the children's shouting? There is no answer.

Is it really this way? Do you want to protest that it doesn't seem this way? As with vision it is possible to look harder into one's own experience of sound and the results can be quite strange. Thinking about the chiming clocks, and listening as sounds come and go, the once-obvious linear stream begins to disappear.

Looking Harder

I have suggested that we need to look hard into our own experience, but what does this mean? How can we look? If the models sketched above are correct then looking means putting in a probe and this precipitates a backwards stream. So we cannot catch ourselves not seeming to be having a stream of consciousness. As William James so aptly put it 'The attempt at introspective analysis in these cases is in fact like seizing a spinning top to catch its motion, or trying to turn up the gas quickly enough to see how the darkness looks' (James, 1890, i, p. 244).

The modern equivalent is the metaphor of the fridge door. Is the light always on inside the fridge? You may keep opening the door, as quickly as you can, but you can never catch it out — every time you open it, the light is on.

Things, however, are not quite that bad for the stream of consciousness. We do, after all, have those obvious examples such as the chiming clock and the meaningless half a word to go on. And we can build on this. But it takes practice.

What kind of practice? A good start is calming the mind. There are many meditation traditions whose aim is to see the mind for what it really is, and all of these begin with calming the mind. You might say that at first it is more like a raging torrent or even a stormy ocean than a stream. To see whether there even is a stream we need to slow everything down. This is not easy. Indeed, it can take many years of diligent practice, though some people seem to be able to do it much more easily than others. Nevertheless, with a calm mind it is easier to concentrate, and to concentrate for longer.

Now we can ask 'What am I hearing now?'. At first, there seems always to be an answer. 'I am hearing the traffic' or 'I am hearing myself ask the question in my head', but with practice the answer becomes less obvious. It is possible to pick up the threads of various sounds (the clock ticking, the traffic, ones own breathing, the people shouting across the road) and notice in each case that you seem to have been hearing it for some time. When you get good at this it seems obvious that you can give more than one answer to the question 'what was I hearing at time t?'. When you can do this there no longer seems to be a single stream of sounds.

My purpose here is not to say that this new way of hearing is right, or even better than the previous way. After all, I might be inventing some idiosyncratic delusion of my own. My intention is to show that there are other ways of experiencing the world, and finding them can help us throw off the false assumptions that are holding back our study of consciousness. If we can find a personal way out of always believing we are experiencing a stream of consciousness, then we are less likely to keep getting stuck in the Cartesian Theatre.

I asked at the outset 'What is all this? What is all this stuff — all this experience that I seem to be having, all the time?'. I have now arrived at the answer that all this stuff is a grand illusion. This has not solved the problems of consciousness, but at least it tells us that there is no point trying to explain the difference between things that are in consciousness and those that are not because there is no such difference. And it is a waste of time trying to explain the contents of the stream of consciousness because the stream of consciousness does not exist.

References

Baars, B.J. (1988), *A Cognitive Theory of Consciousness* (Cambridge: Cambridge University Press).

Baars, B.J. (1997), *In the Theatre of Consciousness: The Workspace of the Mind* (New York: OUP).

Blackmore, S.J., Brelstaff, G., Nelson, K. and Troscianko, T. (1995), 'Is the richness of our visual world an illusion? Transsaccadic memory for complex scenes', *Perception*, **24**, pp. 1075–81.

Chalmers, D.J. (1995), 'Facing up to the problem of consciousness', *Journal of Consciousness Studies*, **2** (3), pp. 200–19.

Clark, A. (1997), *Being There: Putting Brain, Body, and World Together Again* (Cambridge, MA: MIT Press).

Crick, F. (1994), *The Astonishing Hypothesis* (New York, Scribner's).

Damasio, A. (1999), *The Feeling of What Happens* (London: Heinemann).

Dehaene, S. and Naccache, L. (2001), 'Towards a cognitive neuroscience of consciousness: Basic evidence and a workspace framework', *Cognition*, **79**, pp. 1–37.

Dennett, D.C. (1991), *Consciousness Explained* (London: Little, Brown & Co).

Edelman, G.M. & Tononi, G. (2000), *Consciousness: How Matter Becomes Imagination* (London: Penguin).

James, W. (1890), *The Principles of Psychology* (London: MacMillan).

Kanwisher, N. (2001), 'Neural events and perceptual awareness', *Cognition*, **79**, pp. 89–113.

Karn, K. and Hayhoe, M. (2000), 'Memory representations guide targeting eye movements in a natural task', *Visual Cognition*, **7**, pp. 673–703.

Levin, D.T., Momen, N. and Drivdahl, S.B. (2000), 'Change blindness blindness: The metacognitive error of overestimating change-detection ability', *Visual Cognition*, **7**, pp. 397–412.

Levin, D.T. and Simons, D.J. (1997), 'Failure to detect changes to attended objects in moton pictures', *Psychonomic Bulletin and Review*, **4**, pp. 501–6.

Lindberg, D.C. (1976), *Theories of Vision from Al-Kindi to Kepler* (University of Chicago Press).

Mack, A. and Rock, I. (1998), *Inattentional Blindness* (Cambridge, MA: MIT Press).

Nagel, T. (1986), *The View from Nowhere* (New York; Oxford University Press).

O'Regan, J.K. (1992), 'Solving the "real" mysteries of visual perception: The world as an outside memory', *Canadian Journal of Psychology*, **46**, pp. 461–88.

O'Regan, J.K. and Noë, A. (2001), 'A sensorimotor theory of vision and visual consciousness', *Behavioral and Brain Sciences*, **24** (5).

O'Regan, J.K., Rensink, R.A. and Clark, J.J. (1999), 'Change blindness as a result of "mudsplashes"', *Nature*, **398**, p. 34.

Rensink, R.A. (2000), 'The dynamic representation of scenes', *Visual Cognition*, **7**, pp. 17–42.

Simons, D.J. (2000), 'Current approaches to change blindness', *Visual Cognition*, **7**, pp. 1–15.

Simons, D.J. and Levin, D.T. (1998), 'Failure to detect changes to people during real-world interaction', *Psychonomic Bulletin and Review*, **5**, pp. 644–9.

Varela, F.J. and Shear, J. (ed. 1999), *The View from Within* (Thorverton, UK: Imprint Academic).

Varela, F.J., Thomson, E. and Rosch, E. (1991), *The Embodied Mind* (London: MIT Press).

Bruce Bridgeman

The Grand Illusion
and Petit Illusions

Interactions of Perception and Sensory Coding

The Grand Illusion, the experience of a rich phenomenal visual world supported by a poor internal representation of that world, is echoed by petit illusions of the same sort. We can be aware of several aspects of an object or pattern, even when they are inconsistent with one another, because different neurological mechanisms code the various aspects separately. They are bound not by an internal linkage, but by the structure of the world itself. Illusions exploit this principle by introducing inconsistencies into normally consistent patterns of stimulation.

The Grand Illusion (Noë & O'Regan, 2000; Noë *et al.*, 2000; O'Regan & Noë, 2001) is a disturbing contrast between what the visual system offers and what the viewer perceives. To most people, the visual world appears in sharp, vivid focus and full colour throughout its extent. It takes a lecture demonstration of the limits of peripheral vision to convince astonished undergraduates that their internal representation of the visual world is much poorer than it seems, that acuity for both form and colour drop off rapidly with distance from the fovea. This mismatch between high-quality perception and low-quality sensory information is what defines the Grand Illusion. Illusions have a long history in the study of perception, predating even the experimental phase of the discipline. They are of interest not as entertaining parlour tricks, but for what they reveal about the normal processes of perception. Most illusions are not grand, but are restricted to a particular aspect of an object or pattern's appearance.

The Design of Sensory Systems

If the visual system had been designed all at once, like a stereo or a computer, engineers might have given it a geometric engine to map all the spatial relationships that would be needed, and a powerful, general pattern recognizer to compare input with stored information. Inside the brain, however, we find not a single visual area but more than twenty (Felleman and Van Essen, 1991).

Journal of Consciousness Studies, **9**, No. 5–6, 2002, pp. 29–34

Similarly, the brain uses not general solutions but a welter of limited algorithms and heuristics that deal with limited problems. Instead of general solutions, the brain offers a bag of 'cheap tricks' to apply to problems of pattern recognition (Ramachandran, 1990). Each trick applies in only a limited setting. Normally, a cheap trick can be expressed in a few words, requiring no mathematics.

An example of such a trick is the familiar experience of seeing a bump on a surface, such as a rivet, that is illuminated from above. The bump in the surface appears convex only as long as you assume that the illumination is coming from above. If you can convince yourself that the illumination is coming from below, the bump will pop in and appear as a concavity on the surface. The brain's default assumption is that illumination comes from above, as it normally does in the natural world, and this source of information can be used to interpret patterns in the world. The cheap trick might read something like 'if the top of a disturbance in a surface is darker, there is a dimple'. It complements 'if the top of a disturbance in a surface is lighter, there is a bump'.

Another cheap trick specifies that all objects are three-dimensional, for even the most meagre information will demand a three-dimensional solution. Try interpreting the surface in Fig. 1 as a two-dimensional surface.

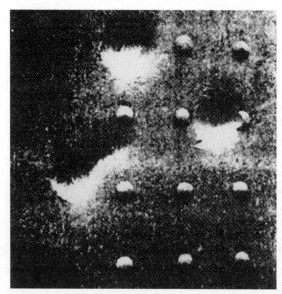

Figure 1. A surface with dimples and bumps, defined only by shading by a localized illuminant.

Application to Illusions

Some cheap tricks are so simple that they sound ridiculous. An ecologically generalized version of the Ebbinghaus illusion, illustrated in Fig. 2, is based on two simple rules: First, the smallest of a bunch of things is pretty small, and second, the biggest of a bunch of things is pretty big. The smallest thing in the top array is the smaller circle, while the biggest thing in the bottom array is the larger circle. It doesn't sound like sophisticated pattern processing, or even good kindergarten wisdom, but it usually works. Only in simplified, systematically biased environments like that in Fig. 1 do the generalizations lead us astray.

The visual system relies on an assumption of a random or near-random distribution of sizes of objects to make this trick work. In the case of the Ebbinghaus illusion, the normally safe assumption of randomness is systematically violated. The assumption is part of a rich tradition in psychology discussing the role of generic or non-accidental views, a perceptual 'cosmological principle', related to a concept used by cosmologists to emphasize that their data should be interpreted as though there is nothing unique about the position of the earth in the cosmos. We circle an average star, at an average location in an average galaxy.

Similarly, there is an assumption built into every visual system that there is nothing unique about the station point of the eye. It is unlikely, after all, that we should just happen to find ourselves at the start of a continuously changing texture density, or looking at a cube from the one angle at which it projects as a hexagon. More likely, the texture density is uniform and it is distance that causes the retinally projected sizes of texture elements to change in a non-random way

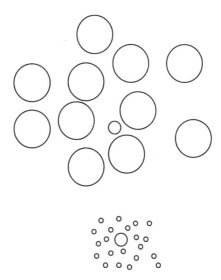

Figure 2. A modification of the traditional Ebbinghaus illusion, using irregular textures rather than circular arrays of inducing objects. The small circle in the top cluster and the large circle in the bottom cluster are the same size.

across the visual field. A projection of a hexagon on the retina is more likely to be a hexagon seen from a generic angle than a cube seen from a unique station point.

Another violation of structural assumptions occurs in the Poggendorff and the Müller–Lyer illusions (Fig. 3). These illusions reveal a dual nature of perception — on one hand, we can perfectly well perceive the fine structure of the illusion figures, even at the vertices where the illusions must originate. On the other hand, we perceive the illusions as though this fine structure were not resolvable. The inconsistency between the fine structure and the gross structure in these figures violates assumptions of consistency upon which the visual system normally relies to interpret the visual world.

Illusions as Inconsistent Codings

These illusions rely not on easily discernable cheap tricks, but on the tenuous relationship between awareness and the neural coding of sensory properties. Explaining the source of the illusions requires a brief diversion into the

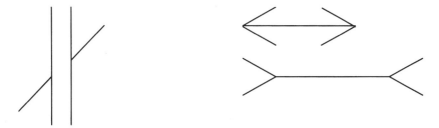

Figure 3. The Poggendorff illusion (left) and the Müller–Lyer illusion (right).

physiology of information coding in the visual cortex. Each neuron in that cortex responds to a region of space, a 'receptive field'. The structure of the receptive field is like the structure of ripples in a pond just after an elongated object is dropped into it: waves and troughs (excitatory and inhibitory regions) alternate, and decrease in magnitude away from the centre. Neurons respond best to elongated patterns; all receptive fields have about the same shape but their sizes vary. The size of a receptive field is measured in spatial frequency, the number of cycles of waves and troughs one encounters in a degree of visual angle; thus their unit is cycles/degree. In humans, the smallest receptive fields are sensitive to about 30 cycles/degree, the largest to perhaps 0.1 cycles/degree. Each neuron's receptive field can be characterized by its orientation, spatial frequency, and position in the visual field.

The dominant explanation for the mechanism of the Müller–Lyer and Poggendorff illusions is that the positions of the critical vertices are coded by low spatial frequency 'blob' detectors, visual neurons whose receptive fields are very large. The receptive fields coding the lengths of the Müller–Lyer figure's lines, for example, must be large enough to encompass the entire lengths of the lines. Receptive fields sensitive to such low spatial frequencies cannot encode the details of the geometry at the vertices in the illusion; they see only the gross structure of the figure. Since the gross structure of the fins-out figure really is longer than the gross structure of the fins-in figure, the illusion in a sense is not an illusion at all — it is literally present in the low spatial frequency domain (Ginsburg, 1984). Because the receptive field optimally sensitive to the fins-out line really is larger, we perceive that line as longer.

In the meantime, other receptive fields of higher spatial frequency are accurately coding the fine details of the geometry around the fins of the figure. For the fins-out figure we can use the higher spatial frequency information to see that the horizontal line whose length we are to judge does not reach through the entire extent of the line. But that line appears longer nonetheless. We are in a sense both aware and unaware that the length of the line is confounded with the extraneous length added by the fins. The 'blob' coding necessary to judge the length of the lines does not interfere with the fine coding necessary to perceive the geometry of the vertices. Both properties are available simultaneously, even though they are contradictory.

This illusion occurs because we use different information to make different judgments about the same scene. Normally, the visual information at all scales is consistent (another cheap trick), but the illusions are designed to violate this assumption. We have a petit illusion in that we can see the fine detail, and therefore know everything about the figure. Knowledge about the size of the figure, though, comes from receptive fields that are too large to detect the detail. The result is an illusion that the detail is available, but it is available only in a special way — to inspect the local geometry. If we need to know about the big picture, the details are lost. Since local and global structures are consistent in most normal perceptual situations, there is no pressure to link the independent processing of details and of gross features.

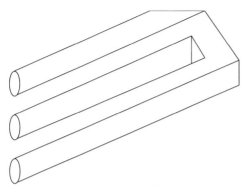

Figure 4. A variant of the 'devil's pitchfork'. A self-consistent structure on one side maps into a different self-consistent structure on the other.

The Poggendorff illusion has a similar explanation. The details of the geometry at the vertices are coded by small, high-spatial-frequency- receptive fields that are not deceived by the angles. Judgments about the positions of the lines, though, are biased by the asymmetric geometry, so that the low-spatial-frequency-receptive fields that best respond to the vertex regions do not line up. Again, the perceived pattern is really present in the figure, but only in the low spatial frequencies (Morgan, 1999; Bridgeman, 2001). Like all stimulus patterns, this one is analyzed not only by low-spatial-frequency filtering but also by other visual-processing algorithms, such as frames of reference, that affect the strength of the illusion (Spivey-Knowlton and Bridgeman, 1993).

Other visual experiences show how perception can be deceived at a higher level after the positions of lines and edges are already established. Figure 4, a version of the well-known 'devil's pitchfork', shows that the visual system uses the local geometry of lines and edges to infer visual structure. Since local geometry and global structure always agree for real-world objects, the strategy works very well. If the local geometry is violated at a more global level, however, the resulting 'impossible' figure cannot be resolved. The pitchfork relies on the poverty of line-drawing representations where figure and ground are identical uniform areas separated only by lines. A perceived surface that is figure because of its local geometric structure in one location becomes ground at another. The visual system reaches no conclusion about the figure because the cheap tricks that might resolve the ambiguity are exhausted. Normally, local-level solutions to the identity of an object will apply throughout the object, leaving simultaneous but contradictory interpretations of the figure at its two ends. The visual system's ability to interpret a consistent three-dimensional geometric object from a few two-dimensional lines enhances our ability to see consistent objects with little sensory input, and backfires only in contrived 'impossible' figures such as this one.

Such petit illusions are ubiquitous in perception, not only in vision but in other modalities as well. In audition, for instance, we hear melodies, timbres, patterns, even though at any instant there is only a single dimension, a momentary air pressure, in the stimulus. The rest of the auditory world is made available by temporal integration and structuring in the auditory system, aided by top-down expectations about what is present.

For instance, a gradually rising tone can begin very quietly at the bottom of a fixed tonal range, gradually increase in amplitude, and then decrease in amplitude as it reaches the top of the tonal range. As it begins to fade away, a second gradually rising tone begins quietly at the bottom of the tonal range, reaching its maximum amplitude as the first tone disappears. A third tone replaces the second in the same way and the process repeats indefinitely. The resulting and rather disturbing perception is of a tone that gradually rises forever, a consequence of the auditory cheap trick of sampling all of the sound available in a short time interval and judging whether the frequency is increasing, steady, or decreasing. The answer is always 'increasing' because the gradual replacement of one tone by another is too slow for this simple mechanism to pick up. In the world of real sounds the cheap trick works very well; it takes a contrived laboratory experience to deceive it.

Conclusion — Grand and Petit Illusions Unified

The disconnections that create grand and petit illusions usually do not bother us. Why not? In the normal visual world, the various ways of describing a sensory experience are consistent with one another. They are linked not by internal checks on consistency but by the structure of the world itself. What we had thought was a binding within us turns out to have been all around us all along in the structure of the world itself.

Applied to the grand illusion, this analysis relies on the consistency of the properties of the real world to give the impression of completeness. Since the world is assumed to be complete — a non-sensory assumption — the sensory systems have only the job of sampling the complete world at particular locations and along particular dimensions. The perception of a rich perceptual world, then, can result from failure to violate the completeness assumption. If I assume that the world is rich with detail at all scales, and my senses do not contradict my assumption, I can continue to perceive a rich world even while sampling only bits and pieces of it. In the same way, the petit illusions arise from the assumption of self- consistency of particular objects and patterns in the world. An observer can use local information to sample these objects with the confidence that the local solutions will apply to the whole object. Though contrived situations violate the consistency assumption and lead perception astray, in the real world the assumption serves us very well.

References

Bridgeman, B. (2001), 'Polarity reversal does not destroy the Poggendorff illusion', *Optic Express*, **9**, p. GV13.

Felleman, D.J. and Van Essen, D.C. (1991), 'Distributed hierarchical processing in the primate cerebral cortex', *Cerebral Cortex*, **1**, pp. 1–47.

Ginsburg, A. (1984), 'Visual form perception based on biological filtering', in *Sensory Experience, Adaptation, and Perception*, ed. L. Spillman and B. Wooten (Hillsdale, NJ: Lawrence Erlbaum).

Morgan, M.J. (1999), 'The Poggendorff illusion: a bias in the estimation of the orientation of virtual lines by second-stage filters', *Vision Research*, **39**, pp. 2361–80.

Noë, A. and O'Regan, A. (2000), 'Perception, attention and the grand illusion', *Psyche*, **6** (15) URL: http://psyche.cs.monash.edu.au/v6/psyche-6-15-noe.html

Noë, A., Thompson, E., Pessoa, L. (2000), 'Beyond the grand illusion: what change blindness really teaches us about vision', *Visual Cognition*, **7** (1/2/3), pp. 93–106.

O'Regan, J.K. and Noë, A. (2001), 'A sensorimotor account of vision and visual consciousness', *Behavioral and Brain Sciences*, **24** (5).

Ramachandran, V.S. (1990), 'Interactions between motion, depth, color and form: The utilitarian theory of perception', in *Vision: Coding and Efficiency*, ed. C. Blakemore (Cambridge: CUP).

Spivey-Knowlton, M. and Bridgeman, B. (1993), 'Spatial context affects the Poggendorff illusion', *Perception & Psychophysics*, **53**, pp. 467–74.

Eric Schwitzgebel

How Well Do We Know Our Own Conscious Experience?

The Case of Visual Imagery[1]

Philosophers tend to assume that we have excellent knowledge of our own current conscious experience or 'phenomenology'. I argue that our knowledge of one aspect of our experience, the experience of visual imagery, is actually rather poor. Precedent for this position is found among the introspective psychologists of the late nineteenth and early twentieth centuries. Two main arguments are advanced toward the conclusion that our knowledge of our own imagery is poor. First, the reader is asked to form a visual image, and it is expected that answering questions about certain basic features of that experience will be difficult. If so, it seems reasonable to suppose that people could be mistaken about those basic features of their own imagery. Second, it is observed that although people give widely variable reports about their own experiences of visual imagery, differences in report do not systematically correlate with differences on tests of skills that psychologists have often supposed to require visual imagery, such as mental rotation, visual creativity, and visual memory.

The guiding question of this special issue is 'Is the Visual World a Grand Illusion?' There are at least two distinct scenarios on which the answer to this question might be yes. The visual world might justly be called a 'grand illusion' if the properties we would naïvely attribute to the world on the basis of our visual experience are very different from the properties of the world as it really is, independently of our visual experience. Or we might call the visual world a grand illusion if our visual experiences are significantly at odds with our judgments about them, regardless of how things stand in the world beyond. In the latter case, the visual

[1] For helpful discussion of the issues in this paper, I would like to thank Mason Cash, Jonathan Cohen, Dillon Emerick, Bill Faw, Jim Garson, Mike Gordon, Russ Hurlburt, Peter Mandik, Stuart McKelvie, Alva Noë, Pauline Price, Wade Savage, the audience at the 2001 Society for Philosophy and Psychology meeting, and especially Nigel Thomas. Similar themes are pursued in Schwitzgebel & Gordon (2000) and Schwitzgebel (forthcoming), both available at http://faculty.ucr.edu/~eschwitz.

world is an illusion in the sense that nothing like the visual world as we naïvely take it to be actually exists; the stream of visual consciousness that flows through us has quite a different character.

In this paper, I will argue for a limited version of the second scenario, but pertaining to our *visual imagery* experience rather than to ordinary visual perception. In particular, I will argue that normal people in favourable circumstances make gross and enduring errors about the nature of their visual imagery experiences, i.e., that at least some people persistently and radically mistake the phenomenal character of their visual imagery. Perhaps support for this view will also indirectly lend plausibility to the corresponding thesis regarding visual experience in perception.

In taking this position, I stand at odds with much of the philosophical tradition that regards people as having some especially accurate 'privileged access' to their own current conscious experience or 'phenomenology'. In the middle of the twentieth century, especially in the analytic tradition, the dominant view appears to have been that we have infallible or 'incorrigible' access to, or are entitled to certainty about, our current conscious experience (for example, Lewis, 1946; Ewing, 1951; Ayer, 1963; Shoemaker, 1963; Rorty, 1970; see also Chalmers, forthcoming, and Gertler, 2001, for restricted contemporary articulations of this view). Although this view has fallen under attack in recent decades, most philosophers seem still to hold to some fairly robust notion of privileged access: Even if we are not infallible judges of our current conscious experience, it is generally assumed that we are nonetheless excellent, and circumstances must be unusually challenging in some respect for us to go seriously wrong. The putative examples of mistakes about conscious experience offered by philosophers have for the most part been limited to marginal or science-fiction cases, or cases of psychological stress or abnormality; or the mistakes have been hypothesized to be made only for a moment or near the threshold of discriminability; or (especially in the many citations of Nisbett & Wilson, 1977) the mistakes have been limited to the *causes* of our experiences rather than the experiences themselves (for example, Armstrong, 1963; Churchland, 1988; Hill, 1991; Audi, 1993; Kornblith, 1998). Few philosophers have offered examples, as I aim to do in this paper, of normal people in calm circumstances of quiet attention making radical mistakes about central features of their current conscious experience.[2]

My position, of course, depends on there being facts about our phenomenology or stream of consciousness about which it is possible to be right or wrong, and in particular that there are such facts about our visual imagery experiences. It also assumes that calling an experience 'conscious' is not tantamount to saying that one is aware of that experience in the sense that being aware of something implies that one is right about it. Additionally, I should make clear that the kinds of mistakes I

---

[2]   Dennett (1991) is a possible exception. Some of his examples seem to be interpretable as examples of mistakes about our own phenomenology, yet he also wants to grant that 'heterophenomenological' reports are incorrigible descriptions of 'what it's like' for the subject (see also Dennett, 2000). The Churchlands and Hilary Kornblith may also endorse the possibility of gross mistakes about conscious experience even in favourable circumstances; but if so, their examples do not show it, since they tend to be limited in the ways described above.

have in mind are not merely linguistic mistakes, admitted by all parties to this debate, that turn on difficulties of expression or the misconstrual of terms; and that I accept the mainstream view that our access to our own experiences is in some respects fundamentally different in kind from our access to other people's — though I insist that such difference in kind does not imply any special accuracy.

In some respects, the position I endorse traces back to the introspective psychology of the late nineteenth and early twentieth centuries. It was not uncommon for psychologists in this period to begin their textbooks with cautions about the difficulty of accurate introspection (for example, Külpe, 1893/1895; Titchener, 1900; 1901), or even to challenge each other's work by suggesting that their opponents failed accurately to introspect (for example, James, 1884; Angell, 1897; Woodworth, 1906; Titchener, 1915). Many felt that introspection was a skill that could improve substantially with dedicated cultivation (for example, in the course plotted by Titchener's 1902 lab manual) and that the reports of untutored introspectors should be treated warily. With all this I heartily agree. However, many introspective psychologists appear to have put too much faith in their own well-trained introspective capacities, which may have been more subject to bias than they thought (Boring, 1953); and some of them did not distinguish sufficiently between the conscious experiences revealed by introspection and the cognitive processes that we might now take to cause or underlie those experiences (especially in the English language literature: see Danziger, 1980).

Imagery was of central importance to introspective psychologists, and they thought that even well-trained introspectors could make serious mistakes about it. In the 'imageless thought' controversy of that period, for example, Külpe, Binet, Stout and their followers claimed that thought was possible without imagery, a view that Titchener and others adamantly denied (for contemporary reviews of this debate, see Angell, 1911; Ogden, 1911). Each side felt that the other was making serious introspective mistakes about the presence or absence of imagery in their thought.[3] Perky (1910) even seemed to show that well-trained introspectors could be tricked into making the most fundamental mistake about imagery, the mistake of confusing it with genuine sensory experience (of a dim, hazy, shimmering light source).

An earlier debate, more familiar to most philosophers, also apparently reflecting fundamental disagreement about the experience of imagery, was the debate between Locke and Berkeley about abstract ideas. Locke seems to have felt that he could form an image of a triangle that is 'neither oblique, nor rectangle, neither equilateral, equicrural, nor scalenon; but all and none of these at once' (1689/1975, p. 596).[4] Berkeley denied that he had the capacity to generate any such images (1710/1965). While Berkeley leaves open the possibility that

---

[3] But see Monson & Hurlburt (1993) for an argument that the introspective psychologists agreed in their introspections more than they thought they did.

[4] Since Locke says 'idea', not 'image', it is possible to interpret him as thinking of the idea of the triangle as non-imagistic. However, the standard view of Locke seems to be that ideas, on his view, are always imagistic (although not always *visually* imagistic). In any case, James (1890/1981) and Huxley (1895) clearly acknowledge the possibility of images with vague or indeterminate features, so they could substitute for Locke as opponents to Berkeley if necessary.

Locke's imagery is just very different from his own, it is evident that Berkeley felt the more plausible view to be that his own failure to experience abstract images was universal and that Locke simply got it wrong about his own conscious experience.

I believe that the participants in these historical debates were right to mistrust their opponents' reports of their imagery experiences: Imagery is difficult to introspect accurately, and even in favourable circumstances people can make large mistakes about their own current, conscious imagery. In arguing for this position, I will focus exclusively on visual imagery, as opposed to auditory, motor, or other types of imagery, since visual imagery has been the most broadly discussed. My argument has three main elements. First, I will ask the reader to reflect on her own experience of visual imagery; it is expected that answering even some fairly basic questions about that experience will be difficult. Second, I will describe the wide variability in narrative descriptions of imagery experiences, variability so extreme as to, I think, plausibly generate suspicions about the accuracy of those descriptions. Third, I will argue that psychologists have generally failed to find reliable relationships between differences in subjective reports of imagery and performance on cognitive tasks that plausibly require imagery. I will conclude by discussing some alternative explanations for the failure to find such relationships, including the possibility that unclear standards of reporting are to blame.

I: Hard Questions about the Experience of Visual Imagery

Let me ask you to reflect, then, on your own phenomenology as you form and maintain a visual image. Form a visual image of some familiar object, such as the front of your house. If you are now visualizing this, you presumably are having a conscious experience of imagery.[5] Let me now ask you some questions about that experience.

How much of the scene are you able vividly to visualize at once? Can you keep the image of your chimney vividly in mind at the same time you vividly imagine (or 'image') your front door? Or does the image of your chimney fade as your attention shifts to the door? If there is a focal part of your image, how much detail does it have? How stable is it? Supposing that you are not able to image the entire front of your house with equal clarity at once, does your image gradually fade away toward the periphery, or does it do so abruptly? Is there any imagery at all outside the immediate region of focus? If the image fades gradually away toward the periphery, does one lose colours before shapes? Do the peripheral elements of the image have colour at all before you think to assign a colour to them? Do any parts of the image? If some parts of the image have indeterminate colour before a colour is assigned, how is that indeterminacy experienced — as grey? — or is it not experienced at all? If images gradually fade from the centre and it is not a

---

[5] Often, I will call this conscious experience simply the 'experience' of imagery or of visual imagery. To my ear, the word 'experience' implies consciousness, although I know some do not hear it that way (for example, Carruthers, 1992), allowing for the possibility of 'unconscious experiences'. In the final section of this paper, I will briefly discuss the possibility of unconscious imagery (whether 'experienced' or not).

matter of the colour fading, what exactly are the half-faded images like? Are the shapes themselves somehow indeterminate, *contra* Berkeley? How much is visual imagery experience like the experience of seeing a picture, or having phosphenes, or afterimages, or dreams, or daydreams?

Most people of whom I ask such questions at some point stumble or feel uncertainty. They seem like *hard* questions — questions one stands a reasonable likelihood of getting wrong, even in circumstances of calm attention. Some readers, I am sure, will feel confident in answering all of these questions, and they may judge that all others should feel the same way. But if you feel as I do the difficulty and potential for error in at least some of these questions — if you think people could easily come to answer them incorrectly — then you are granting the possibility of normal, patient, reflective people in favourable circumstances making significant mistakes about their own current conscious experiences.

Many of these questions play on uncertainty about experience at the periphery of attention. Necessarily, the periphery is elusive: As soon as you move your attention toward the periphery to determine what it is like, the periphery moves somewhere else. Nevertheless, the periphery appears to constitute a significant part, if not the bulk, of our conscious experience (or if not, so much the better for my thesis, since many people attest to conscious awareness of things outside the focus of attention); so if you are wrong about the periphery, you are wrong about a major part of your conscious experience.

It has been objected to me in conversation that my asking such a barrage of questions artificially induces bewilderment in my respondents, either because some of my questions build in false presuppositions (for example, in assuming that images have a focal and peripheral region) or because attention to the questions detracts from the difficult task of maintaining a single, constant image. However, even if a respondent's confusion is a consequence of the format of my questions, it is nonetheless confusion about his own current conscious experience. That the confusion is artificially induced only undermines my thesis to the extent that it implies that he has not been reflecting on his experience in favourable circumstances. I put forward a large number of questions because not everyone will feel uncertainty about the same things, but I imagine that for any respondent we could cull out the questions he finds most difficult and return to them later at leisure. In my own case, at least, the outcome of such a procedure is not very different from the outcome when I consider a barrage of questions.

I also want to emphasize that I have no difficulty with the view that there is a level of detail beyond which it is inappropriate to ask questions. There may be no determinate answer to the question of how many speckles are on the speckled hen you are now imagining, just as there is no determinate answer to the question of exactly how tall Hamlet is. My questions are meant to generate uncertainty not about the number of bricks in the imagined chimney but about the higher-level questions, such as exactly how much detail the image specifies — whether there is or is not a determinate number of bricks.[6]

---

[6] I suppose it is possible that there is no determinate fact whether there is a determinate number of bricks or not. This position is, of course, distinct from the position that there is no determinate number of

II: Variability in Narrative Responses to Questions about Imagery

Since people differ substantially in their perceptual and cognitive abilities, it is reasonable to suppose that they will also differ in their visual imagery. However, as I will describe in this section, narrative reports of imagery vary widely even among apparently normal people — so much, I suggest, that we may reasonably be led to doubt the veracity of at least some of those reports. The ancient Chinese philosopher Mengzi says, 'When someone makes a shoe for a foot he has not seen, I am sure he will not produce a basket' (Lau, 1970) — for most traits, human variation exists within certain limits of normality.

In the 1870s, Francis Galton (1880; 1907) asked subjects to visualize a scene, such as their breakfast table as they sat down to it in the morning, and to describe various features of their resulting imagery, including its vividness, colour and breadth of field. He formally surveyed several hundred men and boys and gathered anecdotal reports from a variety of sources. This classic collection of narrative reports about imagery has to my knowledge remained unduplicated through the present (no doubt in part due to our current preference for quantifiable and easily replicable measures), and I shall rely on it as my primary evidence of the variability in narrative reports about imagery.[7]

Galton's respondents populate the full range from people who claim to have no imagery whatsoever to people who claim to have imagery as vivid and detailed as ordinary vision (or even more so), with a considerable number of apparently normal respondents at each extreme. Here are some quotes from subjects at the high end of the scale: 'The image that arises in my mind is perfectly clear. . . . I can see in my mind's eye just as well as if I was beholding the scene with my real eye' (1880, p. 310); 'All clear and bright; all the objects seem to me well defined at the same time' (1880, p. 305); 'The mental image appears to correspond in all respects with reality. I think it is as clear as the actual scene' (ibid.). Several respondents claim to be able to visualize an object from more than one angle at

---

bricks, and it has not to my knowledge been widely discussed. Such a position might arise from a pragmatic antirealism about visual imagery, on which talk about visual imagery is a useful fiction, and thus should not be abandoned altogether, but on which there is no fact of the matter whether a fiction that posits a determinate number of speckles is more useful than a fiction that does not; or it might arise from a view on which visual images are insufficiently stable to support predications about certain of their features over even the smallest duration of attention; or it may grow from some other motivation. If one accepts some such species of higher-level indeterminism about visual imagery, one might deploy it to explain why my respondents are so often baffled — but this explanation must be handled delicately if it is meant to preserve the view that the introspection of visual imagery is largely accurate, since many people are quite confident in their (diverse, and on this view not determinately true) judgments about their imagery experiences, and since the view may suggest a phenomenology of imagery at odds with what most ordinary people would accept.

[7] One might legitimately doubt the replicability of Galton's results. For example, it seems unlikely that a majority of scientists would now claim to have no visual imagery (see below and footnote 8). This presents no difficulty for my thesis, and in fact supports it, since if people's reports about their imagery experiences in one era conflict with those in another, and if it is reasonable to suppose that the underlying experiences themselves are similar, we can conclude that at least some of the reports must be in error. In any case, rich variability in subjective reports of imagery is readily rediscoverable by anyone who takes the time to seek it among his acquaintances, as I have done. You might be surprised by some of the things people will say if you give them free rein for a few minutes with open-ended questions.

once. For example, one of them says 'My mental field of vision is larger than the normal one. In the former I appear to see everything from some commanding point of view, which at once embraces every object and all sides of every object' (1880, p. 314).[8] Galton also claims that he knows

> many cases of persons mentally reading off scores when playing the pianoforte, or manuscript when they are making speeches. One statesman has assured me that a certain hesitation in utterance which he has at times is due to his being plagued by the image of the manuscript speech with its original erasures and corrections. He cannot lay the ghost, and he puzzles in trying to decipher it (1907, p. 67).

Other subjects say: 'My powers are zero. To my consciousness there is almost no association of memory with objective visual impressions. I recollect the breakfast table, but do not see it' (1880, p. 306); 'No power of visualizing' (ibid.); 'My impressions are in all respects so dim, vague and transient, that I doubt whether they can reasonably be called images' (ibid.). William James, who cites Galton favourably and at length in *Principles of Psychology* (1890/1981), claims that his own powers of visual imagery are very feeble, that he 'can seldom call to mind even a single letter of the alphabet in purely retinal terms. I must trace the letter by running my mental eye over its contour in order that the image of it shall have any distinctness at all' (p. 708).

One of Galton's subjects, a scientist, embarks on a critique of Galton's questionnaire itself:

> These questions presuppose assent to some sort of a proposition regarding the 'mind's eye' and the 'images' which it sees. . . . This points to some initial fallacy. . . . It is only by a figure of speech that I can describe my recollection of a scene as a 'mental image' which I can 'see' with my 'mind's eye'. . . . I do not see it . . . any more than a man sees the thousand lines of Sophocles which under due pressure he is ready to repeat (1880, p. 302, ellipses Galton's).

In fact, Galton says that 'the great majority of men of science' with whom he interacted at the start of his investigations 'protested that mental imagery was unknown to them, and they looked on me as fanciful and fantastic in supposing that the words "mental imagery" really expressed what I believed everybody supposed them to mean' (1880, p. 302). Since Galton found little such scepticism among non-scientists, and even a willingness to declare their imagery completely distinct and full of detail in the face of sceptical responses by him, Galton concludes that, contrary to what one might have expected, scientists tend to 'have feeble powers of visual representation' relative to the rest of the population (1880, p. 304).[9]

---

[8] Jorge Luis Borges describes a similar phenomenon in a fictional character obsessed with a coin he calls a 'Zahir': 'There was a time when I could visualize the obverse, and then the reverse. Now I see them simultaneously. This is not as though the Zahir were crystal, because it is not a matter of one face being superimposed upon another; rather, it is as though my eyesight were spherical, with the Zahir in the center' (Borges, 1962, p. 163).

[9] In contrast, Isaac & Marks (1994) find that the vividness of visual imagery claimed by physics students is at least as great as that of students in other majors, as measured by Marks' (1973) Vividness of Visual Imagery Questionnaire (VVIQ). For more on the VVIQ, see section three of this paper.

Although Galton and James assume that these self-reports accurately reflect a surprising variation in the quantity and quality of visual imagery, I think it is not unreasonable to view the reports with a certain degree of suspicion. At least, before accepting the existence of such extreme variability in the visual imagery of normal people, it seems sensible to ask whether self-reported high and low imagers differ significantly in their success on cognitive tasks that are plausibly aided by the use of visual imagery. Accordingly, James R. Angell (1910), in discussing the imagery literature of his time, stresses the importance of looking for correlations between what he calls 'objective methods' of measuring imagery, in which success or failure on a task depends on the nature of a subject's imagery, and 'subjective methods' in which a subject reports features of her imagery.[10] If the correlation between objective and subjective methods is poor, it is plausible to suppose that the differences in subjective reports are differences in report only, not reflecting real differences in visual imagery experience. And if differences in imaging ability are as vast as they would seem to be from the reports of Galton's subjects, one should expect vast corresponding differences in tasks requiring the use of imagery — differences like the difference between a prodigy and a normal person, or between a normal person and a person with severe deficiencies. Antecedently, it seems plausible to doubt that such differences will be prevalent in normal populations.[11]

III: Recent Attempts to Relate Differences in Subjective Report with Performance on Imagery Tasks

A great body of studies comparing subjective and objective measures of visual imagery has been amassed in the last several decades, with largely discouraging results that I will briefly review here. As I suggested at the end of the previous section, I think such results undermine the credibility of subjective reports of imagery experience.

Through the 1970s, tests calling for numerical or categorical self-ratings of visual imagery experience (such as Betts' [1909] Questionnaire upon Mental Imagery, Sheehan's [1967] shortened version of that questionnaire, Gordon's [1949] Test of Visual Imagery Control, and Marks' [1973] Vividness of Visual Imagery Questionnaire) failed for the most part to correlate with performance on cognitive tasks that researchers had thought plausibly to involve imagery. Early reviews of these questionnaires thus tended to be primarily negative (for example, Ernest, 1977; J. Richardson, 1980), leading Paivio (1986), otherwise a great

---

[10] Despite some concerns about the values and assumptions implicit in the use of the terms 'objective' and 'subjective' (see Lloyd, 1994; 1995), I will employ the same usage in this matter.

[11] If one looks at the self-descriptions of established prodigies, one does find that they sometimes claim to have detailed visual imagery of the sort that could explain their special talents (see, for example, cases described in Luria, 1965/1968; Stromeyer & Psotka, 1970; Sacks, 1995). In such cases, the subjective reports have at least a prima facie plausibility, although it is also possible that in some cases the prodigies are confabulating details of their imagery to explain what they know to be unusual performances.

defender of the importance of visual imagery, to declare that 'self-report measures of imagery tend to be uncorrelated with objective performance tests' (p. 117).

More recently, McKelvie (1995) conducted a very detailed review and meta-analysis of the literature on the most widely tested visual imagery questionnaire, Marks' (1973) Vividness of Visual Imagery Questionnaire (VVIQ), which prompts subjects to form visual images and asks them to rank the vividness of those images on a scale from 1 ('Perfectly clear and as vivid as normal vision') to 5 ('No image at all, you only "know" that you are thinking of the object').[12] Although McKelvie reaches a tentatively positive assessment of the VVIQ, the picture he paints is nonetheless negative in a number of important respects. For example, perhaps the three most obvious sorts of tests on which psychologists historically expected good visualizers to excel (judging from where the bulk of research has been done) are tests involving the spatial transformation of visualized objects, such as mental rotation tasks; tests of visual creativity; and tests of visual memory. McKelvie's meta-analysis finds no significant relationship between scores on the VVIQ and tests of skill at spatial transformation or mental rotation (even Marks [1999], generally quick to defend the importance of his questionnaire, concedes the latter); he finds no significant relationship between the VVIQ and tests of visual creativity for people of normal IQ. (see also Antonietti et al., 1997);[13] and he finds only spotty relationships between the VVIQ and tests of visual memory. On the other hand, McKelvie finds strong relationships between VVIQ scores and self-reports of imagery on other questionnaires;[14] tests of hypnotic susceptibility (but see Crawford & Allen, 1996; Kogon et al., 1998); tests involving Gestalt completion of incomplete figures; and tests of motor and physiological control (but see Eton et al., 1998). One can guess how visual imagery might be important for these tasks, but it is worrisome that we don't see significant differences in performance on the more obvious sorts of tasks as well.

Assessing these results, McKelvie concludes that '[o]n balance . . . the evidence favours the construct validity of the VVIQ, with a more definitive conclusion awaiting further research' (p. 93). Supposing we grant this weakly positive assessment of the VVIQ, it is still true to say that researchers have generally failed to find the dramatic performance differences between self-reported high

[12] See also A. Richardson (1994) for a more positive but less thorough review that doesn't confine itself to the VVIQ (and doesn't undertake a meta-analysis).

[13] McKelvie does find three studies that suggest a relationship between VVIQ scores and visual creativity for subjects of high IQ. Interestingly, he finds a parallel result for *verbal* creativity: no relationship to the VVIQ unless subjects are specially selected for high IQ. What to make of these findings is unclear.

[14] However, McKelvie also notes that the relationship between the VVIQ and other visual imagery questionnaires is in some cases no stronger than the relationship between the VVIQ and self-report measures of *non-visual* imagery. In fact, McKelvie's meta-analysis finds the VVIQ to correlate more highly with the Vividness of Movement Imagery Questionnaire (Isaac et al., 1986) and the Vividness of Auditory Imagery Questionnaire (Kunzendorf, 1982) (combined mean correlation coefficient 0.677) than with any other self-report measures involving visual imagery (see also Antonietti et al., 1997; Eton et al., 1998) — a fact that, as McKelvie observes, raises concerns about the discriminative validity of the VVIQ. It is somewhat surprising that McKelvie doesn't make more of this issue, but I will not pursue the matter further here.

and low visualizers that one might have expected on the basis of the differences in narrative report described by Galton, and consequently that the reports of Galton's subjects remain to a significant extent unjustified.[15]

However, concerns might be raised even about McKelvie's weakly positive assessment. Although reports of correlations between the VVIQ and performance on various cognitive tasks presumably involving imagery have continued to appear since 1995 (Crawford & Allen, 1996; Wallace *et al.*, 1996; Campos & Fernández, 1997; Tomes & Katz, 1997; Campos & Fernández, 1998; Keogh & Markham, 1998; Winograd *et al.*, 1998; Riske *et al.*, 2000; Walczyk & Taylor, 2000), negative findings have also continued to appear with roughly equal frequency (Antonietti *et al.*, 1997; Campos & Pérez, 1997; Campos *et al.*, 1997; Eton *et al.*, 1998; Wilkinson & Hyman, 1998; Antonietti, 1999; Heaps & Nash, 1999; Kunzendorf *et al.*, 2000; Tomes & Katz, 2000). There are multiple reasons, independent of the validity of the VVIQ as a measure of visual imagery, to expect some positive findings. Psychological variables tend to correlate, sometimes robustly, for a whole variety of reasons apart from those hypothesized by the experimenter (Meehl, 1990); and it is widely recognized in psychology that positive findings, whatever their cause, are more likely to be pursued and published than negative findings (Chara [1992] addresses this issue in the VVIQ literature in particular). It is also widely recognized that when the procedure of a study is not wholly straightforward, the results are often influenced by the experimenter's expectations (Intons-Peterson [1983] has shown experimentally how experimenter biases can influence imagery reports in particular). In other words, a disorganized smattering of reported correlations is what we should expect if the VVIQ does not accurately measure visual imagery; and, apart from the correlations with other self-report measures, that is largely what we find. As Slee (1995) emphasizes in her commentary on McKelvie (1995), research on the VVIQ does not seem to fall into the pattern of finding mostly positive relationships with skills there is good theoretical reason to believe are aided by vivid visual imagery and finding mostly weak or negative relationships with skills there is good theoretical reason not to believe are so aided, as would be expected if the VVIQ were an accurate measure of imagery vividness.

Another widely tested area in which one might hope to find a correlation between subjective report and cognitive test is in eidetic imagery, sometimes popularly (but in the view of many theoreticians inaccurately) referred to as 'photographic memory'. Eidetic imagery has been characterized as imagery of prior but now absent visual stimulation, in some respects like afterimages, but

---

[15] It should be noted, however, that McKelvie finds less variability in imagery reports than one might expect from reading Galton, McKelvie's meta-analysis yielding a mean VVIQ score of 2.307 and a standard deviation of 0.692. Demand characteristics of the survey may explain some of this clustering toward the low (vivid) end of the scale. As Ahsen (1990) notes, the survey begins by asking the subject to 'think of some relative or friend' and then to 'consider carefully the picture that comes before your mind's eye', the latter phrase implying that a picture-like image will be experienced. However, Galton's survey employs similar language. It is possible the narrative format of Galton's questionnaire was more encouraging of extreme responses than are the Likert scales of the VVIQ or that cultural differences explain the apparent decline in variability of self-reports of imagery (see footnote 7).

distinguished from afterimages by being positively coloured, while afterimages have colours complementary of the objects perceived, and by being motionless and scannable, while afterimages move about the visual field as the eye saccades (Haber & Haber, 1964; Jaensch, 1930).[16] The presence of eidetic imagery is measured primarily by subjective report (although many recent researchers, following Haber & Haber, 1964, also check that direction of gaze corresponds with the relative location of the details being reported) and is attributed primarily to children. Often, eidetic images are described as being very detailed (for example, Allport, 1924; Jaensch, 1930; but see Leask et al., 1969). Early researchers on eidetic imagery sometimes claimed to find a variety of differences between eidetikers and non-eidetikers in personality, perception and cognition, but the methodology was often obscure or inconsistent (for critical reviews, see Allport, 1928; Klüver, 1933; Gray & Gummerman, 1975). For example, Gray and Gummerman (1975) state that depending in part on the methodology of the study, frequency estimates of eidetic imagery among children were extremely variable, spanning the full range from zero to 100%. Later, more careful research begun and inspired by Ralph Haber and his colleagues in the 1960s (Haber & Haber, 1964; Leask et al., 1969) resolved some of these methodological inconsistencies, but at the price of most of the positive results — so much so that in 1979 Haber concedes that 'extensive research has failed to demonstrate consistent correlates between the presence of eidetic imagery and any cognitive, intellectual, neurological or emotional measure' (p. 583).[17]

Overall, self-reports of imagery experience tend to relate poorly, or at best unsystematically, to objective measures of visual imagery. Although I have not shown this to be the case for narrative reports of the sort catalogued by Galton, I see no reason for special optimism about that case. Accordingly, I am inclined to draw the general conclusion that differences in imagery reports do not reliably reflect differences in imagery experience.[18] I take this fact to lend plausibility to

[16] My focus in this discussion is on what has come to be called 'typographic eidetic imagery' as opposed to 'structural eidetic imagery' of the sort described by Ahsen (1977) and Marks & McKellar (1982), since it is in typographical eidetic imagery that individual differences have been most broadly studied.

[17] Subsequent research on the visual memory of eidetikers has continued to be variable, Kaylor & Davidson (1979), Paine (1980), and Miller & Peacock (1982) finding somewhat better memory performance among eidetikers, Wasinger et al. (1982) finding no difference, and A. Richardson & DiFrancesco (1985) finding a non-significant trend. Glickson et al. (1999) suggest a connection between eidetic imagery and synaesthesia; Kunzendorf (1984) finds electroretinogram differences and differences in control of heart rate and hand temperature between eidetikers and non-eidetikers; Matsuoka (1989) finds eidetikers to report more absorption in sensory and imaginative experiences. For retrospective personal reports of frustration in searching for strong correlations between eidetic imagery and objective tasks see Furst (1979) and Sommer (1980).

[18] Besides looking at numerically scaled visual imagery questionnaires and reports of eidetic imagery, it would be useful to look at studies of 'non-imagers': people who claim to have no visual imagery whatsoever. However, studies of non-imagers are very difficult to find, despite Galton's claim (cited above) that the 'great majority of men of science' claimed that 'mental imagery was unknown to them'. Perhaps people who claim to be non-imagers are less common these days (across a number of studies, McKelvie [1995] reports a mean score of approximately 3, the midpoint of the VVIQ's 5-point scale, for 'poor visualizers', typically defined as either bottom half or bottom third) — but unless human cognition has changed significantly since the late nineteenth century, it is hard to see how the percentage of genuine non-imagers could have declined. (See also Faw, 1997.) Russell

my thesis that people can be, and often are, grossly mistaken about their own current visual imagery experiences.

IV: Alternative Explanations for the Failure of Self-reports to Correlate with Performance on Tests Apparently Requiring Imagery

Since we cannot directly measure another person's visual imagery experiences, we must rely on indirect evidence if we are to reach the conclusion that people can be mistaken in their reports about those experiences. Briefly, my strategy has been to support the plausibility of the view that people can be mistaken about their own imagery experiences by, first, inducing the reader into uncertainty about her own visual imagery, second, describing the strikingly wide variability in narrative reports of visual imagery experience, and third, arguing that there is little if any systematic relationship between people's self-ratings of visual imagery and their performance on cognitive tasks that plausibly employ visual imagery. I will conclude by addressing what seem to me the most plausible challenges to my inference from the lack of relationship between subjective and objective measures of visual imagery to the conclusion that subjects are grossly mistaken about their own imagery experiences.

(1) *The methods of eliciting the subjective reports do not capture the aspects of imagery relevant to performance on cognitive tests.* One version of this objection is raised by Ahsen (1985; 1986; 1987) who suggests that vividness is irrelevant, or even detrimental, to some of the functions of imagery. This suggestion has substantial plausibility: For example, in rotating an imagined figure to see if it matches another figure on the page, what would seem to matter is the gross morphology of the figure, not its vividness. Still, however well this version of the objection works against vividness measures like the VVIQ and Betts' (1909) Questionnaire upon Mental Imagery, the problem with subjective measures is broader than that. For example, the most prominent subjective visual imagery measure that does not focus on vividness, Gordon's (1949) Test of Visual Imagery Control, does not appear to correlate appreciably better than the VVIQ with performance on cognitive tasks such as spatial reasoning and creativity tasks (Ernest, 1977; Hiscock, 1978; J. Richardson, 1980; Lorenz & Neisser, 1985; Antonietti *et al.*, 1997; González *et al.*, 1997). Ahsen's argument also does not address non-imagers or people with imagery as weak as James claims his to be, since a certain minimal level of detail would seem to be required for success on the cognitive tasks, assuming those tasks genuinely to require imagery. Perhaps there are systemic difficulties with all the major visual imagery questionnaires, but someone who wishes to mount this sort of argument at least owes us an explanation as to why a century of trying hasn't yielded anything demonstrably better.

Hurlburt (personal communication, April 2002) says that several self-described non-imagers reported visual imagery when subjected to his experience sampling technique. On a related note, see Thomas' (1989) interesting account of the behaviorist John Watson's shift from claiming that he had vivid visual imagery to claiming that he had none.

(2) *Visual imagery is of no use in most of the cognitive tasks that have been studied in relation to subjective reports of visual imagery.* The extreme version of this view is that imagery is cognitively epiphenomenal: Some people have powerful, vivid and lifelike imagery and others have no imagery whatsoever, but despite this dramatic difference their cognitive abilities differ very little. In this case, we need attribute no errors in reporting: Galton's subjects could each be accurately describing his own imagery. That the differences do not show up in cognitive tests is simply a consequence of the irrelevance of imagery to cognition. I do not want to delve into the complex debate on this subject (see Paivio, 1971; 1986; Pylyshyn, 1973; forthcoming; Kosslyn, 1980; 1994; Block, 1981) other than to note the awkwardness of any position that posits a major faculty that would seem to have a fairly obvious range of purposes but in fact has little purpose at all and little effect on behaviour apart from the power to generate reports. The awkwardness is compounded if one takes subjective reports of imagery with the uncritical credence of Galton and James, since subjects will often claim to have *used* imagery in a particular way to solve a problem. To the extent one wishes to mitigate extreme epiphenomenalism by allowing that visual imagery serves *some* important general functions, it becomes mysterious why correlations have not been found between measures like the VVIQ and success on any but a disorganized smattering of tasks.

(3) *Both self-reported good and poor visualizers use imagery, but only good visualizers experience that imagery consciously.* This position is a variation of the second alternative, except that what is epiphenomenal is not the imagery itself but the conscious experience of it. We don't ordinarily think of imagery as unconscious, but perhaps a suitably functional approach to imagery can give some sense to the idea of an unconscious image (as in Paivio, 1971). However, unless conscious experience in general is epiphenomenal (an unpopular position: recent discussions include Flanagan, 1992; Chalmers, 1996; Nichols & Grantham, 2001), one would expect to see differences between the cognitive performance of people whose imagery is unconscious, or largely so, and that of people whose imagery is more fully conscious. As I have argued, such differences are for the most part not to be found. Locating the top of the scale also creates challenges for the proponent of this alternative. To fully credit subjects' reports on this view, we would have to take reports of extremely detailed and vivid imagery as the benchmark of fully conscious imagery and assume that every subject has imagery at roughly that level of detail. Otherwise, one must either grant that there are substantial differences in the level of imagery detail between subjects (and then one is stuck back with the original problem of explaining the lack of correlation between subjective measures of imagery and cognitive tests) or grant that the subjects at the top of Galton's scale have overdescribed their imagery, in which case one has granted just the sort of error for which I am arguing. But if everyone's imagery has the level of detail described in the most optimistic and extreme reports of imagery, then it is surprising that we don't all perform substantially better on imagery tasks.

(4) *Variation in subjects' responses to questions about their imagery is due to difficulties in expression rather than misapprehension of their conscious experience.* Even granting that differences in imagery reports do not reliably reflect differences in imagery experience, it does not necessarily follow that we are poor introspectors of our own visual imagery, since it is possible that the lack of correlation is a consequence entirely of difficulties of communication — that although subjects know their own imagery experiences quite well, putting that knowledge into words is so difficult that the self-reports are nearly useless.

Consider Marks' VVIQ again. Marks tops the scale with the phrase 'perfectly clear and as vivid as normal vision'. What does this mean? At least two distinct problems arise in interpreting this phrase (for similar concerns, see J. Richardson, 1980; Cornoldi, 1995). The first is simply in understanding what it is for a visual image to be vivid. Vividness has been associated with precision of outline, amount of detail, brightness, saliency, 'liveliness' and other factors (Cornoldi *et al.*, 1992; McKelvie, 1995). Even if a subject has excellent introspective knowledge of his imagery experience, in assessing the 'vividness' of his imagery he may weigh these factors differently than do other subjects. The second difficulty is in comparing clarity and vividness across different types of experience. When I visit the optometrist and she asks me if what I see through one lens is as clear as what I see through another, I feel I understand the question. Since I am comparing one perceptual visual experience to another, what it is to be 'clear' remains the same across the cases; but if I am asked to compare the clarity of my vision without glasses to the clarity of an orchestra heard through a wall, the matter is not so straightforward. Although the experience of visual imagery and the experience of visual perception likely have important commonalities, significant differences also exist between the two, which make it unclear what the criteria are for saying that a visual image is as clear and vivid as normal vision.

Also, consider Galton's sceptical scientist who declares that there is a fallacy in supposing the existence of a 'mind's eye' that 'sees' images. If one takes 'sees' in a literal sense here, this scientist is surely right: There is no homunculus who literally sees the images you form. Yet there seems also to be a looser or metaphorical sense of 'seeing' on which it is permissible to say that we see our visual imagery. One might thus think the difference Galton finds between scientists' and non-scientists' reactions to his questions has more to do with the strictness with which they take the word 'see' than with any real difference in their imagery or any genuine mistake about the experience of imagery.

It is thus reasonable to suppose that some of the variation between reports is due to the lack of clear standards for vividness or even for the presence or absence of an image. If subjects can accurately compare the vividness of one image to another, that provides additional support for this view, since it suggests that the problem is not in the introspection of the images themselves but in the comparison of those introspected images to some external standard. To develop this point it would be necessary to conduct studies that examine the relationship between a subject's ratings of particular images' vividness (or some other introspectible image property)[19] and the effectiveness of those images in support of that subject's performance on particular cognitive tasks — perhaps with special attention to whether a subject's idiosyncratic ratings predict performance as well as do her typical ratings. Most studies of the relevance of imagery to cognitive performance do not use the subjects' own ratings of their imagery experience. Exceptions include Bower (1972), whose subjects more accurately recalled word pairs for which they had formed an image they rated as highly vivid than word pairs for which they had formed an image they rated as less vivid, and Walczyk (1995), who finds a significant correlation between how vivid a subject claims her memory image of a particular familiar object to be and the accuracy of that subject's memory of that object. However, in Walczyk's case, at least, the direction of causation is unclear: Is the memory accurate because the image is vivid, or is the subject reporting a vivid image because she knows that she has an accurate memory? More extensive research is needed before any firm conclusions can be drawn.

Although the lack of clear standards of subjective report likely accounts for some of the variation between reports, I think it plausible that there is substantial genuine introspective error as well. Not all the concerns I have raised about vividness translate equally well to other descriptions of visual imagery, such as those deployed in Gordon's (1949) Test of Visual Imagery Control (which simply asks subjects whether they can imagine certain sorts of situations) and measures of eidetic imagery, and these relate no better to objective performance than the VVIQ; nor is all the vast variation among Galton's respondents confined to variation in vividness. And although there may be some merit to treating Galton's sceptical scientist as a mere quibbler over words, it seems unlikely that all Galton's purported non-imagers were quibblers of that sort. Galton clearly is inquiring about their visual imagery: If they were aware of distinct conscious experiences of visual imagery in contemplating their mornings' breakfast tables, distinguishable from memory that is not visually imagistic, it would have been perverse for them not to mention it, regardless of any disagreement about the phrasing of Galton's questions. Moreover, some respondents explicitly deny having any such distinctive experience. Perhaps some of Galton's scientific respondents allowed their reports to be unduly influenced by their theoretical positions, but if we treat their avowals as nonetheless sincere, this possibility in no way undermines my thesis. Mistakes are no less mistakes for having been theoretically informed. In fact, even among non-scientists, implicit or explicit views about the nature of mental imagery may be one of the major sources of introspective error.

Finally, in introspecting my own imagery, I do not find myself in the position of feeling that I know exactly what the experience is like, fumbling only because I am unable to put my knowledge clearly into words or because I am unsure of the

---

[19] There is some evidence that bizarre imagery is easier to recall than imagery of ordinary scenes (see Einstein & McDaniel, 1987, for a review), but bizarreness seems to be more a feature of one's reaction to an image or one's assessment of the likelihood of the situation depicted in an image than an intrinsic, introspectible feature of the imagery itself.

standards of reporting. Rather, I am unsure about the *experience itself*, about how much detail is filled in at any particular time, about how narrowly the imagery experience confines itself to what is in the scope of my immediate attention, about how much visual imagery is like visual perception. Given that this feeling of uncertainty is not limited to matters of linguistic formulation, it would be odd to suppose that I and others who can be brought to a similar uncertainty by probative questioning can only make mistakes of linguistic formulation. The introspection of visual imagery feels difficult if one sets to it conscientiously. We should not be surprised if people go easily awry.

V: Conclusion

I have conducted this brief examination of our introspective knowledge of visual imagery to promote the more general thesis that we can be, and often are, grossly mistaken about our own current conscious experiences even in favourable circumstances of quiet attention. I do not take myself to have here established that general thesis, which pertains to all of conscious experience, but only to have provided some considerations favouring it in one domain.

Since at least the time of Descartes, theoreticians have widely assumed that nothing is more secure than level-headed judgments about current conscious experience. A similar assumption informs and pervades our commonsense understanding of the mind, as revealed by the surprise or disbelief commonly exhibited in the face of apparent psychological or philosophical examples of even moderate mistakes about conscious experience, and sometimes by our ordinary conversation. If, as I believe, this widespread assumption turns out to be incorrect, we must abandon not only research paradigms in psychology and consciousness studies that depend too trustingly on introspection, and foundationalist and anti-sceptical views in epistemology that take knowledge of immediate experience as a starting point, but also some of our ordinary assumptions about our knowledge of our own mental lives and what it's like to be ourselves. Human judgment about anything as fluid, changeable, skittish and chaotic as conscious experience is bound to error and confusion.

References

Ahsen, A. (1977), 'Eidetics: An overview', *Journal of Mental Imagery*, **1**, pp. 5–38.
Ahsen, A. (1985), 'Unvividness paradox', *Journal of Mental Imagery*, **9**, pp. 1–18.
Ahsen, A. (1986), 'Prologue to unvividness paradox', *Journal of Mental Imagery*, **10**, pp. 1–8.
Ahsen, A. (1987), 'Epilogue to unvividness paradox', *Journal of Mental Imagery*, **11**, pp. 13–60.
Ahsen, A. (1990), 'AA-VVIQ and imagery paradigm: Vividness and unvividness issue in VVIQ research paradigms', *Journal of Mental Imagery*, **14**, pp. 1–58.
Allport, G.W. (1924), 'Eidetic imagery', *British Journal of Psychology*, **15**, pp. 99–120.
Allport, G.W. (1928), 'The eidetic image and the after-image', *American Journal of Psychology*, **40**, pp. 418–25.
Angell, J.R. (1897), 'Thought and imagery', *Philosophical Review*, **6**, pp. 646–51.
Angell, J.R. (1910), 'Methods for the determination of mental imagery', *Psychological Monographs*, **13**, pp. 61–108.
Angell, J.R. (1911), 'Imageless thought', *Psychological Review*, **18**, pp. 295–323.
Antonietti, A. (1999), 'Can students predict when imagery will allow them to discover the problem solution?', *European Journal of Cognitive Psychology*, **11**, pp. 407–28.

Antonietti, A., Bologna, D. and Lupi, G. (1997), 'Creative synthesis of visual images is not associated with individual differences', *Perceptual and Motor Skills*, **85**, pp. 881–2.

Armstrong, D.M. (1963), 'Is introspective knowledge incorrigible?', *Philosophical Review*, **72**, pp. 417–32.

Audi, R. (1993), *The Structure of Justification* (Cambridge: Cambridge University Press).

Ayer, A.J. (1963), *The Concept of a Person* (New York: St. Martin's).

Berkeley, G. (1710/1965), 'A Treatise Concerning the Principles of Human Knowledge', in *Principles, Dialogues, and Philosophical Correspondence*, ed. C.M. Turbayne (New York: Macmillan).

Betts, G.H. (1909), *The Distribution and Functions of Mental Imagery* (New York: Teachers College, Columbia).

Block, N. (ed. 1981), *Imagery* (Cambridge, MA: MIT).

Boring, E.G. (1953), 'A history of introspection', *Psychological Bulletin*, **50**, pp. 169–89.

Bower, G.H. (1972), 'Mental imagery and associative learning', in *Cognition in Learning and Memory*, ed. L.W. Gregg (New York: John Wiley & Sons).

Campos, A. and Fernández (1997), 'Imagen mental e intervalo de retención en el recuerdo de series', *Estudios de Psicología*, **58**, pp. 105–12.

Campos, A. and Fernández (1998), 'La imagen mental en el sistema de enlace', *Revista de Psicología*, **16**, pp. 3–17.

Campos, A. and Pérez, M.J. (1997), 'Mnemonic images and associated pair recall', *Journal of Mental Imagery*, **21**, pp. 73–82.

Campos, A., Pérez, M.J. and González, M.A. (1997), 'The interactiveness of paired images is affected by image bizarreness and image vividness', *Imagination, Cognition and Personality*, **16**, pp. 301–7.

Carruthers, P. (1992), *The Animals Issue* (Cambridge: Cambridge).

Chalmers, D.J. (1996), *The Conscious Mind* (New York: Oxford).

Chalmers, D.J. (forthcoming), 'The content and epistemology of phenomenal belief', in *Aspects of Consciousness*, ed. Q. Smith and A. Jokic (Oxford: Oxford).

Chara, P.J. (1992), 'Some concluding thoughts on the debate about the Vividness of Visual Imagery Questionnaire', *Perceptual & Motor Skills*, **75**, pp. 947–54.

Churchland, P.M. (1988), *Matter and Consciousness*, Rev. Ed. (Cambridge, MA: MIT).

Cornoldi, C. (1995), 'Imagery and meta-imagery in the VVIQ', *Journal of Mental Imagery*, **19**, pp. 131–6.

Cornoldi, C., De Beni, R., Cavedon, A., Mazzoni, G., Giusberti, F. and Marucci, F. (1992), 'How can a vivid image be described? Characteristics influencing vividness judgments and the relationship between vividness and memory', *Journal of Mental Imagery*, **16**, pp. 89–108.

Crawford, H.J. and Allen, S.N. (1996), 'Paired-associate learning and recall of high and low imagery words: Moderating effects of hypnosis, hypnotic susceptibility level and visualization abilities', *American Journal of Psychology*, **109**, pp. 353–72.

Danziger, K. (1980), 'The history of introspection reconsidered', *Journal of the History of the Behavioral Sciences*, **16**, pp. 241–62.

Dennett, D.C. (1991), *Consciousness Explained* (Boston: Little, Brown and Co.).

Dennett, D.C. (2000), 'The case for Rorts', in *Rorty and His Critics*, ed. R.B. Brandom (Malden, MA: Blackwell).

Einstein, G.O. and McDaniel, M.A. (1987), 'Distinctiveness and the mnemonic benefits of bizarre imagery', in *Imagery and Related Mnemonic Processes*, ed. M.A. McDaniel and M. Pressley (New York: Springer-Verlag).

Ernest, C.H. (1977), 'Imagery ability and cognition: A critical review', *Journal of Mental Imagery*, **2**, pp. 181–216.

Eton, D.T., Gilner, F.H. and Munz, D.C. (1998), 'The measurement of imagery vividness: A test of the reliability and validity of the Vividness of Visual Imagery Questionnaire and the Vividness of Movement Imagery Questionnaire', *Journal of Mental Imagery*, **22**, pp. 125–36.

Ewing, A.C. (1951), *The Fundamental Questions of Philosophy* (London: Routledge & Kegan Paul).

Faw, Bill (1997), 'Outlining a brain model of mental imaging abilities', *Neuroscience and Biobehavioral Reviews*, **21**, pp. 283–8.

Flanagan, O. (1992), *Consciousness Reconsidered* (Cambridge, MA: MIT).

Furst, C.J. (1979), 'The inside and outside of eidetic imagery', *Behavioral and Brain Sciences*, **2**, pp. 602–3.

Galton, F. (1880), 'Statistics of mental imagery', *Mind*, **5**, pp. 301–18.

Galton, F. (1907), *Inquiries into Human Faculty and Its Development* (London: J.M. Dent).

Gertler, B. (2001), 'Introspecting phenomenal states', *Philosophy and Phenomenological Research*, **62**, pp. 305–28.

Glicksohn, J., Steinbach, I. and Elimalach-Malmilyan, S. (1999), 'Cognitive dedifferentiation in eidetics and synaesthesia: Hunting for the ghost once more', *Perception*, **28**, pp. 109–20.

González, M., Campos, A. and Pérez, M.J. (1997), 'Mental imagery and creative thinking', *Journal of Psychology*, **131**, pp. 357–64.

Gordon, R. (1949), 'An investigation into some of the factors that favour the formation of stereotyped images', *British Journal of Psychology*, **40**, pp. 156–67.

Gray, C.R. and Gummerman, K. (1975), 'The enigmatic eidetic image: A critical examination of methods, data, and theories', *Psychological Bulletin*, **82**, pp. 383–407.

Haber, R.N. (1979), 'Twenty years of haunting eidetic imagery: Where's the ghost?', *Behavioral and Brain Sciences*, **2**, pp. 583–629.

Haber, R.N. and Haber, R.B. (1964), 'Eidetic imagery: I. Frequency', *Perceptual & Motor Skills*, **19**, pp. 131–8.

Heaps, C. and Nash, M. (1999), 'Individual differences in imagination inflation', *Psychonomic Bulletin & Review*, **6**, pp. 313–18

Hill, C.S. (1991), *Sensations* (Cambridge: Cambridge).

Hiscock, M. (1978), 'Imagery assessment through self-report: What do imagery questionnaires measure?', *Journal of Consulting and Clinical Psychology*, **46**, pp. 223–30.

Huxley, T.H. (1895), *Hume* (London: Macmillan).

Intons-Peterson, M.J. (1983), 'Imagery paradigms: How vulnerable are they to experimenters' expectations?', *Journal of Experimental Psychology: Human Perception and Performance*, **9**, pp. 394–412.

Isaac, A.R. and Marks, D.F. (1994), 'Individual differences in mental imagery experience: Developmental changes and specialization', *British Journal of Psychology*, **85**, pp. 479–500.

Isaac, A., Marks, D.F. and Russell, D.G. (1986), 'An instrument for assessing imagery of movement: The Vividness of Movement Imagery Questionnaire (VMIQ)', *Journal of Mental Imagery*, 10, pp. 23–30.

Jaensch, E.R. (1930), *Eidetic Imagery*, trans. O. Oeser (London: Kegan Paul).

James, W. (1884), 'On Some Omissions of Introspective Psychology', *Mind*, O.S., **9**, pp. 1–26.

James, W. (1890/1981), *The Principles of Psychology* (Cambridge, MA: Harvard).

Kaylor, C.W. and Davidson, R.S. (1979), 'Accuracy of recall as a function of eidetic imagery', *Perceptual and Motor Skills*, **48**, pp. 1143–8.

Keogh, L. and Markham, R. (1998), 'Judgements of other people's memory reports: Differences in reports as a function of imagery vividness', *Applied Cognitive Psychology*, **12**, pp. 159–71.

Klüver, H. (1933), 'Eidetic imagery', in *A Handbook of Child Psychology*, 2nd Ed. 2, ed. C. Murchison (New York: Russell & Russell), pp. 699–722.

Kogon, M.M., Jasiukaitis, P., Berardi, A., Gupta, M., Kosslyn, S.M. and Spiegel, D. (1998), 'Imagery and hypnotizability revisited', *International Journal of Clinical & Experimental Hypnosis*, **46**, pp. 363–70.

Kornblith, H. (1998), 'What is it like to be me?', *Australasian Journal of Philosophy*, **76**, pp. 48–60.

Kosslyn, S.M. (1980), *Image and Mind* (Cambridge, MA: Harvard).

Kosslyn, S.M. (1994), *Image and Brain* (Cambridge, MA: MIT).

Külpe, O. (1893/1895), *Outlines of Psychology*, trans. E.B. Titchener (London: Swan Sonnenschein).

Kunzendorf, R.G. (1982), 'Mental images, appreciation of grammatical patterns, and creativity', *Journal of Mental Imagery*, **6**, pp. 183–202.

Kunzendorf, R.G. (1984), 'Centrifugal effects of eidetic imaging on flash electroretinograms and autonomic responses', *Journal of Mental Imagery*, **8**, pp. 67–76.

Kunzendorf, R.G., Young, K., Beecy, T. and Beals, K. (2000), 'Is visual thinking 'imageless thought'?', *Perceptual and Motor Skills*, **91**, pp. 981–2.

Lau, D.C. (1970), *Mencius* (London: Penguin).

Leask, J., Haber, R.N. and Haber, R.B. (1969), 'Eidetic imagery in children: II Longitudinal and experimental results', *Psychonomic Monograph Supplements*, **3**, pp. 25–48.

Lewis, C.I. (1946), *An Analysis of Knowledge and Valuation* (La Salle, IL: Open Court).

Lloyd, E.A. (1994), 'The secret life of objectivity', unpublished MS.

Lloyd, E.A. (1995), 'Objectivity and the double standard for feminist epistemologies', *Synthese*, **104**, pp. 351–81.

Locke, J. (1689/1975), *An Essay Concerning Human Understanding*, Ed. P.H. Nidditch (Oxford: Clarendon).

Lorenz, C. and Neisser, U. (1985), 'Factors of imagery and event recall', *Memory & Cognition*, **13**, pp. 494–500.

Luria, A.R. (1965/1968), *The Mind of a Mnemonist* (New York: Basic Books).

Marks, D.F. (1973), 'Visual imagery differences in the recall of pictures', *British Journal of Psychology*, **64**, pp. 17–24.

Marks, D.F. (1999), 'Consciousness, mental imagery, and action', *British Journal of Psychology*, **90**, pp. 567–85.

Marks, D.F. and McKellar, P. (1982), 'The nature and function of eidetic imagery', *Journal of Mental Imagery*, **6**, pp. 1–124.

Matsuoka, K. (1989), 'Imagery vividness, verbalizer–visualizer, and fantasy-proneness in young adult eidetikers', *Tohoku Psychologica Folia*, **48**, pp. 25–32.

McKelvie, S.J. (1995), 'The VVIQ as a psychometric test of individual differences in visual imagery vividness: A critical quantitative review and plea for direction', *Journal of Mental Imagery*, **19**, pp. 1–106.

Meehl, P.E. (1990), 'Why summaries of research on psychological theories are often uninterpretable', *Psychological Reports*, **66**, pp. 195–244.

Miller, S. and Peacock, R. (1982), 'Evidence for the uniqueness of eidetic imagery', *Perceptual and Motor Skills*, **55**, pp. 1219–33.

Monson, C.K. & Hurlburt, R.T. (1993), 'A comment to suspend the introspection controversy: Intro-specting subjects did agree about "imageless thought"', in *Sampling Inner Experience in Disturbed Affect* (New York: Plenum).

Nichols, S. and Grantham, R. (2001), 'Adaptive complexity and phenomenal consciousness', *Philoso-phy of Science*, **67**, pp. 648–70.

Nisbett, R.E. and Wilson, T.D. (1977), 'Telling more than we can know: Verbal reports on mental pro-cesses', *Psychological Review*, **84**, pp. 231–59.

Ogden, R.M. (1911), 'Imageless thought: Resume and critique', *Psychological Bulletin*, **8**, pp. 183–97.

Paine, P.A. (1980), 'Eidetic imagery and recall accuracy in preschool children', *Journal of Psychology*, **105**, pp. 253–8.

Paivio, A. (1971), *Imagery and Verbal Processes* (New York: Holt, Rinehart, and Winston).

Paivio, A. (1986), *Mental Representations: A Dual Coding Approach* (New York: Oxford).

Perky, C.W. (1910), 'An experimental study of imagination', *American Journal of Psychology*, **21**, pp. 422–52.

Pylyshyn, Z.W. (1973), 'What the mind's eye tells the mind's brain: A critique of mental imagery', *Psy-chological Bulletin*, **80**, pp. 1–24.

Pylyshyn, Z.W. (forthcoming), 'Mental imagery: In search of a theory', *Behavioral and Brain Sciences*.

Richardson, A. (1994), *Individual Differences in Imaging* (Amityville, NY: Baywood).

Richardson, A. and Di Francesco, J. (1985), 'Stability, accuracy, and eye movements in eidetic imagery', *Australian Journal of Psychology*, **37**, pp. 51–64.

Richardson, J.T.E. (1980), *Mental Imagery and Human Memory* (New York: St. Martin's).

Riske, M.E., Wallace, B. and Allen, P.A. (2000), 'Imagining ability and eyewitness accuracy', Journal of Mental Imagery, **24**, pp. 137–48.

Rorty, R. (1970), 'Incorrigibility as the mark of the mental', *Journal of Philosophy*, **67**, pp. 399–424.

Sacks, O. (1995), An *Anthropologist on Mars* (New York: Random House).

Schwitzgebel, E. (forthcoming), 'Why did we think we dreamed in black and white?', *Studies in History and Philosophy of Science*.

Schwitzgebel, E. & Gordon, M.S. (2000), 'How well do we know our own conscious experience? The case of human echolocation', *Philosophical Topics*, **28**, pp. 235–46.

Sheehan, P.W. (1967), 'A shortened form of Betts' questionnaire upon mental imagery', *Journal of Clin-ical Psychology*, **23**, pp. 386–9.

Shoemaker, S. (1963), *Self-Knowledge and Self-Identity* (Ithaca: Cornell).

Slee, J.A. (1995), 'Vividness is in the mind (but not necessarily in the mind's eye) of the cognizer', *Jour-nal of Mental Imagery*, **19**, pp. 190–93.

Sommer, R. (1980), 'Strategies for imagery research', *Journal of Mental Imagery*, **4**, pp. 115–21.

Stromeyer III, C.F. and Psotka, J. (1970), 'The detailed texture of eidetic images', *Nature*, **225**, pp. 346–9.

Thomas, N. (1989), 'Experience and theory as determinants of attitudes toward mental representation: The case of Knight Dunlap and the vanishing images of J.B. Watson', *American Journal of Psychol-ogy*, **102**, pp. 395–412.

Titchener, E.B. (1900), *A Primer of Psychology* (New York: Macmillan).

Titchener, E.B. (1901), *An Outline of Psychology*, New Ed. (New York: Macmillan).

Titchener, E.B. (1902), *Experimental Psychology: A Manual of Laboratory Practice* (New York: Macmillan).

Titchener, E.B. (1915), *A Text-Book of Psychology* (New York: Macmillan).

Tomes, J.L. and Katz, A.N. (1997), 'Habitual susceptibility to misinformation and individual differences in eyewitness memory', *Applied Cognitive Psychology*, **11**, pp. 233–51.

Tomes, J.L. and Katz, A.N. (2000), 'Confidence–accuracy relations for real and suggested events', *Mem-ory*, **8**, pp. 273–83.

Walczyk, J.J. (1995), 'Between versus within-subjects assessments of image vividness', *Journal of Men-tal Imagery*, **19**, pp. 161–76.

Walczyk, J.J. and Taylor, R.W. (2000), 'Reverse-spelling, the VVIQ, and mental imagery', *Journal of Mental Imagery*, **24**, pp. 177–88.

Wallace, B., Allen, P.A. and Propper, R.E. (1996), 'Hypnotic susceptibility, imaging ability, and ana-gram-solving activity', *International Journal of Clinical and Experimental Hypnosis*, **44**, pp. 324–37.

Wasinger, K., Zelhart, P.F. and Markley, R.P. (1982), 'Memory for random shapes and eidetic ability', *Perceptual and Motor Skills*, **55**, pp. 1076–8.

Wilkinson, C. and Hyman Jr., I.E. (1998), 'Individual differences related to two types of memory errors: Word lists may not generalize to autobiographical memory', *Applied Cognitive Psychology*, **12**, pp. S29–S46.

Winograd, E., Peluso, J.P. and Glover, T.A. (1998), 'Individual differences in susceptibility to memory illusions', *Applied Cognitive Psychology*, **12**, pp. S5–S27.

Woodworth, R.S. (1906), 'Imageless thought', *The Journal of Philosophy, Psychology, and Scientific Methods*, **3**, pp. 701–8.

Dana H. Ballard

Our Perception of the World Has To Be an Illusion

*Our seamless perception of the world depends very much on the slow time scales used by conscious perception. Time scales longer than one second are needed to assemble conscious experience. At time scales shorter than one second, this seamlessness quickly deteriorates. Numerous experiments reveal the fragmentary nature of the visual information used to construct visual experience. Models of how the brain manages these fragments use the construct of a **routine**, which is a task-specific fragment of a sensory-motor program. This paper provides an overview of some of the experiments that test these models. Its aim is to show how the structures that they elucidate constrain the understanding of conscious perception.*

I: Introduction

A fundamental goal of visual science is to have a satisfying explanation of the seamlessness of perception (O'Regan, 1992). We can be sure that the brain extracts information necessary to sub-serve behaviours. So one possibility is that the seamless experience of seeing is a byproduct of this extraction process. How does the information extraction process work? The principal current hypothesis is that the brain creates image-like structures from incoming data and *attends* to the parts that are relevant for the demands of current thought patterns. Research debate has focused on the details of just what it means to attend. One intuitive notion is that, temporally at least, the analysis process should be 'bottom-up'. That is, the image arrives first and then alerts relevant analysis processes. Although we can design experiments that produce this temporal order, there are two principal reasons for rejecting the bottom-up idea as a complete explanation. The first is that of time. Given the slow nature of brain circuitry, it is inefficient to pay the price of having the image drive the selection of goals. Second, there are too many possible goals for the image by itself to be helpful in choosing among them. Of course, when an image is flashed on a blank screen subjects can do a task, but they first have to have had the task explained to them, either verbally in the case of humans or in large numbers of trials with reward contingencies in the case of other primates.

Journal of Consciousness Studies, **9**, No. 5–6, 2002, pp. 54–71

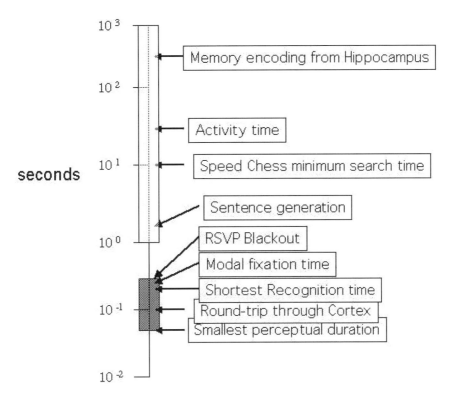

Figure 1. Timescales for understanding brain function are shown in seconds. Most of our appreciation for seamless perception and cognition occurs at times larger than one second. However most of the important computational phenomena take place at times between 50 and 300 milliseconds (ms). (i) RSVP: rapid serial presentations cannot be analysed faster than 250 ms. (ii) Modal eye fixation times are 150–200ms. (iii) The shortest measured recognition time is about 190ms (EEG). (iv) An estimate for the round trip through the cortex is 100ms.

Given that bottom-up processing cannot handle the demands of processing, one way out is the compromise of an integrative process that combines the goals of a task with the initial representation of an image. Depending on the situation, it may be possible to obtain evidence for the goals being set up first or the image representation being set up first. Traditional experiments that flash the stimulus tend to bias the results in favour of the image representation being first. The key question is: what happens under normal viewing? In this case, the evidence is accumulating towards an agenda-first or top-down organization. The most obvious advantage for this organization is time. Setting up the goals first can speed and economize on the representation of the image data. Furthermore, given that the goals are needed to represent the image, and that these are constantly varying, we usefully cannot represent the image until the last moment, saving enormous amounts of memory. This works because of the stability of the world. It effectively serves as the repository for information around us.

The idea of the human's perception requiring the embedding of the human within the world deserves elaboration. One useful way to think of the world is as an enormous computational resource: it provides a wealth of information on the effects on actions and rewards. Similarly, the body, serving as the interface between the world and brain, provides additional essential computational resources for the behaviours that are important to an animal's survival. Parenthetically, what we mean by 'brain' is really the forebrain and what we mean by body includes the spinal cord system that drives it. The computational power of the body can be unappreciated, but remember that a cat without most of its forebrain can still walk on a treadmill with minimal assistance and step over obstacles.

What this means is that:

(1) The brain need not repeat the computational work done by the world and body. Therefore we should expect the representations of the brain to be simpler.
(2) The body can be seen as the interface between the brain and the world that the brain's behavioural programs compete for. The body serves as the arbiter of neural computation (Damasio, 1995).

The idea that perception depends on embodiment, or the interaction of humans with the world, is credited to Merleau-Ponty (1992) but has also found favour with Arnheim (1967). More recently this point has been argued by O'Regan (1992). The embodied view is that the environment and perceiver should not be separated but should be viewed as an integrated system with the perceiver using the world as an external memory. Properties of the world are computed as needed. Because their computation can be done much faster than the time of perceptual awareness, it appears that they are always 'there'.

The difference between the time needed to experience conscious perception and that required to compute the information that form its ingredients is the central focus of the paper. Let us explore this difference in more detail.

The timescale of conscious awareness is relatively slow, taking on the order of seconds. We do not notice television frame rates of one thirtieth of a second, and most of the time we are unaware of our eye movements even though they occur at about every 300 milliseconds. Although perception is slow, there is still precious

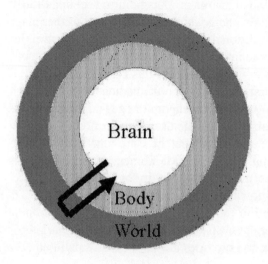

Figure 2.

The embodied cognition hypothesis

The brain directs the search for rewards for its host by directed interactions with the world via the body. The structure of the body and the world provides the brain with vast amounts of computational resources that greatly simplify the brain's task.

As an analogy, the brain just has to 'play' the body in the musical sense by generating the 'notes'. The body interprets the notes and provides the 'music'.

little time for our brains to synthesize any encoding of experience. The neural time scale must be longer than one millisecond as the neural code is signaled with discrete spikes that take one millisecond to produce. If we assume that there is an additional factor of ten to organize the spikes in neural circuitry, then the representations used in visual awareness must be synthesized within a timescale that has access to only two orders of magnitude.

How does the brain produce perceptual experience using these two orders of magnitude? We know that the brain that produces the sensation of seamless experience works in a fragmentary manner from numerous experiments.

(1) In rapid serial visual presentation (RSVP), subjects can recognize faces from a series of faces presented at the rate of one every 70 milliseconds. However when asked to recognize a person's face that comes after another specific person, their performance degrades sharply when the faces are separated by 300 milliseconds or less (Biederman, 1998; Subramaniam, Biederman *et al.*, 2000).

(2) When subjects are asked to discriminate pictures of plants from animals, their electro-encephalograph shows differences at 190 milliseconds (VanRullen and Thorpe, 2001).

(3) In examining scenes, subjects use discrete eye fixations, each lasting about 100–300 milliseconds (Yarbus, 1967).

(4) From numerous measurements it is known that the time to complete a circuit of the cortical memory is about 100ms. This figure is also reinforced by the fact that decision making needs more time than this.

In contrast, at timescales longer than a second the world appears seamless, even though there are important temporal scales. Sentences take several seconds, speed chess requires at least an average of ten seconds per move, classes are organized around one hour, and learning new memories takes several episodes of many seconds during sleep. Figure 1 summarizes these points, showing a sharp boundary at about one second. The processes that operate on a timescale shorter than a second have a discrete character whose progress can be experimentally measured. Processes longer than one second are the ones we associate with seamless experience. Given the huge disparity in the nature of these two sets of processes, it would be very unlikely that a single model would work for both descriptive levels.

It might be the case that seamless perception is produced in a straightforward way of creating an internal picture, but, as has been argued many times, this conjecture can be readily dismissed as it produces an immediate problem of infinite regress: that picture has to be looked at and interpreted, etc. Thus the alternative that we are left with is that visual processing works in some less direct way to produce the experience of seeing from a temporal image sequence.

II: The Importance of Gaze

The human eye is distinguished among primates as having the most pronounced fovea. The human fovea is a small region in the retina of approximately one degree across at the centre of gaze where the resolution about 100 times that of the far periphery. Consequently, human vision relies extensively on the ability to make very fast eye movements (saccades) to orient the high-acuity foveal region of the eye over targets of interest in a visual scene.

Given the enormous increase in foveal acuity, it is easy to succumb to the idea that the primary function of gaze is to provide increased resolution. However, resolution *per se* is far from the only determinant of gaze location. Starting from Yarbus' classical work (Yarbus, 1967), many studies have suggested that gaze changes are directed according to the ongoing cognitive demands of the task at hand. The task-specific use of gaze is best understood for reading text where the eyes fixate almost every word, sometimes skipping over small function words. In addition, saccade size during reading is modulated according to the specific nature of the pattern recognition task at hand (Kowler and Kowler, 1987). Tasks requiring comparison of complex patterns also elicit characteristic saccades back and forth between the patterns. In copying of a model block pattern on a board, subjects have been shown to employ fixations for accessing crucial information during different stages of the task (Ballard *et al.*, 1995). In natural language processing, fixations can reflect the instantaneous parsing of a spoken sentence in the current visual context (Tanenhaus *et al.*, 1995). The role of gaze has been studied by in a variety of natural visuo-motor tasks such as driving, music reading and playing ping pong (Land and Hayhoe, to appear). In each case, gaze was found to play a central *functional* role, closely linked to the immediate task demands. All these tasks have very different kinds of fixation targets, sometimes only defined in terms of functional needs. For example, in driving around a bend, subjects fixate the tangent point of the curve to control steering angle, and in ping-pong, subjects fixate the bounce point in advance, in order to estimate the ball's trajectory.

All the above examples show the intimate relation between gaze location and the ongoing task, so it is natural to ask if there is a relation between gaze and attention. At one time it was believed that it was possible to dissociate these two, but more recent results suggest that gaze and attention are intimately linked (Deubel, 2000) and almost impossible to dissociate. Gaze follows attentional locus. One possibility for confusion is that changing gaze is a slow process compared to the time to extract information from the retina, so that in some cases gaze does not have time to follow attentional locus, providing an impression that they are more separable than is actually the case. However in situations where fovea resolution is required for the information extraction process, they are invariably linked. Thus gaze is a central element of the embodiment hypothesis. Seamless perception is a function of the ability of vision to extract information that guides behaviour and gaze is an indicator of the progress of this information extraction process.

III: Visual Routines

A key property of gaze location is that it is predominately discrete. The eyes typically focus on a specific point in space for a specific time. This is variable, but the modal fixation time is about 200 milliseconds.

Thus a research agenda for the embodiment stance is a specific model of how properties are computed by the brain during the short fixation interval. Since there are vast numbers of properties that one wants to compute, one way to be able to produce them is to use computational primitives that can be composed. The idea of computational primitives was suggested by Pat Carpenter and Marcel Just, but the first model that used computational primitives was proposed by Kosslyn (Kosslyn and Shwartz, 1977). Ullman is usually credited with describing the rationale for the composition of primitives that he termed *visual routines*. The basic idea of visual routines is simple. The computation of properties of the visual world can be described in terms of programs that are compositions of primitive programs. The primitive programs are each designed to compute some very specific property of the image, such as whether there is a specific colour at a specific point. Abstractly, the input to a routine is an image and the output is a predicate. Getting the primitive that biology might use is a difficult problem and it may be that the visual routines research progress was stalled initially because Ullman's first suggestions were not the right ones.

Rather than guess the right routines, it is easier to gather evidence that visual routines might be being used at all. Kosslyn has shown that the times taken to answer visual questions about landmarks on a map vary with the distance between the landmarks. In a neural recording experiment, neurons in striate cortex show enhanced responses for cells that are important to the task. Moreover, cases where two operations are called for take longer to display the enhanced response than cases that call for one operation (Roelfsema, Spekreijse *et al.*, 2000; Lamme, Heeger *et al.*, 2001). The experiment is very innovative and is described in Figure 3.

Additional evidence can be seen in a visual search experiment by Zelinsky *et al.* Subjects searching for an object have very different search paths when they have had time to memorize the location of an object compared to cases when they have to find the object using only its appearance. In the first case gaze can be transferred to the object with a single saccade. The second case typically requires three or more saccades and a curved trajectory. This provides a dramatic demonstration of the difference between slow time-scale perception and the fast time-scale of visual routines. Subjects are of course unaware that their search patterns are different between the two cases. Yet the circumstances of the experiment force them to use very different methods and this is reflected in the gaze trajectories. Typical saccade patterns for the two cases are shown in Figure 4.

Human subjects show remarkable insensitivity to changes in a display introduced during saccades or some other brief transient. This phenomenon has recently received extensive study as 'change blindness'. Visual routines provide a straightforward interpretation of these phenomena. One important property of a visual routine is that it must execute quickly. Thus an obvious suggestion is that one can only be aware of the properties of the world that are being tested by the routines that are running. Changes that do not impact these routines should not be noticed. Simons, reviewing the change blindness literature, suggests that there may be several causes of change blindness, since in different experiments subjects can report the representation before the change, the representation after the change, or a combination of the two. However the visual routines paradigm has a simple interpretation: the report is based on *when* the routine is run. Treisch *et al.*, provide recent evidence for this interpretation. Their block sorting experiment was done in a virtual reality environment using force feedback to pick up blocks and put them on moving conveyor belts. Subjects used sets of blocks consisting of two different sizes. On some of the block moves, the size of the block was changed. Three groups of subjects each had different instructions as shown in the following Table.

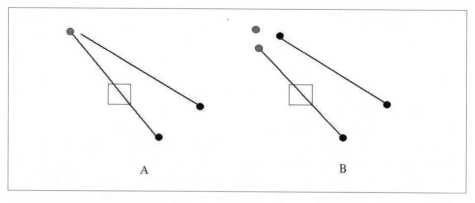

Figure 3. A schematic of Roelfsema et al. experiment providing evidence for visual routines.

A monkey has to make a saccade to the end of one of the two lines, starting from the point indicated by the arrow. Since it takes time to move the eyes, the response of a neuron lying on the path of the lower line can be studied in this interval. In A, the line is specified as the one connected to the starting point. In B, the line is specified as the one that has the same initial color as the starting point. Recordings show that the response of the neuron whose receptive field is localized to the rectangle is later in case B than case A. The suggestion is that the reason is that two visual routines are needed in B, one for the color and one for curve tracing.

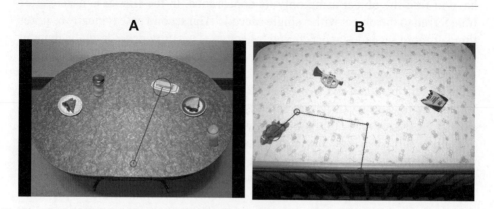

Figure 4. Evidence for visual routines in visual search

(A) Subjects preview a scene of objects in a venue for one second. Next, they see a small image of a target object. Then they see the original scene. In this case they can make a saccade directly to the object. (B) Without the preview they must find the object by its appearance and produced curved eye movement traces typically containing three or more saccades.

INSTRUCTIONS	% CHANGES REPORTED
'Pick up the blocks in front-to-back order and put them on the near conveyor belt.'	25
'Pick up the tall blocks first and put them all on the near conveyor belt.'	35
'Put the tall blocks on the near conveyor belt and then the small blocks on the far conveyor belt.'	57

The sensitivity to size changes is correlated with the importance of size to the task. One might wonder why the results are graded instead of all-or-nothing. If subjects should either run the size change routine or not, they would presumably have noted all or none of the size changes respectively. One answer could be that the size change procedure takes very little time so that the time when it is run is smaller than the time to transfer a block to the conveyor belt. Noticing the change depends on having the routine running when the change occurs. Another possible answer is that checking the size is probabilistic. So that it may or may not be done and the exigency is scaled with the task goals.

In any case the principal result is that subjects do not notice size changes, even when they are task relevant. A startling result is that some size changes are missed even when the subjects are fixating the block during the moment of the change. This provides some of the strongest evidence for the visual routines hypothesis. The suggestion is that gaze location is not the determiner of change detection. Change detection is a function of the instantaneous predicate being extracted by the visual routine.

IV: The Computational Demands of Visual Routines

Visual routines can require prodigious amounts of computation, which translates into prodigious amounts of circuitry in the brain. Salgian (Salgian and Ballard, 1998) modeled the use of a looming reflex for following a car in a simulated automobile driving task. When following a car the relative speed of the followed car is signaled visually by differential changes in looming. Salgian designed a neural circuit to detect these changes. The principle is straightforward: if the following car is gaining the visual image of the followed car will expand. Thus one strategy for detecting this is to sample images in time and then expand the previous image and compare it to the current image. If it matches, a looming is detected, and the following car must slow down. A similar computation can be done to detect a need to speed up. Although detecting looming might seem simple in principle, the realization of this algorithm requires much computation. In comparing the image one cannot compare the image samples directly because similar colours in whole areas produce too many false matches and a consequent false looming detection signal. Thus the matches have to be made somehow more unique. One way to do this is to not match image samples, but to match local features of each image sample. The area around an image sample varies and this variation can be detected by local spatial filters similar to those found in visual cortex.

A summary of the computation in looming detection is as follows. For every point in the image local features are use to replace the sample by a vector of measurements. The vector image is then compared to the corresponding image from a later time. Each feature is produced by the convolution of the image with a fixed image template. If the template is a modest 10 by 10 and the image is 1000 by 1000 and there are 25 templates, then the amount of multiplications that have to be done is 2.5×10^9. Another factor of ten is needed to handle normalization and comparison operations. If these operations are placed onto neural circuitry in the most obvious way the multiplications can be done with synapses, but the design of just this one operation still needs 250 million neurons or 1% of those available. Furthermore the templates used are typically standard edge detectors. If this strategy were to be extended to other features such as colour and texture and motion, another order of magnitude of neurons would be required.

One important question relates to the brain's parallel computing capabilities. Could it be the case that the brain can run many routines at the same time? At this time we cannot have a definitive answer to this question, but a good guess is that the number of simultaneous routines that can run is low and in fact is related to the capacity of working memory (Baddeley, 1986). Working memory is often studied in terms of the number of items that can be remembered in the short term, but is just as easily and perhaps more usefully conceived as the number of simultaneous routines that can be run. This number is Miller's famous 7 plus or minus 2, which more recently has been revised downward to about 4 (Miller, 1968). A possible reason for this low number is related to the fact that visual routines are likely to use massive amounts of similar neural circuitry. If this is the case, there must be some way to keep them from interfering with each other. This has been first characterized as the binding problem: if a neuron is active there seems to be no straightforward way to limit which computation it is participating in (von der Malsburg, 1995). Thus if 'red', 'blue', 'circle' and 'square' neurons are active, do we mean a red square and a blue circle or a blue square and a red circle? One obvious way to limit interference is to limit the number of routines that can be active simultaneously. The reinterpretation of the problem in terms of processing rather than data makes sense because we know that the brain has such limitations. The original interpretation of needing the properties in the world to cohere in the neural representation is unnecessary since they already have such coherence in the world itself.

The Salgian model is a synthetic model, so that we cannot be sure that the brain does not have a more clever way to minimize the requirements than the straightforward one assume here. However there is a wealth of information on early cortical representations, and the detailed characterizations of receptive fields suggest that precisely the kinds of neurons needed for pattern matching do exist in the required quantities. These facts are encouraging when synthetic experiments provide us with estimates of the circuitry required and these estimates suggest that the requirements are comparable.

V: The Human Brain as an Operating System?

Our overall theme is that below the time scale of one second, the substrate that produces seamless perception is fragmentary, and consists of a sequence of goal-directed tests conducted by visual routines. How is the brain anatomy organized in order support fragmentary constructions of experience? To support the visual routines model, there must be neural mechanisms not only to run the visual routines but also sequence through routines and choose new routines. Where could these mechanisms exist in the brain and how would they be represented? One line of emerging evidence suggests that the forebrain, which consists of anatomically and functionally distinct parts containing the basal ganglia, hippocampus and cortex, operates as a unit, with the different parts doing different jobs of scheduling and running routines.

The leading candidate for doing the main computation of visual routines is the cortex. However there are different models of the ways that the visual routine computations can be carried out. One of the leading candidates is that of an attractor (Hopfield, 1994). The cortex represents a set of constraints that are distributed in the different synaptic strengths of neural connections and are combined to produce a state that consists of a firing pattern of neurons across the whole of cortex. The attractor model is a nice fit to the observed timing relationships in cortex in that the time to communicate between all of the neurons is very fast, on the order of a few milliseconds. Since this time is small compared to the time of a visual routine, it is extremely likely that the whole of cortex is involved. Data is accumulating to suggest that the attractor model may be realized in terms of neural oscillations (Engel *et al.*, 2001).

Visual routines represent a quantum of computation that uses a huge fraction of the cortex but takes only about 100–200 milliseconds. For ongoing behaviour, successions of routines have to be strung together. Thus there needs to be some kind of sequencing mechanism that keeps track of what routine to run next. The leading candidate for sequencing routines is the basal ganglia. Neurons in the basal ganglia are associated with motor sequencing, but lines of evidence suggest that they are involved in the more general task of sequencing components of a learned program as well. Tanji (2001) showed that when monkeys learn a sequence of button presses, neurons in the basal ganglia learn to code subsets of the sequence. Schultz has shown that neurons in the basal ganglia are sensitive to reward, consistent with learning models that use reinforcement learning signals to predict reward. Surmeier has shown that tonically active neurons in the basal ganglia cease firing at logical breakpoints in a task, implying that they are sensitive to a task's steps (Surmeier, 2001).

The picture of the forebrain that emerges is one of a task-directed device that manages the progress of tasks through a sequence of distinct steps. An analogy would be that of an internal combustion engine in a car. The engine itself uses a set sequence of steps in combustion, but the net result is smooth forward motion. In the same way the sequence of steps in the brain may be the way that we perceive smooth seamless perception.

VI: A Small-Scale Model to Illustrate the Principles

The emergent description of short time scale perception is that it is driven by task-specific, discrete computations, consisting of collections of a small number of visual routines each taking on the order of 100–300 milliseconds to complete. We have outlined just a small portion of a host of experimental evidence for this fragmentary arrangement, but such evidence is in the form of necessary conditions. A successfully tested hypothesis acts as a constraint for the design of an overall system, but does not circumscribe that system. A complementary approach is to attempt to design a complete system using visual routines as an organizing principle. Such systems are necessarily very simple models of human complexity, but they nonetheless can illustrate the soundness of the hypotheses in another way; they provide sufficient conditions for the overall design, which, unlike individual hypotheses, must circumscribe the complete system at the chosen level of description.

Building a model human visual system situated in a body would have been unrealistic just a few decades ago, but recent advances in computer graphics models have provided another way to test the visual routines model: one can build a simulated human or virtual human in a graphics world, program behaviours based on vision in the simulated world and observe the results. This idea was pioneered by Rabie and Terzoupolis (1997), originally in model fish and most recently in model humanoids. Sprague and Ballard (2001) also use virtual humanoids as a platform for studying methods of attention in visual processing.

Basic computer vision research has made great progress in recent years. However, there is still little understanding of how to effectively utilize visual information to subserve the goals of mobile agents in dynamic environments. The central difficulty is that there is no general-purpose model of attention; most studies invariably tackle a single well-defined problem related to an observed property of attention. The more central question is: how is it possible to achieve behavioural generality, when computational feasibility demands the use of special purpose vision algorithms? The visual routines paradigm provides a possible answer to this question. The visual routines approach suggests that visual processing is built on top of a library of simple visual operators. Generality is achieved by composing multiple visual operators into task specific visual routines. The crucial property of the visual routines approach is that vision is procedural; when the performance of some task requires a piece of information, a visual routine is run that collects that information. This is an efficient approach because only the necessary visual processing is performed.

The challenge in designing a system based on visual routines lies in scheduling the routines to support ongoing behaviour. The approach is to restate behaviour-based control as a resource allocation problem. In particular, Sprague and Ballard consider individual behaviours to be analogous to threads of execution in a computer operating system. Behaviours, like computer processes, compete for a finite amount of processor time and for control of other limited resources. This competition takes the form of a set of auctions, where each behaviour places bids for the resources it needs. The model is illustrated using a humanoid that walks along a sidewalk in an urban environment. Besides staying on the sidewalk, the humanoid must also avoid obstacles.

The virtual humanoid simulation environment is composed of several different software components. The visual environment is a highly detailed 3D model of a small town including buildings, roads, and vehicles. The real world is not purely visual. In reality, objects collide, have mass, and in general, are governed by the laws of physics. A realistic simulation should have these characteristics as well. In order to provide our virtual world with physics, we use a physics simulation package that provides stable and fast kinematic simulation and contact detection. The graphical humanoid agent itself is built on Boston Dynamic's DI-Guy. DI-Guy provides visually realistic and highly efficient human motion generation based on motion capture. The disadvantage of motion capture based animation is that characters are limited to a library of pre-recorded motions. This does not allow for the closed loop control that is necessary for tasks involving hand-eye coordination. This limitation can be overcome by constructing an articulated arm driven by simple endpoint control. The arm is thus able to physically interact with the environment.

The visual routines are implemented with programs. Each routine has access to the video display from the humanoid's point of view and computes a specific property. The visual routine control architecture borrows heavily from ideas developed in the robotic agents community. In particular, the small autonomous robots developed for the autonomous vehicle soccer competition Robo-Cup have incorporated ideas of resource competition and state-dependent control of actuators. The virtual human extends these ideas to two levels of competition. Visual routines can compete for gaze resources in order to update their measurements of task relevant information. A separate round of competition is used to determine which of the running routines will control the body, as shown in Figure 5.

Behaviours must move between the regions in Figure 5 in order for the agent to accomplish his long term goals. Each of these transitions represents a different task that must be handled by the architecture. We will focus on the two innermost circles: selecting behaviours to run, and determining which behaviours should be given control of the body.

The set of relevant behaviours will generally evolve over the course of seconds or minutes as the agent's overall situation changes. However, there is also a need for a mechanism to select behaviours to execute at a finer time scale. This corresponds to moving moving a behaviour from 'Active' to 'Control' in Figure 5. Each of the agent's active behaviours is responsible for tracking some aspect of the environment and responding to it appropriately. Depending on the information that is being tracked, a given behaviour may need to run more or less frequently. For example, for walking in an urban environment, a sidewalk following behaviour can be run infrequently, because the sidewalk's relative position will remain fairly constant.

The goal of the attentional mechanism is to ensure that each active behaviour gets a large enough time slot to meet its own goals. More specifically a 'scheduler' chooses a single behaviour at every video frame and allows that behaviour

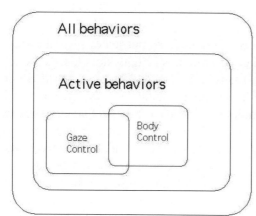

Figure 5.
The basic organization of behaviours
The outermost area contains the entire possible repertoire, most of which will be irrelevant at any given time. The area, 'active behaviours', contains all of the behaviours that are appropriate for the current task goals. The number is limited to working memory capacity. The area labelled 'Body Control' contains the behaviour(s) currently using the body and the area labelled 'Gaze Control' the behaviours that are controlling gaze position. The fact that these are a subset of all of the active behaviours is a consequence of the fact that the body is an even more scarce resource than working memory.

to execute. The frame rate of the simulation is approximately 12Hz, so the scheduler is run about 12 times per second. When a behaviour is chosen to run, it is allowed to move the eyes, and it is given exclusive access to the agent's visual input.

The scheduler is based on a probabilistic algorithm. Probabilistic scheduling is a simple but elegant mechanism, that allows proportional share resource distribution, and avoids starving processes. It works as follows: each process is allocated a probability based on exigency. The scheduler randomly selects one process from the entire current probability distribution and that process is then allowed to run. A dynamic prioritization mechanism allows behaviours to bid for parts of the body based on their perceived need. At each video frame all behaviors place in a bid in the range from zero to one indicating what share of the processor they would like to have. The architecture analyses all of these bids, and computes appropriate probabilities. Then the scheduler is run, the winning behaviour is given an opportunity to update its probability, and the process starts over. At present the architecture assigns probabilities in direct proportion to the behaviours relative bid. For example, if one behaviour bids twice as high as another, it will have twice the probability of being chosen.

If each behaviour is allowed to take control of the entire body every time it is chosen by the scheduler, then the agent will be susceptible to dithering; control of the body may rapidly alternate between multiple behaviours in such a way that no behaviour is able to accomplish its goal. In order to avoid this, control of locomotion resources are allocated separately from gaze. At each frame behaviours place bids for control of the body, and the behaviour that bids highest is given control for an appropriate interval. In addition to reducing dithering, this mechanism is desirable because it allows separate allocation of gaze and locomotion bodily resources; it may not always be the case that the behaviour that needs gaze the most also has the greatest need to control the body.

Putting a behaviour in control of the body is equivalent to moving it from 'Running' to 'Locomotion Control' in Figure 5. 'In Control' is not a proper subset of 'Running' because a behaviour maintains control of the body as long as its bid is highest, even if it is not actively gathering data from the environment.

The results of using this architecture are shown in the simple sidewalk navigation task. In this task the humanoid must walk along a sidewalk while simultaneously meeting two goals: avoiding a number of moving obstacles, and maintaining a constant distance from the street. Each of these goals is guided by an independent visual routine. Despite the simplicity of this task, it contains many of the challenging aspects of human vision, including time constraints, and conflicting priorities.

Figure 6 shows an example of the virtual humanoid performing the sidewalk navigation task. It can be seen that the agent is able to successfully avoid all obstacles, while staying close to the desired path. The next two figures examine the interaction of the two behaviours in some detail. The two vertical black lines in Figure 6 indicate the time period that will be examined in Figures 7 and 8.

Figure 8 shows the frame-by-frame leg bids placed by the two behaviours during the time period under consideration. Initially there are no obstacles nearby, and the sidewalk following routine has control of the agent. As the agent approaches each obstacle, the obstacle avoidance routine begins to ramp up its bid for control of the legs until it eventually takes control. Each time the obstacle avoidance behaviour takes over, the agent is pulled away from the path preferred by the sidewalk following behaviour. The sidewalk following behaviour responds by increasing its own bid.

The humanoid simulation is extremely oversimplified but it does provide us a concrete illustration of a model for the way the brain can interact with the body. Visual routines can use gaze to update measurements, and on a longer timescale, can direct the motion of the body in navigation and avoidance behaviours. The advantage of having a synthetic model is that in some sense we have a complete description of the requirements to do the task. Whether they are in fact done this way is still an open question, but the challenge of a competing description would be to reproduce the observed behaviours with the same or better fidelity. In any case the model suggests that complex behaviours may be possible by scheduling a handful of routines every 300 milliseconds. The exact number of such routines

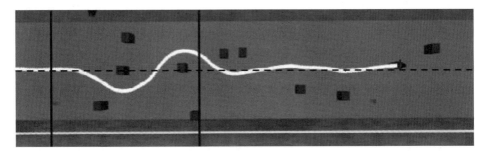

Figure 6. An overhead view of the virtual humanoid performing the sidewalk navigation task

The curving white line indicates the agent's path. The dotted horizontal line indicates the preferred path for the sidewalk following behaviour. The agent finds a reasonable compromise between staying on the preferred path and avoiding obstacles.

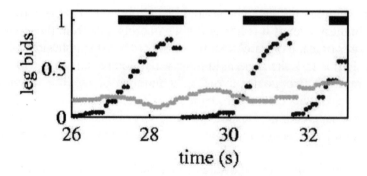

Figure 7. Bidding for control of gaze

A frame-by-frame trace of the bids for the control of gaze. Black points are the obstacle avoidance bids, and gray points are the sidewalk-following bids. Black bars at the top of the figure indicate the time periods during which the obstacle avoidance behavior has taken control by placing the highest bid; white spaces correspond to sidewalk-following. 'Control' corresponds to looking at a point appropriate for the winning behavior. Figure 4 shows the overall behavior during this time period. (From Sprague, 2001 #108.)

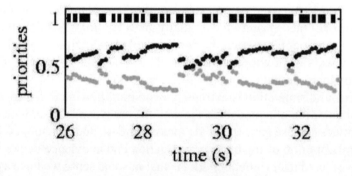

Figure 8. Bidding for control of the legs

The frame-by-frame trace of the bids placed for control of the legs by the two behaviors. The black points are the obstacle avoidance bids, and the gray points are the sidewalk following bids. The black bars at the top of the figure indicate the time periods during which the obstacle avoidance behavior has taken control by placing the highest bid. (From Sprague, 2001 #108.)

is open to experimentation. Naturally if it were very large then the model is unlikely to have much explanatory force, but the suggestion is that the number of routines is dictated by the capacity of working memory: that rather than seven plus or minus two 'items' we should think of seven plus or minus two routines. In this model, successful behaviour depends of the ability to have the right seven running at the right moment.

VII: The Grand Illusion Revisited

We have argued that the seamlessness of perception is grounded in a time scale of one second. What can be said about perception at this level? One of the most astonishing observations is the extent to which our perceptions are inventions. This is nowhere more apparent than in the study of patients who report phantom limbs. Such patients will swear that an amputated arm is still present and functional. Ramachandran's studies suggest that the problem might be that the part of the cortex that normally looked after the limb has been remapped to other body stimuli (Ramachandran and Blakesee, 1998). So the brain's representation of the arm looks still functional internally. But whatever the precise explanation, it is amazing that patients can override the visual image of a truncated arm along with its history.

In the case of phantom limbs patients think that they have something that they do not. Much more frequently subjects have no sensation of something that is missing. Split brain patients, whose corpus callosum has be cut to alleviate symptoms of epilepsy, do not notice anything is amiss, despite numerous tests that show that their abilities to coordinate information between the hemispheres has been impaired. Similarly, parietal patients can neglect one half of their visual field without realizing it. One has the distinct impression that conscious perceptions and the brain would behave like Alice's Cheshire cat: as more and more of the brain was damaged, perceptions would incrementally fade.

Perhaps the best description of conscious perception is Norretrander's description of the 'user illusion' (Norretranders, 1999). On a computer screen when we drag a file to the trash icon and deposit it with appropriate sound effects, we are dealing with a very abstract model of a complicated process that is nothing at all like this simple iconic description. Yet the simple description serves and is extremely satisfying be cause it interprets the complex process in terms of everyday experience. In the light of the complex perceptual mechanisms underlying brain machinery, this metaphor is a very satisfying description of the experience of seeing. Even though it must be an illusion, it is very satisfying one as it melds seamlessly with the structure of our everyday behaviours.

However to go further in understanding, we are forced to use a short time scale and on this time scale the descriptions that we can entertain are more detailed and completely at odds with our perceptions. On a finer scale there is overwhelming evidence that the interactions between the brain and visual world are extremely fragmented. This idea is not new: Humphreys makes it a central point that computing useful information takes a definite amount of time and so we cannot continuously be keeping up with the environment. Thus we are force to pick and choose the relationships in the environment that we focus on (Humphreys, 1993).

One of the most obvious and compelling arguments for fragmented perception is that of eye movements. The point of gaze is very tightly associated with our attentional focus and, since it switches to different targets at the rate of about three gazes per second, it reveals the rate of our fragmentary processing. To put it in other terms, we could fancifully entertain perceptual seamlessness as resulting from an interpolation of the environment; the temporal grain of eye movements of 1/3 of a second strongly suggests that the interpolation is not across image-like structures but some more abstract representation.

More evidence for the importance of gaze comes from Baron-Cohen's studies of autism in children (Baron-Cohen et al., 1997). Autistic children who have problems distinguishing what another person knows when it is different from their own self-knowledge. Importantly, they also have problems recognizing the direction of eye gaze in other people. Thus having a complete theory of mind of another person is correlated with being able to interpret that person's direction of gaze.

Of course seeing depends on a functioning brain. Furthermore on short time scale we can see the progression of neural representation of visual processing as the changing in firing patterns between neurons. But a finer distinction that can be made is that how different parts of the brain operate in concert during visual processing. We know that the basal ganglia contain representations of sequences in a task and reward signals related to those steps. We know that the cortex contains an elaborate memory for visual details such as faces, expressions, visual motions etc. We know that the hippocampus is essential for encoding those memories and that such encoding occurs during sleep.

VIII: Prospects for a Reductionistic Understanding of Consciousness

Ultimately we will have to have a comprehensive theory of visual processing that addresses conscious perception. But at the moment there are just models of various components. We have argued that the most promising avenue of a complete description of what the brain *does* lies at the short time scale level. What we term seeing is manifested in the brain as being able to predict the consequences of actions (Wolpert *et al.*, 2001). Visual actions take the form of routines designed to extract specific features from the image. The brain's functions can be described algorithmically in terms of Markov models that capture the state changes in a task and visual routines that extract information to characterize that state itself.

It may be much more difficult to have a satisfying explanation of visual processing at the longer time scale. The problem is that what we mean scientifically by satisfying is a reductionist explanation and it may well be that the experience of seeing is not readily isolated to any specific brain component or mechanism. However we have seen that there are several neural mechanisms that are correlated with conscious experience so the matter is far from settled at this point.

If one were to take an optimistic stance, and hold out for such a reductionistic explanation, one important cautionary fact to keep in mind is that almost any way of measuring the bandwidth of consciousness comes up with very small estimates. For example Norretranders' estimate of consciousness is 40 bits per second. Compare this with the spike rate of all the neurons in the cortex together of 10^{12} bits per second or more. Given this huge disparity, the effort needed to 'run' consciousness may be easily be dwarfed by that used to run just one routine. This provides a cautionary note for the efforts to find direct neural correlates of conscious perception (Rees *et al.*, 2002).

To review this final point, the computational capacity of conscious perception is probably very small after everything else is in place. From the standpoint of building a constructive model of the brain, the small 'cost' of consciousness in perception has at least one major consequence. Given its tiny bandwidth, a 'consciousness routine' necessarily works with only a summary of the brain's state. This summary depends crucially on a host of details that are expensive in themselves to compute but, for the most part, are inaccessible to conscious experience.

Refrences

Arnheim, R. (1967), *Visual Thinking* (University of California Press).

Baddeley, A. (1986), *Working Memory* (Oxford: Clarendon Press).

Ballard, D.H., Hayhoe, M.M., *et al.* (1995), 'Memory representations in natural tasks', *Journal of Cognitive Science*, **7**, pp. 723–67.

Baron-Cohen, S., Tooby, J., *et al.* (1997), *Mindblindness* (Cambridge, MA: MIT Press).

Biederman, I. (1998), *Visual Recognition of Repeated Images.* KTH Summer Workshop on Computer Vision, Stockholm.

Damasio, A.R. (1995), *Descartes' Error: Emotion, Reason, and the Human Brain* (Avon Books).

Deubel, H. (2000), 'Saccades, attention and subjective gaze', **29** (2-2 Suppl. S).

Engel, A.K., Fries, P., *et al.* (2001), 'Dynamic predictions: Oscillations and synchrony in top-down processing', *Nature Reviews Neuroscience*, **2**, pp. 704–16.

Hopfield, J.J. (1994), 'Neurons, dynamics and computation', *Physics Today*, **47**, pp. 40–7.

Humphreys, G.W. (1993), *Consciousness: Psychological and Philosophical Essays* (Oxford: OUP).

Kosslyn, S.M. and Schwartz, S.P. (1977), 'A simulation of mental imagery', *Cognitive Science*, **1**, pp. 265–95.

Kowler, E. and A.S. (1987), 'Reading twisted text: Implications for the role of saccades', *Vision Research*, **20**, pp. 45–60.

Lamme, V.A.F., Heeger, D.J., *et al.* (2001), 'The role of early visual areas in cognitive aspects of vision', *Society for Neuroscience Abstracts*, **27**.

Land, M. and Hayhoe, M.M. (to appear), 'In what ways do eye movements contribute to everyday activities?', *Vision Research* (Special Issue on Eye Movements and Vision in the Natural World).

Merleau-Ponty, M. (1992), *Phenomenolgy of Perception* (London: Routledge).

Miller, G.A. (1968), *The Psychology of Communication: Seven Essays* (London: Penguin).

Norretranders, T. (1999), *The User Illusion: Cutting Consciousness Down to Size* (Viking Press).

O'Regan, J.K. (1992), 'Solving the "real" mysteries of visual perception: The world as an outside memory', *Canadian J. Psychology*, **46**, pp. 461–88.

Rabie, T.F. and Terzopoulis, D. (1997), 'Active vision in artificial animals', *Journal of Computer Vision Research*, **1**, pp. 2–19.

Ramachandran, V.S. and Blakesee, S. (1998), *Phantoms in the Brain: Probing the Mysteries of the Human Mind* (William and Morrow & Co.).

Rees, G., Kreiman, G., *et al.* (2002), 'Neural correlates of consciousness in humans', *Nature Reviews Neuroscience*, **3** (4), pp. 261–70.

Roelfsema, P.R., Spekreijse, H. *et al.* (2000), 'The implementation of visual routines', *Vision Resarch*, **40**, pp. 10–12.

Salgian, G. and Ballard, D.H. (1998), *Visual Routines for Autonomous Driving.* 6th International Conference on Computer Vision (ICCV-98), Bombay, India.

Sprague, N. and Ballard, D.H. (2001), *A Visual Control Architecture for an Artificial Humanoid.* IEEE-RAS International Conference on Humanoid Robots, Tokyo, Japan.

Subramaniam, S., Biederman, I., *et al.* (2000), 'Accurate identification but no priming and chance recognition memory for pictures in RSVP sequences', *Visual Cognition*, **7**, pp. 511–35.

Surmeier, D.J. (2001), 'The colenergic interneuron: Tantalizing new results in basal ganglia research',

Tanenhaus, M.K., Spivey-Knowlton, K.M., *et al.* (1995), 'Intergration of visual and linguistic information in spoken language comprehension', *Science*, **268**, pp. 632–34.

Tanji, J. (2001), 'Sequential organization of multiple movements: Involvement of cortical motor areas', *Annual Review of Neuroscience*, **24**, pp. 631–51.

VanRullen, R. and Thorpe, S. (2001), 'The time course of visual processing: From early perception to decision-making', *Journal of Cognitive Neuroscience*, **13**, pp. 454–61.

von der Malsburg, C. (1995), 'Binding in models of perception and brain function', *Current Opinion in Neurobiology*, **5**, pp. 520–6.

Wolpert, D.M., Ghahramani, Z., *et al.* (2001), 'Perspectives and problems in motor learning', *Trends in Cognitive Sciences*,

Yarbus, A.I. (1967), *Eye Movements and Vision* (New York: Plenum Press).

Temre N. Davies
Donald D. Hoffman
Antonio M. Rodriguez

Visual Worlds

Construction Or Reconstruction?

Psychophysical studies of change blindness indicate that, at any instant, human observers are aware of detail in few parts of the visual field. Such results suggest, to some theorists, that human vision reconstructs only a few portions of the visual scene and that, to bridge the resulting representational gaps, it often lets physical objects serve as their own short-term memory. We propose that human vision reconstructs no portion of the visual scene, and that it never lets physical objects serve as their own short-term memory.

Introduction

According to the standard account, vision is a process of reconstruction. From images at the eyes, human vision reconstructs those properties of the physical world that are useful to the viewer (Marr, 1982). The task of vision, on this account, is the inverse of the task of computer graphics.

A graphics expert starts with a 3D specification of a scene, the positions and shapes of all its objects, the reflectance functions of all its surfaces, and the extent, position, and spectral composition of all its light sources. Then from any vantage point, and assuming any camera model, the expert can render an image of the scene using techniques such as ray tracing. Although rendering is computationally expensive, it enjoys the simplifying property that it is mathematically well-posed: a solution almost always exists, is unique, and varies continuously with changes in the scene or camera.

The task of vision, on the standard account, is just the opposite. Vision starts with a rendered image, or a pair of rendered images, or even a dynamically changing pair of rendered images. The visual system must then reconstruct the physical scene, including the positions and shapes of all its objects, the reflectance functions of all its surfaces, and the extent, position, and spectral composition of all its light sources. As Yuille and Bülthoff (1996, p. 123) put it,

'We define vision as perceptual inference, the estimation of scene properties from an image or a sequence of images.' In particular, they are interested 'to model the individual visual cues for estimating the depth and material properties of objects . . .' (p. 124). So on the standard account, the scene consists of physical objects and their material properties, and the more accurately human vision can estimate depth and material properties from images, the better it can reconstruct the scene and its objects. The goal is reliable perception, i.e., to make the estimation as accurate as possible so that the objects and properties reconstructed by the visual system resemble as much as possible their physical counterparts in the scene.

To this end some vision researchers try to systematically measure the distribution of certain properties of the physical world. Once these distributions are accurately measured, they can be compared to the estimations computed by the visual system, to see how accurate the visual estimations are. Maloney and Wandell (1986), for instance, in a paper entitled 'Color constancy: a method for recovering surface spectral reflectance', propose a computational theory for color constancy. In their theory, color constancy is primarily the problem of estimating or recovering surface spectral reflectances. They justify their theory in part by appeals to objective physical measurements of natural terrain reflectances by Krinov (1947), and conclude that their theory can adequately reconstruct natural reflectances.

Visual reconstruction is computationally expensive, and suffers the complicating property that it is mathematically ill-posed: solutions do not always exist, are almost never unique when they do exist, and need not vary continuously with changes in the images. This ill-posedness was well understood by Berkeley, who wrote

> It is, I think, agreed by all that distance, of itself and immediately, cannot be seen. For distance being a line directed endwise to the eye, it projects only one point in the fund of the eye, which point remains invariably the same, whether the distance be longer or shorter (Berkeley, 1709/1963, p. 19).

Berkeley's point is that for any given images at the eyes, there are countless distinct 3D worlds which could have projected to those images.

What is true of depth is true of other properties such as shading, motion, reflectance, illumination, and even object identity: for any given images at the eyes there are countless distinct states of these properties in the world which could have generated those images. The task of vision is ill-posed everywhere you look.

The standard account explains the success of vision, despite the ill-posedness of its task, by positing that the processes of visual reconstruction can be modeled as nondemonstrative inferences, typically unconscious, which exploit regularities of the physical world (Knill and Richards, 1996). This inferential explanation has a long and venerable history, dating back at least to the Islamic scholar Alhazen (965–1039 AD), who wrote:

> For the shape or size of a body, or the transparency of a transparent body, and such like properties of visible objects, are in most cases perceived extremely quickly, and

not immediately, since they are perceived by inference and discernment . . . (Translated by Sabra, 1978, p. 176).

An inferential account of vision was also elaborated by Hermann von Helmholtz (1821–1894) who wrote:

> The psychic activities that lead us to infer that there in front of us at a certain place there is a certain object of a certain character, are generally not conscious activities, but unconscious ones. In their result they are equivalent to a conclusion, . . . it may be permissible to speak of the psychic acts of ordinary perception as unconscious conclusions, thereby making a distinction of some sort between them and the common so-called conscious conclusion (Helmholtz, 1910).

Many regularities of the physical world have been studied, and shown to be in principle capable of leading to unique reconstructions of different aspects of the physical world. For instance, light sources tend to be overhead (Howard *et al.*, 1990), and their spectra are usually linear combinations of just three basis vectors (Maloney, 1985). Surface reflectances tend to change abruptly (Land, 1977), and are often linear combinations of just a few basis vectors (Maloney and Wandell, 1986; Marimont and Wandell, 1992). Many objects move rigidly (Ullman, 1979; Bennett et al., 1989), quasi-rigidly (Ullman, 1984), or piecewise-rigidly (Hoffman and Flinchbaugh, 1982); and they intersect transversally to create parts of more complex objects (Hoffman and Richards, 1984).

The standard account has proven powerful both in theory and in practice. Modeling vision as bayesian inference has led to the construction of numerous computer-vision systems with remarkable performance (Knill and Richards, 1996).

Change Blindness

Although the standard account states that vision reconstructs the physical scene, it doesn't state how much, or which properties, of the scene are reconstructed at any one time. Marr himself was not explicit on this point, but a reasonable interpretation of his theory is that he intended the early stages of reconstruction, which he called the primal sketch and $2^1/_2$ D sketch, to simultaneously encompass the entire visual field. These stages reconstructed the edges, surfaces, reflectances, and viewer-centered depths of the visible world. The last stage, which Marr called the 3D model, reconstructed objects in an object-centered framework, and did not seem intended to encompass the entire visual field at once, but rather to proceed on a small number of objects at a time.

Other theorists, however, have proposed that the reconstruction gives rise to stable and richly detailed representations of the entire visible world (Feldman, 1985; Trehub, 1991). Experimental studies of change blindness suggest that this is false (Rensink, 2000a). In a typical study using the 'flicker' paradigm, a subject is shown a picture of a scene for a few hundred milliseconds, followed by a blank screen for about one hundred milliseconds, followed by the original picture of the scene for a few hundred milliseconds, followed by a blank screen, and so on repeatedly until the subject responds or time runs out (Rensink, O'Regan and Clark, 1997, Rensink, 2000b; see also Phillips, 1974). The subject's task is to decide if the two pictures of the scene are the same or different. The differences can include deleting objects, moving objects, or changing the colours of objects. Subjects typically find this task difficult, and can sometimes require several minutes to discover a major change, such as the deletion of a large object.

This result comes as a surprise to most subjects. It has also come as a surprise to many seasoned vision researchers. Several theories have been proposed to account for it (see Visual Cognition, 2000, volume 7, for several papers and a review). However the dominant theory is that human vision reconstructs certain primitive visual properties over the entire visual field, but that the reconstruction and storage of more advanced properties requires selective attention (Rensink, 2000b) and has a limited capacity of five or six items. Only those five or six items that have been reconstructed and stored in visual short term memory (vSTM) are available for change detection in the flicker paradigm, or for change detection across eye blinks or saccades. Normally the visual system relies on motion or brightness transients to draw its attention to image changes. However saccades, eye blinks, and the blank screens of the flicker paradigm all serve to interfere with the normal processing of transients, and force the visual system to rely only on the few items it has stored in vSTM to detect changes.

The recent literature on negative priming of visual objects indicates, however, that unattended objects can be recognized implicitly and that the visual system can detect changes to these unattended objects, as evidenced by implicit measures such as reaction times (Khurana et al., 2000). This suggests that current theories of change blindness might need to be modified somewhat to account for these negative priming results. In particular, attention is not required to hold object files in coherence over space and time, and unattended object files can persist for days or even weeks (DeShepper and Treisman, 1996). Again, these negative priming results are based on implicit measures of change detection; subjects cannot consciously report the changes that they implicitly report. The conscious reports appear to require attention.

The World As Short Term Memory

If at most five or six items are stored in vSTM, and these are the only aspects of the visual scene that survive eye blinks and saccades, then it seems reasonable to suggest that the visual system relies on the physical world to serve as its own short term memory. Each time that information about the scene is needed, the visual system does not pull the details out of its own internal representation, instead it just looks to the right place in the scene and reconstructs whatever information is needed. The possibility that the world serves as its own short-term memory was suggested long ago by Stroud:

> In the case of vision for mammals, since our illumination is typically continuous sunlight and most of the scenery 'stays put,' the physical object can serve as its own 'short-term memory.' The way we 'remember things best' in the immediate visual present is to 'keep looking at them' (Stroud, 1955, p. 199).

It has also been suggested more recently by O'Regan:

seeing constitutes an active process of probing the external environment as though it were a continuously available external memory (O'Regan, 1992, p. 484).

For this approach to work, the visual system must reconstruct some stable properties of the entire visual scene as part of its early visual processing, so that this information can be used to direct attention to those parts of the scene which need to be reconstructed in greater detail. An architecture for doing this has been proposed by Rensink (2000a).

These points are all easily accommodated by the standard theory. The key idea remains that vision reconstructs useful properties of the physical world. The only modification required is to note that vision is selective in what it reconstructs. Reconstruction proceeds primarily on an as-needed basis. And only five or six items are reconstructed in detail at any one time. We never feel bothered or limited by having details on such few items at a time, for the simple reason that we can quickly get details whenever and wherever we need them by simply redirecting our attention. As a result, as Noë (2000, p. 203) puts it, 'It seems to us as if all the detail is in the environment, which is where, in fact it is.'

Is It Reconstruction Or Just Construction?

One aspect of the standard account that deserves closer scrutiny is its claim that visual representations of a physical scene are, in whole or in part, reconstructions. It doesn't claim merely that they are constructions, but makes the stronger claim that they are reconstructions. A reconstruction, as most vision researchers use the term, means a construction with the further property of resemblance. To say that the visual system reconstructs the cats I see before me means that it constructs representations of cats that resemble, in relevant respects, the real physical cats. To say that the visual system reconstructs, or recovers, the 3D shape of the cats is to say that it constructs representations of the 3D shapes of the cats that correctly match, to within some useful tolerance, the real 3D shapes of the physical cats. To say that it recovers the colours of the cats is to say that it constructs representations of their colours that correctly match, to within some useful tolerance, the real colours.

Such claims of matching or resemblance are stronger than necessary, and stronger than is justified. First we will consider why they are stronger than necessary, and then why they are stronger than is justified.

Reconstruction Is Stronger Than Necessary

Consider the visual processes involved in watching a movie, such as The Score, on the big screen. The visual system of the viewer constructs a multitude of objects and people—the vault, the priceless sceptre, Marlon Brando, Robert Deniro, Ed Norton. But would it be correct to say that the visual system reconstructs these objects and people? It would seem not, since these objects and people are not literally in front of the viewer. Instead, the viewer looks at a white screen with changing coloured lights projected onto it.

Now one might maintain that, although the objects and people are not literally before the movie viewer, it still makes sense to say that the viewer reconstructs them. For at some point in the filming of the movie those objects and people were literally before the camera, and the camera served merely as a convenient surrogate for the viewer's own eye.

Then consider a viewer watching a completely animated film, such as Shrek. In this case the objects and creatures that the viewer sees never were literally before the camera. The viewer constructs these objects and creatures, but could not reconstruct them because they don't literally exist.

Take this one step further, and consider interactive virtual reality games, in which the viewer dons a helmet and body suit, and proceeds to fight virtual aliens, explore virtual worlds, or toss a virtual softball to the virtual image of another person who has also donned a helmet and body suit. Again all the objects and people that the viewer constructs are not reconstructions. There are no literal aliens that the viewer interacts with, and therefore no aliens to be reconstructed. What the viewer interacts with is a supercomputer and megabytes of software. The visual constructions of the viewer in no way resemble the diodes and resistors of the supercomputer that houses the software of the virtual-reality game. Nor do they resemble the lines of C++ and OpenGL code that constitute the software.

And this is no problem at all for the viewer. To successfully fight virtual aliens, viewers don't need that their visual constructions are in fact reconstructions, all they need is for their visual constructions to be useful guides for their subsequent actions. One could in principle successfully fight those aliens by studying the C++ code of the virtual-reality game and then setting the correct values in the correct registers. But the visual constructions of the viewers allow them to bypass all the nasty code, even to be ignorant of the existence of code, and still successfully interact with that code in a way that lets them defeat the virtual aliens. Useful constructions are necessary for survival in virtual worlds or the real world; reconstructions are not.

One might argue that the viewer's constructions in the virtual-reality game are reconstructions, not of physical objects directly before the viewer but of the objects that were in the mind of the game designer. And these in turn were the game designer's reconstructions of objects in the physical world. But suppose that the game maker did not directly code the objects in the game, but instead coded a genetic algorithm that probabilistically evolved the flora, fauna, and inanimate objects of the game. Then even the game maker would be surprised at the creatures that eventually evolved in the game, just as Richard Dawkins (1986) was surprised by the 'biomorph' shapes that evolved from his own genetic algorithm.

In this case of the blind game maker, the viewer is not reconstructing the objects in the mind of the game maker. Instead both the viewer and maker are constructing de novo the objects they experience when they don a helmet.

One might still argue that, although these novel visual objects are not reconstructions, nevertheless the parts of which they are made are not novel, and thus these parts are reconstructions. The novel objects are merely novel combinations of familiar, and reconstructed, parts.

This argument is more difficult to counter. Examples of objects that cannot be reconstructions will not counter it. For instance, consider the 'devil's triangle' devised by Oscar Reutersvärd (1984) in 1934:

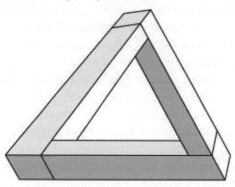

It is fairly straightforward to build a 3D structure out of wood which, when photographed from exactly the right angle, gives rise to this image (Gregory, 1970, p. 56). However, the 3D 'object' that our visual systems construct when viewing this figure is physically impossible, i.e., it could not be built out of wood. Therefore it could not be a reconstruction. However, the individual parts of which it is made are perceived individually as 3D shapes that are physically possible. So one can argue that although the entire devil's triangle could not be a reconstruction, its parts could be.

But our claim in this section is not that reconstruction is impossible, just that it is a stronger condition than is necessary: construction, without reconstruction, will suffice. For this purpose, the devil's triangle establishes that there are some perceptual objects, namely the 'impossible objects,' that cannot be reconstructions. They must simply be constructions. This demonstrates that at least some perceptual constructions are not reconstructions. Reconstruction is not a necessary property of visual constructions. Why require that object parts be reconstructions if the objects themselves are not reconstructions?

Another case in which some constructions cannot be reconstructions occurs in colour perception. Some women are, genetically, tetrachromats rather than trichromats. They have four distinct colour pigments rather than the normal three. Careful psychophysical studies combined with genetic assays have found that these women perceive a richer world of colour than do the rest of us (Jameson, Highnote, and Wasserman, 2001). So if two observers, one a tetrachromat and one a trichromat, both see a peacock, the colours they construct are different. Therefore, assuming that the peacock has definite colours to be reconstructed, at least one of the two observers must not be reconstructing the colours of the peacock. And if at least one of them is merely constructing, not reconstructing, the colours of the peacock, it is surely in the cards that they both might be merely constructing, not reconstructing, these colours. Again, reconstruction is not necessary.

This same style of argument holds for photographic negation. If an image is shown in photographic negative, the patterns of shading that it displays are not, in general, depictions of physically possible illuminations of 3D objects. That is, there is no set of 3D objects and illuminations that could project to the given image. Therefore there are no physically possible worlds that could be reconstructions from that image. But observers nevertheless construct interpretations of these images as illuminated scenes of 3D objects (Subramaniam and Biederman, 1997), although negated faces may pose special problems (Liu, Collin, and Chaudhuri, 2000). Such constructions from negated images cannot be reconstructions. And once again this suggests that if some constructions are not reconstructions, then perhaps no constructions are attempts at reconstruction.

A further problem for reconstruction is synesthesia, an unusual mixing of the senses (Cytowic, 1993). Some synesthetes hear what they see, others see what they hear. One felt tastes with his hands. The taste of mint, for instance, felt to his hands as smooth, cool columns of glass. Every taste had its systematically associated feel, and he found this quite useful as an aid to creative cooking. However it would be quite a stretch to imagine that the feel of smooth columns of glass in response to eating mint is in any way a reconstruction. It is simply a construction that most of us don't make, but that happens to be quite useful to the one person who does make it.

Reconstruction Is Stronger Than Is Justified

It is one thing to argue that visual reconstruction is more than is necessary to account for our perceptions and for our survival, and that visual constructions will do just fine, but it is quite another to argue that in fact the constructions of vision are not justifiably called reconstructions.

We can use the powerful tools of the standard account itself to argue for this stronger claim. According to the standard account, vision is a process of inference in which the initial premises are images, I, and the conclusions are those properties of the visual scene, S, that the viewer constructs. The viewer determines the probabilities of various scene properties S given the images I, i.e., the viewer determines $P(S|I)$, and then selects those scene properties that satisfy some criterion such as maximizing probability or minimizing risk (Knill and Richards, 1996). The standard formulation of this inference uses Bayes rule:

$$P(S|I) = \frac{P(I|S)P(S)}{P(I)}.$$

In this equation, the term $P(I|S)$ is a markovian kernel often called the 'likelihood function' by Bayesians and the 'rendering function' by vision theorists. It describes the probabilities that various possible images I would be rendered, given that the scene property is S. The computation of these probabilities just is the graphics rendering problem which, as we described earlier, is complex but well posed. The term $P(S)$ is a probability measure called the 'prior'. It describes the biases or assumptions that the viewer brings to the construction process, such as a bias toward rigid 3D objects or toward light sources that are overhead. The term $P(I)$ is simply a normalization factor which can be ignored unless it is zero, in which case continuous formulations of Bayes rule can be employed (Bennett et al., 1996). Finally the term $P(S|I)$ is a markovian kernel called the 'posterior distribution'. It describes, as mentioned above, the probabilities of various scene properties S given the images I.

Now on the standard account the viewer's construction is some function f of the posterior distribution; that is, the construction is $f(P(S|I))$, where f is a function which optimizes some property such as risk. This account is intended to hold not only for vision, but for all perceptual modalities. In each modality the perceiver's constructions, and therefore the perceiver's perceptions, are a function of the relevant posterior distribution.

The issue of reconstruction then becomes: Do the constructions $f(P(S|I))$ resemble or match the corresponding items in the physical world? To get empirical evidence to decide this question, we would need to compare the objective state of the items in the physical world against the constructions $f(P(S|I))$. The problem is that the standard account allows us only one way to get information about the state of the physical world, namely via Bayes rule and $f(P(S|I))$. It does not allow non-inferential access to the objective state of the world. Every time we go to assess the state of the world, we are limited to seeing only what we construct (Bennett, Hoffman, and Prakash, 1989; Knill and Richards, 1996). This remains true even if we extend the range of our senses with various high-tech instruments. What we can perceive by means of those instruments, and of their readings, is limited to what our own senses can construct. It is true that these instruments can extend the range of our senses, e.g., from the visible electromagnetic spectrum to xrays and gamma rays. But they do not let us somehow bypass the inferential apparatus of the visual system and other perceptual systems, and indeed they often require, in addition, the more elaborate inferential apparatus of scientific theory building for their interpretation.

For this reason there is no way, on the standard account of perception, for the viewer to obtain the empirical evidence needed to justify the claim that perceptual constructions are in fact reconstructions.

One might ask how this can be so, since the standard account needs the formal model S before it can even get started. Where does S come from? And isn't S just the information required to determine if our perceptual constructions are in fact reconstructions? Unfortunately not. S does not represent the mind-independent external world. It represents the range of possible constructions available to the observer. Knowing S still leaves wide open the question of whether these constructions are reconstructions.

But doesn't natural selection guarantee that our perceptions are in fact reconstructions? Didn't those whose perceptions were more accurate reconstructions have a reproductive advantage over the rest, with the result, over aeons of evolution, that we are now a race that reconstructs the world quite accurately? Not at all. Natural selection promotes perceptions which guide useful behaviours. Roaches flee light, moths approach light. Neither species need accurately reconstruct the world in any sense; they just need perceptual constructions that usefully guide their behaviour. Arguments from natural selection do justify the claim that our perceptions are useful constructions; they don't justify the claim that they are reconstructions.

The Physical World Is Not A Short-Term Memory

The idea that perceptual constructions are reconstructions, and the idea that the physical world can serve as its own short-term memory, are intimately linked. The reason the physical world could serve as a short-term memory is that the information that is effectively stored in the state of the physical world can be reconstructed as needed by the perceptual system of the observer. As long as the reconstruction can be triggered whenever needed, and as long as it proceeds quickly enough once it is triggered, then there is no reason to waste cortical resources to store what is already in the world. If, for instance, I am walking outside on a moonlit night, there is no need to store the moon in my short-term memory, since I can just look at the moon and quickly reconstruct it whenever I need.

But we have just seen that perceptual constructions need not be reconstructions to be of use for survival, and that there are no empirical grounds to justify the claim that perceptual constructions are reconstructions. Thus there are no empirical grounds to justify the claim that the physical world serves as its own short-term memory. For, in order to justify this claim we would have to show that the constructions of the observer match, within allowed tolerances, the items in the physical world; without such a match, the world cannot serve as a high-fidelity memory. Now of course it is not true in general that the format of what is stored in a memory must match the format of what is ultimately retrieved from that memory. Good memories can use elaborate encoding schemes to improve efficiency in storage. But in the currently published accounts of the world as short-term memory, the assumption is made that vision recovers, i.e., faithfully reconstructs, the items that are in the world. And that assumption is not justified.

Philosophical realists will of course object to this line of argument. A typical objection is that of Musgrave (1989):

> Indeed, some pretty mundane and well-entrenched results of science tell us that the moon (not some hyphenated moon, not even the Kantian moon-in-itself, just the moon) is objective and independent of us: it exists outside of our heads, it was not created by us, it existed before we did, and so forth (Musgrave, 1989, in Curd and Cover, 1998, p. 1221).

Whatever these results of science might be that are supposed to tell us this, they are surely not the results of physics, and especially quantum physics, which have told us instead that we should be extremely careful about our claims to knowledge of the world 'outside of our heads' (Albert, 1992; Barrett, 1999). Indeed the textbook interpretation of quantum theory, the so-called Copenhagen interpretation, maintains that observations of subatomic particles do not reconstruct dynamical physical properties of those particles because, between acts of observation, there are no values to reconstruct. The sciences that most directly bear on the issue of the relation between perception and the world 'outside' are the cognitive science and neuroscience of perception. And pretty mundane and well-entrenched results of these sciences, as we have briefly discussed, tell us a quite different story about the moon (Hoffman, 1998).

The World As A Reliable Trigger

If we reject the concept of the physical world as a short-term memory, then how do we deal with the fact, revealed by change-blindness experiments, that visual short-term memory is limited to five or six items? If the memory is not in the head, and it's not in the physical world, where else can it be?

For an answer, we can consider again the example of the virtual-reality game. When the players have donned their helmets and body suits they find themselves immersed in some new visual world. Perhaps they are in a forest which is filled with various trees, rocks, sticks, leaves, and creatures. A player might look at a particular tree, then look away. If someone else asks what colour were its leaves or what branching structure characterized its limbs, then the player could look back at that same tree to obtain the answer. In this case the player is using the environment as a memory. But there is nothing in that environment that resembles the tree that the player observes. In this example, the environment is some supercomputer with many megabytes of software, but no trees. Yet this treeless environment effectively serves as a memory for the tree, because the player can act on that environment in such a way that the environment, in turn, triggers the player's visual system to construct the tree. The player acts on the environment by means of eye, head, and body movements, which are measured and transmitted to the supercomputer. The environment, in turn, triggers the player to construct the tree by having the supercomputer transmit a carefully crafted spray of photons to the player's helmet. The player is not reconstructing a tree that is in the environment; the player is instead constructing a tree in response to triggers from a treeless environment (Hoffman, 1998).

There is evidence as well from studies of eye movements that the environment triggers the visual system to construct, preattentively, a description of the 'gist' of an entire visual scene with each glance of the eye (De Graef, 1998). This gist describes the kind of visual scene it is, such as a garden scene or a gymnasium scene, and includes a parsing of the scene into objects, with a description of each object that is at least rich enough to determine if the object fits meaningfully into the scene, or if it is instead anomalous, such as a garden hose in a gymnasium. This preattentively constructed scene can then be used by the observer to guide eye movements and focus attention on specific objects in order to make more detailed constructions of these objects (Rensink, 2000b). Again these more detailed constructions are triggered by the interactions of the observer with the environment.

What is the nature of this environment? To investigate this question is a matter for scientific theory building, and beyond the scope of this paper. One theory is a form of naive realism which holds that, in many important respects, this environment is isomorphic to the constructions of observers, and so these constructions are in fact reconstructions of the environment. But as we have seen, this theory is at present not necessary and not justified.

Nevertheless it is natural to ask: If perceptual constructions are just constructions — not reconstructions — how can one account for the consistency of the visual world? I can inspect some portions of a table, turn away for a while, then come back and continue where I had left off. Doesn't this consistency of visual experience have everything to do with the environment serving as an external memory?

Indeed it does, and this is no problem even if we reject reconstruction in favour of construction. One can still retain the notion of an external environment that is mind independent, in the sense that its existence does not depend on the mind or observations of any particular observer. In the virtual-reality example above, the supercomputer with its game software served in this role as the mind-independent environment. The key point is that this environment need not in any way resemble anything in our worlds of visual experience, just as the supercomputer and its software don't resemble the rocks, trees, and creatures of the virtual world that the helmet-laden observer experiences. Those worlds of experience can merely be a useful graphical user interface to the external environment, allowing us to interact effectively with that external environment.

So the environment can serve as an external memory, without needing to resemble anything in our worlds of visual experience. As long as it is mind independent, and allows us to consistently interact with it in a manner that triggers us to create the same visual worlds, it can serve as a source of consistency for our visual worlds, and therefore as a reliable memory.

Of course a mind-independent environment cannot be the only source for the consistency of our visual worlds. Another source is the rule-governed nature of our own constructive processes of perception. Systematic computational and psychophysical studies of human visual perception have uncovered dozens of interacting rules which guide the construction of our visual worlds. Some of these we mentioned earlier, such as trying to construct rigid objects, or modeling light sources and surface reflectances as linear combinations of a small number of basis functions. If the observer interacts with a consistent and mind-independent environment, and if in consequence of the interaction the observer is triggered to engage the same set of rules of construction, then the resulting worlds of visual experience will also be consistent. And all without need of any resemblance relation between the worlds of visual experience and the mind-independent environment.

Even cases of inconsistency in visual experiences can be understood in this framework. Consider, for instance, the well-known Necker cube, published in 1832 by the Swiss naturalist Louis Albert Necker:

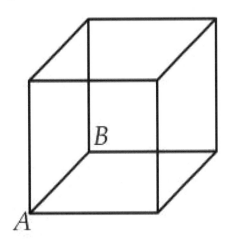

If you look at the figure, you will see a cube, perhaps with the corner labelled A in front. If you look away and then look back at the figure, you might again see a cube with corner A in front. That is an example of consistency of perception, and it can be explained as a result of your application of a consistent set of rules of construction: You see the same cube repeatedly because you engage the same rules repeatedly each time you look.

However, sometimes when you look you might see a different cube, one with corner B in front. This demonstrates a failure of consistency in our worlds of visual experience. But it can also be explained in the construction framework. The rules of construction which create a cube are here being given a trigger which is a tad ambiguous. The rules result in two, rather than just one, 3D construction. Your visual system must pick one or the other construction, and sometimes it switches which one it picks. So the rules that help explain the consistency of visual experience also can account for its occasional multistability, viz., as a consequence of rules leading to multiple constructions. Notice again that the cubes being constructed here are not likely to be reconstructions, since it is highly improbable that there is a cube in a mind-independent physical world that is changing its shape each time your perception of the Necker cube reverses.

After reading this section one might ask, 'What is the deep difference between an external stable trigger and an external memory?' Our answer is 'None'. We are not trying to distinguish between an external stable trigger and an external memory. We do distinguish between two theories of external memory. The first says that external memory is in fact a physical world whose contents resemble the contents of our perceptions. The second says that external memory need not in any way resemble our perceptions, any more than the software and hardware driving a virtual reality display resembles the perceptions of someone immersed in a virtual world. And we are endorsing the second theory.

So What?

So what if perception is construction, and not reconstruction? This might be of interest to philosophers, but what difference does it make to practicing vision scientists? One difference is that the two theories make different empirical predictions. D'zmura, Colantoni, and Seyranian (2000) have created an immersive virtual world with four spatial dimensions and one temporal dimension. Users don a helmet and data glove, and set off exploring this 4D world, finding 4D objects, and chasing and shooting 4D aliens. The entertainment value of such a system is obvious. Once you've battled aliens in 4D, then 3D seems insipid by comparison. But an intellectual question was the primary force driving the creation of the 4D virtual world: Could human users learn to build visual maps of 4D worlds? It is too early to know the answer for sure, but initial results are encouraging.

However, if perception is reconstruction, and if the physical world in fact has only three (uncurled) spatial dimensions, then there is no need to do perceptual research on whether human subjects can learn to perceive and visualize in 4D.

The answer must be that they cannot. Since they can only reconstruct, and since our best theories of physics tell us that there is no 4D world to reconstruct, they can never have 4D perceptions.

But if perception is construction, and not restricted to being merely reconstruction, then it's an open possibility that some human observers might learn to perceive 4D worlds. This is a different empirical prediction than one obtains from the reconstruction theory. Thus, asking if perception is construction or reconstruction is not like asking how many angels can dance on the head of a pin. It makes another difference as well. Giving up the doctrine of reconstruction frees the theorist to consider a much wider range of possibilities for the relationships between perception and the world. One example comes from a practical problem faced by various intelligence agencies. They must daily comb through mountains of books, magazines, newspapers and other media looking for those rare tidbits of information that might prove critical to national security. At present this must ultimately be done by human readers, since only such readers can effectively do the job.

But their job could be made much easier if an artificial intelligence program could first search all the articles for key words, and then organize them and present them graphically in such a way that the human readers would look first at the most interesting and most informative articles. So what is needed is a way to map abstract categories of information, say information about terrorists, bombs, weapons and oil, into a virtual visual world so that the human user can navigate through this virtual world and quickly find the important information. The virtual world might take the appearance of a 3D city with visual icons of oil cans and bearded hoodlums; or it might look like a forest populated with predatory animals and hostile plants; or it might assume whatever other appearance turns out to be an effective guide for the human users. Clearly this mapping need not, indeed in most cases cannot, be an isomorphism between the various important categories of abstract information and the virtual visual worlds that are used to display them; the abstract information might be twenty-dimensional, and the virtual visual world but three-dimensional, precluding an isomorphic map. That is no problem. The virtual worlds need not be reconstructions of the abstract worlds of information to be useful guides. On the contrary, the very usefulness of the virtual worlds derives from the fact that they are not reconstructions, but are instead well-chosen simplifications of some aspects, and exaggerations of others.

Conclusion

The standard account of vision has the observer reconstructing those properties of the physical world that are useful. Change-blindness studies, and their discovery that vSTM is limited to five or six items, constrains the standard account by only allowing the observer to reconstruct five or six items at any one time. This limitation of the vSTM of the observer entails that the memory must be somewhere else, and the physical world seems to be the only candidate.

But the very notion of reconstruction on which this account relies is itself problematic, and careful examination suggests that it is not necessary and not justified. When we reject the notion of reconstruction, and replace it with the more conservative notion of construction, we give up nothing the observer needs for survival. We do give up the idea that the physical world serves as short-term memory which the observer can access when needed to reconstruct the desired items in that world. But we replace it with the more conservative idea that the observer can interact when needed with the environment in such a way that the environment in turn triggers the observer to construct the needed perceptual information.

The move from reconstruction to construction is not a move to solipsism, but merely a move to more modest knowledge claims. To say that perception is reconstruction is to claim that the problem of the relationship between perception and the world is essentially solved, and that the relation is a particularly simple one: a rough isomorphism. To say, more modestly, that perception is construction is to recognize that the problem of the relationship between perception and the world is an open scientific problem with many possible solutions; isomorphism is just one solution, and perhaps not a likely one, given the variety of organisms and their perceptions.

Acknowledgements

This work was supported in part by grant 009083 from the U.S. National Science Foundation to Don Hoffman. We thank Manish Singh and an anonymous reviewer for helpful comments.

References

Albert, D.Z. (1992), *Quantum Mechanics and Experience* (Cambridge, MA: Harvard University Press).

Barrett, J.A. (1999), *The Quantum Mechanics of Minds and Worlds* (New York: Oxford University Press).

Bennett, B.M., Hoffman, D.D., Nicola, J.E. and Prakash, C. (1989), 'Structure from two orthographic views of rigid motion', *Journal of the Optical Society of America, A*, **6**, pp. 1052–69.

Bennett, B.M., Hoffman, D.D. and Prakash, C. (1989), *Observer Mechanics: A formal theory of perception* (New York: Academic Press).

Bennett, B.M., Hoffman, D.D., Prakash, C. and Richman, S. (1996), 'Observer theory, Bayes theory, and psychophysics', in Knill and Richards (1996).

Berkeley, G. (1709/1963), *Works on Vision*, ed. C.M. Turbayne (New York: Bobbs-Merrill).

Dawkins, R. (1986), *The Blind Watchmaker* (New York: Norton).

DeShepper, B. and Treisman, A. (1996), 'Visual memory for novel shapes: Implicit coding without attention', *Journal of Experimental Psychology: Learning, Memory, and Cognition*, **22**, pp. 27–47.

Curd, M. and Cover, J.A. (ed. 1998), *Philosophy of Science: The central issues* (New York: Norton).

Cytowic, R.E. (1993), *The Man Who Tasted Shapes* (New York: Putnam).

De Graef, P. (1998), 'Prefixational object perception in scenes: Objects popping out of schemas', in *Eye Guidance In Reading and Scene Perception*, ed. G. Underwood (New York: Elsevier).

D'Zmura, M., Colantoni, P. and Seyranian, G. (2000), 'Virtual environments with four or more spatial dimensions', *Presence: Teleoperators and Virtual Environments*, **9**, pp. 616–31.

Feldman, J.A. (1985), 'Four frames suffice: a provisional model of vision and space', *Behavioral and Brain Sciences*, **8**, pp. 265–89.

Gregory, R.L. (1970), *The Intelligent Eye* (New York: McGraw-Hill).

von Helmholtz, H.L.F. (1910), *Treatise On Physiological Optics*, trans. J. Southal, 1925, (New York: Dover).

Hoffman, D.D. (1998), *Visual Intelligence: How we create what we see* (New York: Norton).

Hoffman, D.D. and Flinchbaugh, B. (1982), 'The interpretation of biological motion', *Biological Cybernetics*, **42**, pp. 195–204.

Hoffman, D.D. and Richards, W.A. (1984), 'Parts of recognition', *Cognition*, **18**, pp. 65–96.

Howard, I., Bergstrom, S.S. and Ohmi, M. (1990), 'Shape from shading in different frames of reference', *Perception*, **19**, pp. 523–30.

Jameson, K.A., Highnote, S.M. and Wasserman, L.M. (2001), 'Richer color experience in observers with multiple photopigment opsin genes', *Psychonomic Bulletin & Review*, **8**, pp. 244–61.

Khurana, B., Smith, W.C. and Baker, M.T. (2000), 'Not to be and then to be: Visual representation of ignored unfamiliar faces', *Journal of Experimental Psychology: Human Perception & Performance*, **26**, pp. 246–63.

Knill, D.C. and Richards, W.A. (ed. 1996), *Perception as Bayesian Inference* (Cambridge: Cambridge University Press).

Krinov, E.L. (1947), 'Spectral reflectance properties of natural formations', *Technical Translation, National Research Council of Canada TT:439, 1947*.

Land, E.H. (1977), 'The retinex theory of color vision', *Scientific American*, **237**, pp. 108–28.

Liu, C.H., Collin, C.A., and Chaudhuri, A. (2000), 'Does face recognition rely on encoding of 3-D surface? Examining the role of shape-from-shading and shape-from-stereo', *Perception*, **29**, pp. 729–743.

Maloney, L.T. (1985), 'Computational approaches to color constancy', Ph.D. Dissertation, Stanford University (Applied Psychological Laboratory Technical Report 1985-01).

Maloney, L.T. and Wandell, B.A. (1986), 'Color constancy: a method for recovering surface spectral reflectance', *Journal of the Optical Society of America A*, **3**, pp. 29–33.

Marimont, D. and Wandell, B.A. (1992), 'Linear models of surface and illuminant spectra' Journal of the Optical Society of America, A, 9, pp. 1905–1913.

Marr, D. (1982), *Vision: A computational investigation into the human representation and processing of visual information* (San Francisco: Freeman).

Musgrave, A. (1989), 'NOA's Ark — Fine for realism', *Philosophical Quarterly*, **39**, pp. 383–98.

Noë, A. (2000), 'Beyond the grand illusion: What change blindness really teaches us about vision', *Visual Cognition*, **7**, pp. 93–106.

O'Regan, J.K. (1992), 'Solving the "real" mysteries of visual perception: the world as an outside memory', *Canadian Journal of Psychology*, **46**, pp. 461–88.

Phillips, W.A. (1974), 'On the distinction between sensory storage and short-term visual memory', *Perception & Psychophysics*, **16**, pp. 283–90.

Rensink, R.A. (2000a), 'Visual search for change: A probe into the nature of attentional processing' *Visual Cognition*, **7**, pp. 345–76.

Rensink, R.A. (2000b), 'Seeing, sensing, and scrutinizing', *Vision Research*, **40**, pp. 1469–87.

Rensink, R.A., O'Regan, J.K. and Clark, J.J. (1997), 'To see or not to see: The need for attention to perceive changes in scenes', *Psychological Science*, **8**, pp. 368–73.

Reutersvärd, O. (1984), *Unmögliche Figuren: Vom Abenteuer Der Perspektiven* (Munich: Verlag Moos & Partner KG).

Sabra, A.I. (1978), 'Sensation and inference in Alhazen's theory of visual perception', in *Studies in Perception: Interrelations in the history of philosophy and science* ed. P.K. Machamer and R.G. Turnbull (Columbus: Ohio State University Press).

Stroud, J.M. (1955), 'The fine structure of psychological time', in *Information Theory in Psychology: Problems and methods*, ed. H. Quastler (Glencoe, IL: Free Press).

Subramaniam, S. and Biederman, I. (1997), 'Does contrast reversal affect object identification?' *Investigative Ophthalmology & Visual Science*, **38**, pp. S998.

Trehub, A. (1991), *The Cognitive Brain* (Cambridge, MA: MIT Press).

Ullman, S. (1979), *The Interpretation of Visual Motion* (Cambridge, MA: MIT Press).

Ullman, S. (1984), 'Maximizing rigidity: The incremental recovery of 3-D structure from rigid and rubbery motion', *Perception*, **13**, pp. 255–74.

Yuille, A.L. and Bülthoff, H.H. (1996) 'Bayesian decision theory and psychophysics', in Knill and Richards (1996).

Frank H. Durgin

The Tinkerbell Effect

Motion Perception and Illusion

A new motion illusion is discussed in relation to the idea of vision as a Grand Illusion. An experiment shows that this 'Tinkerbell effect' is a good example of a visual illusion supported by low-level stimulus information, but resulting from integration principles probably necessary for normal perception.

Is visual consciousness a Grand Illusion? In one sense, the answer must be 'Of course.' On the other hand, it sure doesn't seem that way (which is why the illusion deserves to be called 'grand'). What visual consciousness seems to be, naively and subjectively, is a direct rendering of visually available information. Taking this naive view too seriously, however, would lead to some unfortunate conclusions. What I propose to argue in this paper is that perceptual awareness pretends to have access to more information than is actually available to visual cognition. The content of visual awareness when it goes 'beyond the information given' is often as accurate as the information-processing goals of 'seeing' require, but its apparent 'directness' can only be understood as an illusion, grand or otherwise.

One way of capturing the nature of visual consciousness was put forth by von Helmholtz in his classic general rule that '. . . such objects are always imagined as being present in the field of vision as would have to be there in order to produce the same impressions on the nervous mechanisms, the eyes being used under ordinary conditions.' (1910/1925, p. 2). What von Helmholtz is saying is not merely that perception involves unconscious inference, but that it is an act of imagination. Perception is an act of imagination based upon the available information.

To illustrate the power of this idea, consider Figure 1, which shows two sub-sampled images of a face. From close up, the distortion produced by sub-sampling is quite evident. But if you stand back a few meters, the pictures will appear to be clear and undistorted. At that distance the blockiness is not visible, but the resulting percept seems to assert more than it can possibly know (but in a way consistent with von Helmholtz's general rule). I call this sort of illusion

Journal of Consciousness Studies, **9**, No. 5–6, 2002, pp. 88–101

Figure 1. Subsampled images. Viewed from a meter or two away, these images appear to be clear pictures. Squinting works too.

the filling-in of visual detail (Durgin, 1998). I don't think the detail itself is filled in anywhere in the brain. Rather, I think the apparent content of visual consciousness often goes beyond what is actually available to visual cognition. It is enough that the relevant face-encoding units in the brain all fire in their characteristic manner as if they were witnessing the clear image of the face. Such firing is indistinguishable from actually witnessing the clear image of the face.

Why do I doubt that the filling in actually occurs anywhere? I doubt this because there are many cases of perceptions where it is clear that the content of visual cognition is a kind of summary of the visual information given, and not a duplication of it. Visual textures are a good example of stimuli that have characteristic appearances but are too complex for full, lossless representation in visual cognition. Despite being based on summary information (cf. Durgin, 1995), visual consciousness seems to assert direct experience in the perception of visual texture. I was personally shaken out of the naive view of perception as direct access to visual information when I discovered, with Dennis Proffitt, the texture density after-effect: After adapting different regions of the visual system to different densities of texture, the perceptual registration of apparent texture density (and element numerosity) can be distorted by a factor of two (Durgin, 1995; Durgin and Proffitt, 1996). If 400 dots can be made to look like 200 dots, one wonders where the missing dots have got to — or whether it makes sense to believe that one is really seeing the actual dots at all — before or after adaptation.

To take a more extreme example, imagine viewing a detuned television set and observing the dynamic visual noise on the screen. Millions of dots change brightness 30 times per second and it feels like we are seeing it all. But for the brain to store those millions of bits of information (or even encode them all past the retina) would be simply ridiculous. Our visual experience presents itself to us as direct, unmediated, and complete. This is an illusion.

It is difficult not to view this as a happy illusion — happy because for normal purposes the visual system can get away with it without harm. I have argued elsewhere that the very goal of the visual system is to support this illusion by doing its best to make itself and its workings invisible (Durgin and Proffitt, 1996).

What cognition wants is information about the world, not about the visual system. Vision's methods work well for the most part.

The present paper concerns a new phenomenon that illustrates the problem of indirectness in motion perception very nicely. The phenomenon generally supports a Helmholtzian framework of perception as imagination. It concerns the illusory perception of coherent motion in dynamic noise. I call it the Tinkerbell effect.

The Tinkerbell Effect

In 1981, while I was still a high-school student, a friend informed me that he had seen a demonstration on television of the ability of psychic powers to influence quantum processes. The theoretical significance of such a demonstration will not be lost on those interested in consciousness, nor did it fail to appeal to my imagination twenty years ago. What had impressed my friend was that, by a collective act of will, the audience members had apparently been able to influence the pattern of quantum activity when displayed as blips of light on a screen. That is, the quantum process that the demonstrator had set up could be perceived as random points of light that flashed around a ring. By inviting the audience to try to make the procession of blips move clockwise, the demonstrator was able to convince his audience that the action of their will influenced the movement of the dots. Whether the demonstrator was a charlatan or simply naive, I do not know. The reason I share this story is to emphasize that perceptual experience really does pretend to be an accurate record of visually available information, and that anyone convinced by such a demonstration would profit from understanding that perceptual experience is mediated, not direct, and that effects of conscious will on conscious perceptual experience should not be mistaken for effects of conscious will on the world itself.

As for myself, it was not until many years later that I realized that the demonstration had very different implications than those originally intended. First of all, this particular visual phenomenon does not even require a quantum-process generator. As I will discuss below, the phenomenon can be experienced with dots projected into pseudo-random positions by what is, in fact, a completely deterministic 'random number' generator on a computer. Thus, the sexy part of the demonstration, purporting to demonstrate the conscious control of *quantum* events, is simply invalid. Second, and more important, it is fairly trivial to show that if one group of observers is asked to try to make the dots move in one direction, while a second group is asked to make the dots go in the opposite direction, both groups will feel that they have succeeded simultaneously. Thus, contrary to the strong native assumption that visual experience is an unmediated conduit of reality, the wilful control of visual motion seems to concern the wilful control of perception, not of the displays themselves.

Because of its resemblance to the audience participation in Peter Pan, I refer to this phenomenon as the Tinkerbell effect. In the stage version of Peter Pan, a fairy named Tinkerbell intentionally drinks poison so as to prevent Peter Pan from drinking it. Sadly, Tinkerbell is left dying, but the audience (normally children) is then asked to demonstrate that they believe in fairies by clapping. Sure enough, they are thereby successful at restoring Tinkerbell to life. In the quantum control demonstration described above, a similar request is made with a similar illusory result. Of course, in the play, the illusory efficacy of the audience is supported by an external event performed by an actor, whereas the illusory perception of coherent directed motion (in actually random motion) is nearly entirely in the head of the beholder (in the Cartesian theatre?). Nonetheless, in both cases an illusion of control may be obtained. The question is, how does the head see coherent motion where there isn't any?

Classic Problems of Motion Interpretation and Integration

To begin to answer this question requires consideration of some of the information-processing demands involved in the visual perception of motion, because in order to understand how illusory motion might be perceived, it would be a good idea to understand how real motion is perceived. The two most relevant conceptions in this regard are known as the aperture problem and the correspondence problem.

The aperture problem concerns one way in which motion information is inherently ambiguous. It can be illustrated by the well-known barber pole illusion, in which the stripes of the barber pole appear to move vertically, though the pole itself is rotating horizontally about a vertical axis. A more general case may be observed by moving a piece of paper with diagonal stripes behind a circular aperture. Although the paper may be moved vertically or horizontally, the motion of the stripes will appear perpendicular to their orientation. This corresponds to the local motion signals — and is a good reflection of what motion detectors in the brain might tend to represent. What is therefore actually surprising is that when the aperture is removed, the motion is seen correctly — the local motion signals are somehow combined into a coherent image.

Although an incoherent random dot pattern does not have oriented elements, the visual system is still working with local motion information (i.e., from motion detectors with small receptive fields), which is subject to aperture-problem errors. Thus, it is a requirement of the accurate visual registration of motion that local motion signals must sometimes be reinterpreted by global constraints. That is, as each motion-detection unit in the early stages of processing provides information to a higher level, it is with the understanding that the provided information is ambiguous and subject to error.

A closely related problem is known as the correspondence problem, which assumes that creating the global motion percept depends on matching local image features between successive 'frames' of motion. In a stable pattern that translates between two frames, this matching can be done using high-dimensional feature analysis, but it can become quite problematic when there is added visual noise, or when the elements are highly uniform. Not surprisingly, the correspondence problem becomes more difficult as the displacements between corresponding points in coherent motion become larger (i.e., the points to be matched up are farther apart than other, spurious candidate matches).

Braddick (1974) defined d_{max} as the maximum displacement of a random-dot pattern at which the direction of coherent motion could still be detected. Eagle and Rogers (1996) showed that d_{max} was dependent on the density of elements. In essence, for lower-density displays, larger displacements are acceptable because fewer nearby elements could produce spurious matches. The correspondence problem in motion is probably solved using visual codes that are more abstract than mere texture elements (Glennerster, 1998). For present purposes, it is only important to note that global motion signals can be ambiguous when reliable matches between local elements become difficult to make.

The Tinkerbell effect may arise, in part, because the visual system is designed to organize motion signals that are intrinsically noisy. In order to document the effect and study its properties, Feng He and I conducted an experiment in which we often embedded directional motion signals within an otherwise incoherent sequence of dot patterns. We were particularly interested in addressing the possibility that the perceived speed of motion depended on dot density, because dot density could affect both the distance over which the correspondence problem can be solved and the magnitude (average distance) of the random motion signals that might be generated by the displays.

Measuring the Tinkerbell Effect

Measuring hallucinated motion is somewhat complicated. Our primary goal was to demonstrate that we could get observers to perceive coherent motion of a certain direction in dynamic incoherent dots patterns, but we also wanted to have a fairly precise measure of perceived speed. In order to try to measure perceived speed, we had to make a number of design decisions that will require explanation. For instance, we were particularly interested in using a speed-matching task to assess perceived speed. However, the visual system is notoriously susceptible to motion after-effects (for example, Wöhlgemuth, 1911). Thus, if we required an observer to compare the hallucinated motion to real motion, we ought to be concerned that the real motion would produce strong after-effects that might alter the perceived speed in the target display. To avoid directionally biasing after-effects, we ensured that all motion signals presented were balanced by equal and opposite motion signals. Thus, the speed-matching task employed dynamic dot fields in which half of the signal dots moved clockwise about the annular display and the other half moved counter-clockwise. Visually, this appeared as two overlapping sets of dots moving in opposite directions.

Moreover, because speed perception is affected by the size and contrast of the particular stimulus used, we wanted the target and comparison displays to be as similar as possible. Finally, we were concerned that the task itself appear meaningful to the observers, and therefore chose to embed real motion signals in many of the trials. This allowed us to test whether our observers were sensitive to these embedded motion signals.

Pilot investigations indicated that observers could indeed respond differentially to different speeds if we embedded a weak bi-directional motion stimulus in our otherwise random dynamic dots fields. On the other hand, we were also predicting that denser displays might appear to move more slowly than sparse displays. Our pilot studies had also suggested that effects of density could be found alongside effects of embedded speed provided that the embedded speed signal was not so strong as to overwhelm the possible effects of dots spacing. With this in mind we conducted an experiment to investigate the role of dot density in the Tinkerbell effect.

Methods

Observers: Sixteen college students participated in the experiment in exchange for money or course credit. Of these, one had to be eliminated for failing to follow instructions.

Apparatus: The experiment was conducted using a Cambridge Visual Stimulus Generator driving a Sony GDM-F500T9 display set to a resolution of 800 x 600 pixels refreshed at 100 Hz.

Procedure: Each observer was instructed to judge the speed of coherent motion embedded within an otherwise incoherent dynamic dot stimulus. Note that the observer was not informed that on 40% of the trials, there would be no actual embedded coherent motion. Neither were observers informed about the amount of embedded motion. All stimuli were presented as an annulus of dynamic grey dots on a black background, and each trial was preceded by instructions as to the direction of motion (clockwise or anticlockwise) to be judged. The target stimulus then appeared and stayed on until the observer pressed a button to view the adjustable matcher stimulus (which began at a random speed). If no further button were pressed, the matcher would appear for 800 ms and then the target stimulus would reappear. The subject used two buttons to adjust the speed of the matcher up or down (each button initiated display of the newly adjusted matcher). A third button was used to toggle between the target and matcher stimulus, and a fourth button was used to indicate that the match was now satisfactory. Each observer made matches for 60 target stimuli in about 25 minutes.

Design: The two manipulated variables in the design were the density of the dots (0.08, 0.16, or 0.24 dots per square degree — each square degree was the area of 100 dots, so these numbers can be interpreted directly as percentage filled), and the speed of the embedded motion (180, 360, or 720 degrees per sec, or undefined — for the completely incoherent displays). There were twice as many undefined-speed trials as for each other speed. That is, there were eight undefined speed trials at each level of density, and only four of each of the other three speeds. Half the trials required clockwise judgements and half anticlockwise.

Initial matcher speed was randomly selected among 26 possible values within the range of 4–200 degrees per second. These values were approximately evenly distributed in logarithmic space (each about 15% higher than the next). The order of trials was completely random.

Stimuli: The target motion displays were presented within annuli having an inner radius of 5 degrees and an outer radius of 12 degrees of visual angle (total area was 384 square degrees). In order to blur the edges of the annulus, dot luminance was modulated across the width of the annulus, falling off parabolically toward the edges. On every video frame, the stipulated density of dots was presented (i.e., 30, 60, or 90 dots). All but seven percent of these dots (i.e., all but 2, 4, or 6 dots per frame) were scattered randomly on each frame. The remaining seven percent were correlated with the previous frame (on embedded motion trials) by being offset by 1.8, 3.6, or 7.2 degrees in rotation from dots in the previous frame (half moved clockwise, and half anticlockwise). A new seven percent were correlated on each frame. Note that, because dot speeds were stipulated in terms of angular rotation within the annulus, the middle speed, of 360 degrees per sec, for example, could be represented by a linear displacement of 0.31 to 0.78 degrees of visual angle per frame (31 to 78 degrees of visual angle per second), depending on eccentricity.

The matcher displays were constructed similarly, with density matched to that of the target display. However, in the matcher displays, 50% of the dots on each frame were correlated with dots in the previous frame (25% moving in each direction — this is the maximum correlation possible given that each dot's position is re-randomized after it moves one frame). In addition, the observer controlled the speed of movement. (This speed could be set to zero, or range from 40 to 2000 degrees per second by steps of about 15%.) These matcher displays clearly depicted two transparent scintillating textures moving in opposite directions, and were readily used for making speed-matching judgments for either direction of motion.

Results and Discussion

How readily was the Tinkerbell effect experienced? Of the fifteen observers, twelve were able to perform the task consistently for all displays. Two of the other observers seemed only to see coherent motion (give non-zero matches) in the lowest density conditions, and the third was unable to reliably perceive coherent motion (give non-zero matches) in any condition. The main statistical conclusions from the data are essentially the same whether all fifteen subjects are analyzed together or only the twelve who reliably saw motion in all the displays. So as not to artificially deflate perceived speed of motion for these twelve, graphs and statistical analyses will be reported for them only. Mean perceived rotational speeds as a function of density and of embedded speed are shown in Figure 2.

A 3 (density) x 4 (embedded speed) repeated measures ANOVA was conducted using mean matches from each observer, collapsing across direction of motion. Although our primary concern is with the effect of manipulating dot density, we will first consider the effects of embedding various speeds of coherent dots.

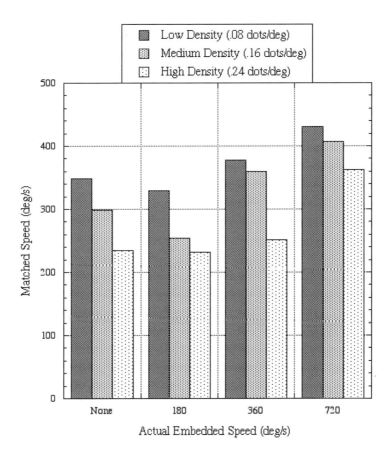

Figure 2. Results of experiment measuring speed of perceived rotation as a function of embedded speed and dot density. Data are average of twelve observers.

Relative speed comparisons

As expected, speed judgments differed as a function of embedded speed, $F(3, 33) = 6.01$, $p < .01$. Planned comparisons showed that the judgments of the highest embedded speed ($M = 400$ deg/s) were reliably higher than those of the lowest embedded speed ($M = 272$ deg/s), $t(11) = 12.8$, $p < .01$. They were also higher than judgments when no coherent motion was embedded ($M = 294$ deg/s), $t(11) = 10.6$, $p < .01$. No other differences among embedded speed conditions were statistically reliable.

Absolute speed comparisons

We originally chose our embedded speeds based on what we expected the illusory speed would be. Our lower two embedded speeds did in fact bracket the mean illusory speed. In the absence of any embedded speed, the mean perceived speed (294 deg/s), was reliably less than 360 deg/s, $t(11) = 2.87$, $p < .05$, but greater than 180 deg/s, $t(11) = 4.98$, $p < .01$. When speeds were embedded, the average judgments of the middle speed ($M = 369$ deg/s) did not differ reliably from the actual embedded speed (360 deg/s), $t(11) = 0.18$, n.s. However, the judgments of the lowest speed ($M = 272$ deg/s) were higher than the actual embedded speed (180 deg/s), $t(11) = 3.50$, $p < .01$, and the judgments of the highest embedded speeds ($M = 400$ deg/s) were much lower than the actual embedded speed (720 deg/s), $t(11) = 7.97$, $p < .01$. Indeed, judgments of the lowest embedded speed were reliably lower than 360 deg/s, $t(11) = 3.34$, $p < .01$, but judgments of the highest embedded speed did not differ reliably from 360 deg/s, $t(11) = 1.00$, n.s. In summary, although there is clear evidence of some sensitivity to embedded speeds (which is impressive given that only 7% of the dots were correlated from frame to frame!), that sensitivity is fairly weak.

Perceived speed as a function of density. In addition to the effect of embedded speed, there was a highly reliable main effect of dot density on perceived speed, $F(2,22) = 6.80$, $p < .01$. We had hypothesized that higher speeds would be perceived for lower densities. Although the mean matched speed for the lowest density (352 deg/s) was not reliably different from that for the middle density (330 deg/s), $t(11) = 0.67$, $p > .10$, each of these was higher than the mean speed for the highest density (271 deg/s), $t(11) = 3.54$, $p < .01$ (30 vs. 90 dots), $t(11) = 2.76$, $p < .05$ (60 vs. 90 dots).

If differences in speed judgments were related directly to differences in density by virtue of the concomitant changes in inter-dot distances, we would expect the three speeds to fall in a ratio of 1: 1.22: 1.73, corresponding to the square roots of the 1:2:3 changes in density. In fact, they fall in ratio of 1.0: 1.22: 1.30. In other words, the speed–density relationship is quantitatively predicted for the higher two densities, but perceived speed falls off from what might be expected for the lowest density / fastest speed.

The limited range of perceived speeds. With respect both to density and to embedded speed predictions, there seemed to be a limited range of perceived speeds. Mean estimates of perceived rotation speed ranged from 232 deg/s in the highest density, lowest embedded speed condition to 430 deg/s in the lowest density, highest embedded speed condition, despite a fourfold change in embedded speed and a threefold change in density. It is not that higher speeds cannot be perceived, however. Pilot studies suggest that if the percentage of dots given embedded speed were increased, a broader (more accurate) range of speed matches would have resulted. However, with only these weak motion signals provided, the range of perceived speeds is apparently curtailed.

General Discussion

The Tinkerbell effect is presented here as a demonstration that conscious visual experience may be very loosely supported by 'sense' impressions, as in the case of dynamic visual noise. It represents a case where a top-down selection of information seems to create a perceptual experience that, while clearly illusory in one sense, masquerades as the true state of the world. The dots truly do seem to move in the direction the observer attempts to see. Our concern has been to measure the speed of that perceived motion and examine its relationship to stimulus factors that might well be expected to influence the motion detection systems. True to von Helmholtz's (1910/1925) dictum, the act of imagination evidenced here is responsive to stimulus factors relevant to normal motion processing.

Although we decided not to ask our subjects to 'control' the motion of the dots, we did require them to 'find' the motion in the direction specified at the outset of the trial. By focussing their attention on matching the rotation speed of the dots we required them to organize the dot motion. Their responses indicate sensitivity both to motion signals that were intentionally embedded, as well as to the effects of element density. While no specific motion integration model is being considered here, the general model is one in which low-level, noisy motion information is treated as the raw materials for an integrative process of imagination.

There are two other motion phenomena that are probably relevant to understanding the motion-processing aspects of the Tinkerbell effect. One of these was reported by MacKay in 1961, and labelled the *omega effect* in 1965. It concerns the spontaneous appearance of directional motion in visual noise confined to a narrow channel. The other was also reported by MacKay (1961), though it is better know as *motion capture*, the name given by its re-discoverers, Ramachandran and Anstis (1983). It concerns the spurious perception of coherent motion in dynamic visual noise when a strong motion signal overlays the noise.

MacKay's omega effect

MacKay (1957) reported that visual noise, when superimposed on near-parallel lines (such as gratings or concentric circles), would seem to stream at right angles to the local orientation of the lines. In addition to this orthogonal streaming, however, MacKay (1961) later noted that, with concentric patterns, there seemed to be slow rotations of the noise within the channels formed by the rings — or even within a single narrow circular channel (only a few minutes of arc in width). MacKay (1965) dubbed this narrow-channel noise drift the 'omega effect' and reported that the period of perceived rotation was fairly consistent across a wide range of annular diameters provided the width of the aperture was increased in proportion to the diameter. (No account of the method of speed estimation is given. The periods of rotation that MacKay reports range from about two to four rotations per second or 90–180 deg/s.) In these demonstrations, MacKay's noise stimuli consisted of visual snow, such as on a detuned television set. MacKay (1965) varied the frame rate of his displays (which had no effect on perceived speed), and reported no effect of varying element size.

It is particularly notable that, in a later study that examined whether various visual noise effects could be produced under conditions of retinal stabilization, MacKay *et al.* (1979, p. 715), reported that 'voluntarily reversible omega motion' was observed. In other words, though the omega effect is presented as unavoidable (unlike the Tinkerbell effect), its direction can be wilfully controlled. It seems reasonable to suppose that the Tinkerbell effect might be a low-signal version of the omega effect. That is, both effects may depend on the same kinds of underlying principles of motion perception systems, but the sparse density and wider channel employed in the present experiments may push the visual system to a more extreme case of signal 'recovery'.

MacKay (1961; 1965) provides little explanation of the omega effect. With modern theories of motion detection, it is fairly easy to construct a rough explanation based on two principles. The first principle is that, within a narrow channel of visual noise, there will be a statistical bias to sense motion signals (temporal image correlations) along the longer axis — so that the possibility of relatively strong motion signals along the channel (as apposed to across them) is fairly well suggested by current theories of motion detection. This principle is illustrated in Figure 3, which shows how the distribution of possible match locations might be biased to lie along the channel. The second principle is that these low-level visual motion signals are organized according to higher-level hypotheses that seek to find a single common motion when possible. Thus, although the visual system is perfectly capable of perceiving overlapping transparent surfaces of dots moving in opposite directions (as in our matcher displays), it seems to organize random noise signals in a narrow channel into a single direction in the omega effect. Evidently, spurious noise 'evidence' of directional motion is not adequate to support two directions simultaneously in the omega effect.

The explanation of the omega-like motion in the Tinkerbell displays used here would have to depend less on the presence of sharp edges, because our annuli

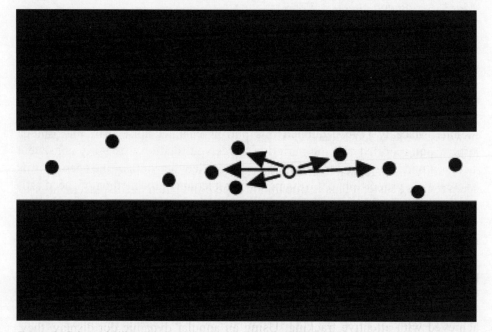

Figure 3. Schematic illustration of how random correspondences within a narrow channel might lead to a directional motion signal along the channel, leading to an omega effect.

were quite wide and the edges were blurred intentionally by ramping down luminance near the edges. Nonetheless, a statistical bias for registering motion signals along the annulus might still play a role in providing bottom-up support for the top-down rotational motion interpretation in the Tinkerbell effect. The important phenomenal difference between omega motion and Tinkerbell motion (that the former is involuntarily perceived whereas the latter is voluntarily perceived) may therefore result from differences of the strength of the bottom-up directional-motion signal. This was presumably much weaker in the displays used here than in those used by MacKay (1961; 1965). To the extent that the Tinkerbell effect is related to the omega effect, the present data showing effects of density variations is an important extension of MacKay's findings. Further exploration is warranted.

Motion capture

There is a second class of motion illusions in which coherence emerges from incoherent visual noise when a strong coherent motion signal is overlaid on the noise. MacKay (1961; 1965) reported that when a wire frame was dragged across dynamic visual noise, the noise seemed to be carried along by the frame. He called this the frame adhesion effect, and he reported it worked with a fingertip as well. Ramachandran and Anstis (1983) described a similar effect produced by superimposing a moving sinusoidal grating atop incoherent dynamic noise. They dubbed this phenomenon 'motion capture', and argued that it showed that the visual system did not bother to solve the correspondence problem in vision when it could substitute a solution from a more readily matched (lower spatial frequency) source.

Ramachandran's (1991) description of motion capture is rather forceful. He states that when the incoherent random dots were 'captured' by the gratings (for example, in the work of Ramachandran and Cavanagh, 1987), the percept is indistinguishable from coherently moving dots superimposed on a grating. He suggests that the visual system simply throws away (or inhibits) the motion information from the dots (in favour of that from the grating or frame). In our lab, however, we have reproduced the displays used by Ramachandran and Cavanagh (1987) and observed that even when capture is achieved, incoherent dot patterns are readily distinguishable from coherently moving dots because they tend to seem to move faster. (This is true up until the point when the displacement is so large that the coherent dot motion is no longer detectable as such.) In other words, our observation is more consistent with the Helmholtzian principle that requires that available data be accounted for rather than all of it being tossed out. Although the visual system need not solve the correspondence problem on a point-by-point basis, local motion-detector systems provide information, nonetheless, about the kinds of possible motion out there.

Culham and Cavanagh (1994) provided evidence that motion capture can be achieved with attentive tracking. Using an annular dynamic dot display, they superimposed a radial grating that moved in ambiguous apparent motion (each frame was 180 degrees out of phase with the next). Motion capture followed the direction of motion tracked by the observers. It is notable that this is very similar to the Tinkerbell effect except that there is no explicit support for tracking in the latter. It is possible that observers in our experiments tended to attentively track random features within the incoherent noise. The important point, again, is that stimulus characteristics of the dot patterns themselves were influential in setting the speed of the resultant perceived motion in our experiments. That is, the Tinkerbell effect clearly feeds off motion information in the display. We have demonstrated this by manipulating embedded coherent signals and dot density, which is a correlate of the average dot displacement.

Supporting the Grand Illusion

The Grand Illusion of perception is the illusion of direct and complete vision. In the change blindness literature, much emphasis is placed on the limited amount of information that can be encoded at one time. At the extreme of information overload comes dynamic visual noise. It is easy to summarize visual noise (for example, in terms of spatial and temporal statistics), but it is a gargantuan task to represent it accurately in detail. Although we seem to see the noise 'in detail', that seeing is certainly not based on representing all the information actually necessary for specifying every flashing pixel. Instead, motion perception summarizes and organizes information. The Tinkerbell effect brings out the Helmholtzian character of perception as an act of imagination fitted to the visually available information. Motion processing, in particular, entails integration processes that can apparently be fooled when enough noise is fed into the system. The resulting perceptions seem to accord well with von Helmholtz's rule of vision discussed in the introduction.

There are a number of behind-the-scene visual and cognitive activities that support (i.e., enable) the Grand Illusion in practice. For example, although visual cognition actually has less information than our conscious experience might lead us to believe, it is also privy to implicit learning strategies that make it much more powerful than a high-resolution camera would be. Included in these are adaptation and calibration processes that keep visual processing efficient (cf., Durgin and Proffitt, 1996), as well as implicit learning of successful oculomotor habits (for example, Durgin, 1999). These kinds of processes provide necessary support for successful visual cognition, and thus help to maintain the illusion that visual cognition is simply direct.

Von Helmholtz's doctrine of perception is best understood in terms of his first general rule of vision. That rule is essentially a version of the Grand Illusion doctrine. It states that perception is an act of imagination based on the available sensory information. The integration of motion information from motion detection systems is a complex problem. The visual system's solution to that problem requires the use of summary information and the integration of inherently ambiguous signals. This leaves the visual system open to systematic errors, such as the hallucination of coherent rotational motion in the Tinkerbell effect. What is particularly notable about the Tinkerbell effect is both that it involves an act of will and that it shows up the difficulties of simply believing ones eyes. Illusions are often helpful in understanding the processes of normal perception. Although the visual system is designed to be a transparent medium for cognition and action to receive accurate information about the world, it is a mediating mechanism, which can only imperfectly capture that information. What is often more interesting than its failures, however, are the intricacies involved in its typical success.

Acknowledgments
This research was supported in part by HHMI and by a faculty research grant from Swarthmore College. I am grateful for the contributions of Fred Bush, Mike Kim, and especially Feng He in designing and conducting the experiment described here.

References

Braddick, O. (1974), 'A short-range process in apparent motion', *Vision Research*, **14**, pp. 519–27.

Culham, J.C. and Cavanagh, P. (1994), 'Motion capture of luminance stimuli by equiluminous colour gratings and by attentive tracking', *Vision Research*, **34**, pp. 2701–6.

Durgin, F.H. (1995), 'Texture density adaptation and the perceived numerosity and distribution of texture', *Journal of Experimental Psychology: Human Perception and Performance*, **21**, pp. 149–69.

Durgin, F.H. (1998), 'Quasimodal encounters of the third kind: The filling in of visual detail', *Behavioural and Brain Sciences* (commentary), **21**, pp. 756–7.

Durgin, F.H. (1999), 'Supporting the "Grand Illusion" of direct perception: Implicit learning in eye-movement control', in *Toward a Science of Consciousness III*, ed. S.R Hameroff, A.W. Kaszniak, and D.J. Chalmers (Cambridge: MIT Press).

Durgin, F.H. and Proffitt, D.R. (1996), 'Visual learning in the perception of texture: Simple and contingent after-effects of texture density', *Spatial Vision*, **9**, pp. 423–74.

Eagle, R.A. and Rogers, B.J. (1996), 'Motion detection is limited by element density not spatial frequency', *Vision Research*, **36**, pp. 545–58.

Glennerster, A. (1998), 'd_{max} for stereopsis and motion in random dot displays', *Vision Research*, **38**, pp. 925–35.

von Helmholtz, H. (1910/1926), *Physiological Optics*, Vol. 3, J.P.C. Southall (trans.) (Menasha, WI: George Banta Publishing Company).

Mackay, D.M. (1957), 'Moving visual images produced by regular stationary patterns', *Nature*, **180**, pp. 1145–6.

Mackay, D.M. (1961), 'Visual effects of non-redundant stimuli', *Nature*, **192**, pp. 739–40.

Mackay, D.M. (1965), 'Visual noise as a tool of research', *Journal of General Psychology*, **72**, pp. 181–97.

MacKay, D.M., Gerrits, H.J. and Stassen, H.P. (1979), 'Interaction of stabilized retinal patterns with spatial visual noise', *Vision Research*, **19**, pp. 713–16.

Ramachandran, V.S. (1991), 'Interactions between motion, depth, color and form: the utilitarian theory of perception', in *Vision: Coding and Efficiency*, ed. C. Blakemore (Cambridge: Cambridge University Press).

Ramachandran, V.S. and Anstis, S.M. (1983), 'Displacement thresholds for coherent apparent motion in random dot patterns', *Vision Research*, **23**, pp. 1719–24.

Ramachandran, V.S. and Cavanagh, P. (1987), 'Motion capture anisotropy', *Vision Research*, **27**, pp. 97–106.

Wöhlegemuth, A. (1911), 'On the after-effect of seen movement', *British Journal of Psychology* (Monograph Suppl. 1).

Arien Mack

Is the Visual World a Grand Illusion?

A Response

The question of whether the visual world is a grand illusion is addressed and answered negatively. The question only arises because of the recent work on Inattentional Blindness (IB), Change Blindness (CB) and the Attentional Blink (AB) which establishes that attention is necessary for perception. It is argued that IB occurs only when attention is narrowly focussed and not when attention is more broadly distributed, which is the more typical attentional state. Under conditions of distributed attention we are likely to have a fuller, if less detailed, impression of the visual scene, which may be why we are so surprised by demonstrations of IB, AB and CB. It is also argued that the question about the possible illusory quality of our perceptual world cannot be avoided by denying that inattention causes blindness and asserting instead that it causes amnesia. This argument is grounded on the similarity between these phenomena and visual neglect and by evidence that priming by the unseen stimuli occurs in each case indicating that the stimuli to which we are functionally blind are processed and represented in implicit memory. The adaptive utility of this information is discussed.

The simplest and most straightforward answer to this question taken literally is no, since, after all, we do see. The real question is not whether all that we believe we see is an illusion, but how much of what is before our eyes we see and why we have the impression that we see it all. Undoubtedly, it has been the recent discoveries and explorations of the phenomena of CB, IB and the AB that have prompted us to seriously worry about this question at all. These phenomena seem to establish that the very presence of an object we are fixated upon may not be perceived if our attention is directed elsewhere. They tell us that large changes in a scene may go undetected unless we happen to be attending to what it is that changes. In addition, these phenomena tell us that we are likely not to see a highly visible target we are searching for if it follows quite quickly on the heels of some other target we also have been looking for because our attention is absorbed by the prior target. These three, related phenomena together not only

Journal of Consciousness Studies, **9**, No. 5–6, 2002, pp. 102–10

seem to have established that there is no perception without attention, but in doing so have led us to wonder why we nevertheless have the impression that we see everything before us when in fact we seem to see only what we are attending to. If we must attend to see, and we cannot attend to everything at once, then it would appear to follow that we do not see everything, and probably only see a small part of all that at any moment is potentially seeable.

One possible way of dealing with or avoiding this apparent puzzle simply is to deny that these phenomena demonstrate that attention is necessary for perception and instead to claim that inattention leads to a failure of memory; that is, it leads to amnesia, not blindness. Were this the case, we would no longer have to worry about why we think we see more than we do, since on this view we don't, although we now would have to figure out why our perceptions are so ephemeral despite the fact that they do not appear to be. As it turns out this is exactly the position taken by several investigators (Moore & Egeth, 1997; Moore, 2001; Wolfe, 1999). These investigators explicitly argue that inattention does not lead to a failure to see, but rather to a failure to remember. It is not that we do not see what is in front of us if we are not attending to it. It is that we do not remember what we have seen. But even if this argument were correct, and it is argued below that it is not, we only would have dodged one bullet, (Why do we think we see less than we see?) to be hit by another, (Why do we immediately forget what we have just seen?). If the question about whether seeing is a grand illusion arises from the apparent clash between our phenomenological experience and the evidence which purports to establish that there is no perception without attention, we may be no better off if it is memory that suffers from inattention since our phenomenal experience is not only of seeing what's there, but also of remembering it. I suspect we do not walk around with the sense that our percepts are momentary and fleeting, although , of course, they might be.

As it turns out though, even if the interpretation of IB, CB and AB as memory failures resolved the question at issue rather than replacing it with another, there are other grounds for rejecting this alternate view of the consequences of inattention. A strong argument against this view lies in the significant similarity between IB and Visual Neglect (VN), a pathological condition caused by damage to the posterior (usually right) parietal cortex which produces a disruption in attentional processing and a consequent failure to perceive objects in the scene opposite the lesion. So for example, if the lesion is in the right hemisphere, objects on the left are 'neglected' (see, for example, Bisiach *et al.*, 1979; Bisiach, 1993; Rafal, 2000). Patients suffering visual or unilateral neglect will fail to orient toward objects on the side opposite the lesion and will appear completely blind to them, although they have suffered no sensory impairment. This is most clearly demonstrated by the fact that if a single object is shown anywhere in the visual field, even in the neglected field, the patient will have no difficulty in seeing it and orienting to it. Since the blindness associated with neglect is caused by the failure to attend — and no one seems to doubt this or to suggest that the lesion in the parietal cortex causes a memory deficit — we would seem to have at least one clear and undisputed instance in which inattention causes blindness. This being the case, the least that follows is that inattention can cause blindness, which lends credibility to the hypothesis that inattention causes blindness more generally. It is, of course, possible to question whether the deficit in attention caused by a parietal lesion has the same affect on perception as inattention which is experimentally induced, but there are enough similarities between neglect and inattentional blindness to suggest that the effects are not so different (Humphrey, 2000).

One of the most striking similarities between IB and VN is that in both there is clear evidence of preattentive processing and encoding of the objects that are not seen and there is similar evidence in the case of the AB. In addition, a recent study establishes that this is true for CB as well (Silverman & Mack, 2001; Silverman, 2001.) Both in the case of unilateral neglect and Balint's syndrome, an even more severe form of attentional deficit caused by bilateral lesions of the posterior parietal lobes or of the parieto–occipital junctions (Farah, 1990; Rafal & Robertson, 1995), there is evidence of priming by the unseen stimuli appearing in the neglected portion of the scene which, of course, means that these stimuli have been processed and encoded and consequently are able to affect subsequent responses. Similarly in the case of IB, there is also evidence that lexical stimuli, whose presence is not detected under conditions of inattention, produce semantic priming (Mack & Rock, 1998) and evidence of the same sort has been reported in the case of the AB (Shapiro *et al.*, 1997) where it has been shown that a target which is undetected because it occurs during the blink is nevertheless capable of priming. Finally, we have recently found evidence of priming by stimuli suffering CB which had not previously been demonstrated (Silverman & Mack, 2001; Silverman, 2001).[1] This last piece of evidence further strengthens the argument for the basic similarity between these various inattention phenomena.

In a series of experiments in which CB was induced using sequenced pairs of 3 x 3 consonant trigram matrices with each matrix presented for 100 msec and separated from its mate by an 80 msec interstimulus interval, observers were asked to report whether the second of the two matrices was the same or different from the first. If they detected a change, they were required to indicate in which of the three rows it had occurred. Change occurred on every trial and consisted of the replacement of one, two or all three letters in a row of the second matrix with new consonants. Following the offset of the second matrix (*changed-to-matrix*), observers indicated whether they had seen a change and in which row it occurred. Once their report was complete, a severely degraded consonant trigram appeared on the screen which they were asked to identify. This degraded trigram was a novel trigram, one of the two trigrams from one of the two unchanged rows of the matrix, the trigram from the original matrix that changed, (*changed-from-trigram*), or the changed trigram from the second matrix, (the *changed-to-trigram*). We reasoned that if the letters from the initial matrix were encoded, then even if change was not detected, both the *changed-from* and the *changed-to*

---

[1] Prior evidence of the encoding of changes that could not be identified was reported by Fernandez-Duque and Thornton (2000).

rows of letters should be correctly identified as frequently as either of the trigrams from the two rows of the matrix that did not change and therefore were presented twice. Finally, we predicted that all of these trigrams would be identified significantly more frequently than the novel trigrams. This, in fact, is exactly what we found. When CB occurred, i.e., when change was not detected, observers were equally good at identifying the degraded, changed-row trigrams as the trigrams from the rows that were unchanged, all of which were correctly identified significantly more often than the novel trigrams. Thus it appears that the stimulus information in CB arrays like that in IB, AB and VN arrays which is neither detected nor is available to consciousness, nevertheless is processed and encoded. This is important because it extends the link between these phenomena and in turn supports the conclusion that they are all inattention phenomena which cause failures to perceive not failures to remember — blindness not amnesia — since in each case the stimuli that are not perceived are encoded in implicit memory .

The upshot of this conclusion is that we cannot dodge the question raised by IB, CB and AB about whether the visual world is a grand illusion by claiming that these phenomena are all instances of memory failure, so the motivating question remains unanswered.

One possible answer which addresses rather than tries to avoid the phenomenological issue raised by the title of this paper might lie in the difference between focussed and distributed attention. When the attention of an observer is strictly or intensely focussed on a particular part of a visual scene as it is in the inattention procedure, then only its object(s) are present in consciousness, but in most ordinary viewing situations attention is not so exclusively focussed. Rather, it tends to be far more broadly distributed, encompassing much of what is present in the scene, which may give rise to our impression that we usually have of seeing a richly articulated visual scene.

If attention is necessary for conscious perception, then distributed attention may be enough to account for our impression that we see much that is there to be seen. The sense we have of seeing the entire scene may derive from the many occasions in which our attention is distributed broadly or is divided and is not exclusively focussed on a single object. Since these states are the most typical and afford a general sense of a complete scene and even may be sufficient for the apprehension of its gist (Potter, 1976; Rensink *et al.*, 1997), this could explain why we are so surprised by demonstrations of inattentional blindness. It is only when attention is highly focussed, as it is in the inattention procedure (Mack & Rock, 1998) or in other procedures in which there is what Lavie and Tsal (1994) and Lavie (1995) have termed a *high perceptual load* that only the object to which attention is directed is perceived, and there is virtually no conscious awareness of any other aspects of the scene. But even though this is not the typical state, it is not one that is restricted to the laboratory. We all have had moments when we were completely absorbed by something we were listening to, looking at, or thinking about during which we were completely unaware of anything else. Even Aristotle offers us a description of such a state, '. . . Persons do not perceive what is brought before their eye, if they are at the time in deep thought, or in a fright, or listening to some loud noise' (See quote on page 250 in Mack & Rock,1998).

But why, if distributed attention affords us a general sense or the gist of a scene, do we still so readily experience change blindness for the changes that occur in the parts of the scene which are not central to its meaning or gist? (It should be clear that we do not ordinarily fail to see change when the change affects an item central to the meaning of the scene.) Perhaps the answer to this is that the parts of the scene that are not central to it and therefore are not meaningful to it quickly become inaccessible to consciousness even if they have been encoded, which makes changes to them difficult to detect. This would be consistent with the evidence that meaning captures attention and accounts for what we are aware of, and with the recent work of Silverman & Mack (2001) showing that changed items in displays in which change is undetected produce priming.

However, even if distributed attention accounts for our sense of seeing everything, there is at least one puzzle that remains. Assuming (1) that attention is necessary for perception, (2) that inattention yields *blindness* and not *amnesia,* and (3) that we generally distribute our attention broadly, which gives us a sense of the scene around us and explains why we are so surprised by the various inattentional blindness phenomena, what purpose is served by the deep processing and encoding of the stimuli to which we have not attended and of which we are consequently unaware? The evidence gained from demonstrations of priming by the unseen stimuli in instances of IB, CB, AB and VN establish that stimuli of which we are unaware are deeply processed and retained, but why and for how long?

To neither question is there a clear answer. At least one set of investigators has presented data suggesting that 'ignored stimuli' may have the capacity to prime after weeks if not months (Treisman & DeSchepper, 1994), even though there seems to have been no further corroboration of this finding. Nevertheless, even the suggestion that this may be the case should force serious consideration of the question 'What use is all this encoded but inaccessible information?'.

One might try here, too, to avoid the question by denying its existence or downplaying the importance of all this apparently stored but inaccessible information revealed by priming. To accomplish this one might simply argue that the deep, preattentive processing of unattended stimuli is a very limited occurrence, that it is limited to very special circumstances and does not ordinarily occur so that our heads are not cluttered with representations of all those things we have not seen. Something like this argument is implicit in the proposal made by Lavie (1995) and Lavie and Tsal (1994) that deep processing and priming only occur for ignored or unattended stimuli when the perceptual load is light. It is also implicit in the recent paper by Rees *et al.* (1999) who not only claim but also appear to demonstrate that there is no automatic processing of the unattended input when the perceptual task is highly demanding. In one condition of their interesting experiment, participants searched for repeated pictures in an RSVP design in which the pictured objects in the stimulus streams were superimposed on letter strings or words. The investigators report finding no difference in the processing of the ignored words and letter strings which should have been evident in the functional imaging record had the ignored words been automatically processed. In addition, subjects subsequently were unable to recognize the unattended stimuli which the investigators took to be further evidence that these stimuli were not encoded. The conclusion that they drew from their data is that the ignored stimuli suffer inattentional blindness rather than inattentional amnesia, but for them inattentional blindness rules out any processing and encoding of the ignored stimuli. However, a recent finding in our own lab raises a question about their conclusion that the ignored stimuli are not semantically analysed, and that in general stimuli to which attention is not directed under conditions of high attentional load are not deeply processed and encoded.

In this experiment we used the Rees *et al.* procedure as well as their stimuli to explore whether a stimulus which captures attention and is normally seen under conditions which produce IB and which also resists the attentional blink would be seen if it were included among the ignored stimuli in their high perceptual load condition.[2] We reasoned that if it was, then this would be evidence of the semantic processing of these ignored stimuli, since if it is the meaning of a stimulus that is responsible for the capture of attention, then its meaning must have to have been analysed in order for it to have been seen. We adapted the Rees *et al.* stimuli so that one of the ignored lexical stimuli was the subject's own name, which has been shown to resist both IB (Mack & Rock, 1998) and the AB (Arnell *et al.*, 1999; Shapiro *et al.*, 1997). Following trials in which observers sought to report all repeated objects in an attended RSVP stimulus string (as in Rees *et al.* these pictured objects were superimposed on letter strings and words), the subjects were shown a list of lexical stimuli (words and non-words), half of which came from the set of unattended stimuli and half of which were novel. They were asked to indicate which of them had been present during the immediately previous trial. A significantly large number of subjects reported having seen their own name, which means that there had to have been some processing and encoding of the ignored stimuli even under these purportedly high load conditions. We are now in the process of exploring whether the ignored and unrecognized word stimuli are capable of priming, which, of course, they should not be, if they are not processed nor encoded as Rees *et al.* have concluded. Preliminary evidence suggests that priming may occur.

Since, as described above, we have already found priming by the initial *to-be-changed stimuli* in a version of change blindness arrays (Silverman & Mack, 2001; Silverman, 2001), where the detection of change would seem to qualify as exacting a high attentional load, this, too, would appear to be additional evidence that the unattended input is processed and encoded even under these conditions, which, of course, leaves us with the question this section began

---

[2] Geraint Rees was generous enough to provide us with his experimental programme that we modified slightly in order to ask whether highly meaningful stimuli were ignored under his high attentional load conditions.

with about the utility of all this stored information which is inaccessible to conscious recall.

Before attempting to suggest a possible answer to this question, it should be noted that the existence of this information raises a special problem for one of the answers given to the question motivating this paper. O'Regan and Noë (2001) propose that the impression of scene completeness stems from our knowledge of sensorimotor contingencies,

> Another way of understanding why our visual phenomenology is of seeing every-thing in front of us derives from the fact that since the slightest flick of the eye or attention allows any part of a visual scene to be processed at will, we have the feel-ing of immediate availability about the whole scene. In other words, despite the fact that we are only processing a small number of details of the scene . . . we really are seeing the *whole* scene. (Section 4.2.)

To quote again from these authors, 'We propose that seeing is a way of acting. It is a particular way of exploring the environment. Activity in internal representa-tions does not generate the experience of seeing. The outside world serves as its own external representation' (Abstract). What sense can this account of perceiv-ing make of the fact that much of what we do not attend to and therefore do not see is nevertheless represented in memory even if it cannot be recalled at will. Their very Gibsonian account of perception, like Gibson's own, gives little weight to memory, and stresses the apprehension of invariant visual–motor contingencies, 'The experience of seeing occurs when the organism masters what we call the governing laws of sensorimotor contingencies' (Abstract). For Gibson, perceiving was a process of apprehending invariances and so it is for Regan and Noë as well. Since neither theory gives much place to stored represen-tations, it makes the question of why these representations exist even for stimuli we have never been aware of all the more puzzling.

A possible answer to the question concerning the utility of all the deeply pro-cessed and stored input that never was perceived and cannot be voluntarily recalled can be derived from the analysis of Inattentional Blindness offered by Mack & Rock (1998).This account proposes that IB is clear evidence that atten-tion is necessary for perception and that without it we are functionally blind. This in turn means that when our attention is highly focussed on some stimulus or task, we are 'blind' to everything else *unless* there is something present that is highly salient and meaningful that captures attention and therefore is detected. In all our research we have found only a few stimuli capable of defeating IB by cap-turing attention. These stimuli, however, are not the simple features which have been shown to pop out in search displays (Treisman & Gelade, 1980) but are quite complex and highly meaningful. The two most reliable of this small group of attention-capturing stimuli are one's own name and the iconic representation of a happy face. Not too surprisingly, these stimuli not only resist IB, but also resist the AB (Shapiro *et al.*, 1997; Arnell *et al.*, 1999; Mack & Silverman, 2000) as well as metacontrast masking (Shelley-Tremblay & Mack, 1999). If, however, these stimuli are even modestly modified, for example, the happy face is trans-formed into a sad face by inverting the line representing the mouth, or a single vowel is changed in one's name, or if either stimuli is inverted, their resistance to IB vanishes and now their presence is *not* detected, strongly suggesting that it is the *meaning* of the stimulus that captures attention and not some lower-level stimulus attribute.[3]

The fact that it is the meaningfulness of a stimulus which captures attention and causes it to be perceived when attention is focussed elsewhere, coupled with the fact that undetected stimuli are capable of semantic priming, appears to tell us that the deep processing and encoding of undetected stimuli is important because without it meaning would be lost and consequently not available to capture attention when it was important that it did so. On this analysis the deep processing and encoding of stimuli to which we are functionally blind because of inattention has high adaptive utility since it allows those stimuli which are important for us to see to be seen even when our attention is deeply absorbed with other objects or tasks.

One final comment concerning the question posed at the outset — why was the question, 'Is the *Visual* World a Grand Illusion?' rather than, 'Is our *Sensory* World in its Entirety a Grand Illusion?' Both preliminary (Mack & Rock, 1998) and anecdotal evidence suggest that inattentional insensitivity extends at least to hearing and touching. We do not hear or feel what we are not attending to any more than we see what we are not attending to. When we are concentrating on writing a paper, there will be interludes in which we are unaware of the music playing on the radio or of the cat purring on the desk. We also will be unaware of the pressure on our bottoms or the smoothness of the surface of the desk, but, of course, if we turn our attention to them, we will perceive them. Why then do we not wonder whether our entire sensory world is a grand illusion? Is it because we do not have the impression that we hear what is there to be heard or that we feel what is there to be felt and makes contact with our bodies? Or is it because we have not invested research time in exploring the effects of inattention on these other sensory modalities? Perhaps it is because we are visually dominant creatures and depend so heavily on seeing that we are likely to be less surprised by inattentional deafness or numbness and therefore are less likely to wonder whether our auditory or tactile worlds are illusory. Whatever the reason, there are grounds for believing that inattentional insensitivity is a general characteristic of all sensory modalities and that the deep, preattentive or inattentive processing that occurs for visual stimuli we are unaware of also occurs in these other sensory systems where meaningfulness also is likely to be the attribute responsible for bringing what we do not perceive because of inattention into awareness. We are likely to hear our names spoken across a crowded room and if we are sleeping, we are likely to be awakened by the crying of our baby that wakes no one else. So while we see, feel and hear only some or even very little of what is present when

---

[3] In a group of experiments reported in *Inattentional Blindness* (Mack & Rock, 1998, pp. 147–51), the question of whether it was our familiarity with these stimuli that was responsible for the capture of attention was explored and answered negatively. Familiarity alone was not sufficient to significantly reduce IB as demonstrated by the finding that neither the word 'The' or 'And', which are the two most frequently appearing words in the English language, were detected significantly more often than 'Tie' and 'Ant'. None of these words were very effective in reducing IB. (The reader is referred to the book for a complete description and discussion of this issue.)

our attention is sharply focussed, what we are not seeing, hearing or feeling is analysed for its meaning, because if it is important, it must capture our attention so that it will be present in the forefront of our consciousness where it needs to be if we are to act appropriately.

References

Arnell, K., Shapiro, K. and Sorensen, R. (1999), 'Reduced repetition blindness for one's own name', *Visual Cognition*, **6**, pp. 609–35.

Bisiach, E. (1993), 'Mental representation in unilateral neglect and related disorders: The Twentieth Bartlett Memorial Lecture', *Quarterly Journal of Experimental Psychology: Human Experimental Psychology*, **46**, pp. 435–561.

Bisiach, E. Luzzatti, T. and Perani, D. (1979), 'Unilateral neglect, representational schema and reality', *Brain*, **102**, pp. 757–65.

Farah, M. (1990) *Visual Agnosia* (Cambridge, MA: MIT Press).

Fernandez-Duque, D. and Thornton, I. (2000), 'Change detection without awareness: Do explicit reports underestimate the representation of change in the visual system?', *Visual Cognition*, **7**, pp. 323–44.

Humphrey, G. (2000), 'Neuropsychological analogies of inattentional blindness', *Psyche: An Interdisciplinary Journal of Research on Consciousness*, **6**.

Lavie, N. (1995), 'Perceptual load as a necessary condition for selective attention', *Journal of Experimental Psychology: Human Perception and Performance*, **21**, pp. 451–68.

Lavie, N. and Tsal, Y. (1994), 'Perceptual load as a major determinant of the locus of visual selection in visual attention', *Perception and Psychophysics*, **56**, pp. 183–197.

Mack, A. and Rock, I. (1998), *Inattentional Blindness* (Cambridge, MA: MIT Press).

Mack, A. and Silverman, M. (2000), *Alteration in the Attentional Blink* (Fort Lauderlade, FL: ARVO).

McGlinchey-Beroth, R., Milberg, W. P., Verfaillie, M., Alexander, M. and Kilduff, P.T. (1992), 'Semantic processing in the neglected field: Evidence from a lexical decision task', *Cognitive Neuropsychology*, **10**, pp. 79–108.

Moore, C. (2001), 'Inattentional blindness: Perception or memory and what does it matter?', *Psyche: An Interdisciplinary Journal of Research on Consciousness*, **7**.

Moore, C. and Egeth H. (1997), 'Perception without attention: Evidence of grouping under conditions of inattention', *Journal of Experimental Psychology: Human Perception and Performance*, **23**, pp. 339–52.

O'Regan, K. and Noë, A. (2001), 'A sensorimotor account of vision and visual consciousness', *Behavioral and Brain Sciences*, **24** (5).

Potter, M. (1976), 'Short-term conceptual memory for pictures', *Journal of Experimental Psychology: Human Learning and Memory*, **2**, pp. 509–22.

Rafal, R. (2000), 'Neglect', in *The Attentive Brain*, ed. R. Parasuranam (Cambridge, MA: MIT Press).

Rafal, R. and Robertson, L. (1995), 'The neurology of visual attention', in *Cognitive Neuroscience*, ed. M. Gazzinga (Cambridge, MA: MIT Press).

Rees, G., Russell, C., Frith, C. and Driver, J. (1999), 'Inattentional blindness versus inattentional amnesia for fixated but ignored words', *Science*, **286**, pp. 2504–07.

Rensink, R., O'Regan, K. and Clark, J. (1997), 'To see or not to see: the need for attention to perceive changes in scenes', *Psychological Science*, **8**, pp. 368–73.

Shapiro, K., Caldwell, J. And Sorensen, R. (1997), 'Personal names and the attentional blink: A visual "cocktail party" effect', *Journal of Experimental Psychology: Human Perception and Performance*, **23**, pp. 504–14.

Shapiro, K., Driver, J., Ward, R. and Sorensen, R. (1997), 'Priming from the attentional blink: A failure to extract visual tokens but not visual types', *Psychological Science*, **8**, pp. 95–100.

Shelley-Tremblay, J. and Mack, A. (1999), 'Metacontrast masking and attention', P*sychological Science*, **8**, pp. 95–100.

Silverman, M. (2001), *Priming by Change Blindness*. Unpublished doctoral dissertation, New York City: New School University.

Silverman, M. and Mack, A. (2001), Priming from change blindness. Poster, Vision Science Meeting, Sarasota, FL, Abstract, B 13.

Treisman, A. and Gelade, G. (1980), 'A feature integration theory of perception', *Cognitive Psychology*, **112**, pp. 97–136.

Wolfe, J. (1999), 'Inattentional amnesia', in *Fleeting Memories*, ed. V. Coltheart (Cambridge, MA: MIT Press).

Daniel T. Levin

Change Blindness Blindness As Visual Metacognition

Many experiments have demonstrated that people fail to detect seemingly large visual changes in their environment. Despite these failures, most people confi- dently predict that they would see changes that are actually almost impossible to see. Therefore, in at least some situations visual experience is demonstrably not what people think it is. This paper describes a line of research suggesting that overconfidence about change detection reflects a deeper metacognitive error (which we refer to as 'change blindness blindness', or CBB) founded on beliefs about attention and the role of meaning as a support for a coherent perceptual experience. Accordingly, CBB does not occur in all situations (subjects can, indeed, make accurate predictions about change detection in some circum- stances), while the scope of the phenomenon remains broad enough to suggest more than a misunderstanding of a small niche of visual experience. I finish by arguing that despite the very small amount of research on visual metacognition, these beliefs are critical to understand.

Although vision is a rich experience, recent research suggests that this richness does not necessarily arise in the way we might think it does. On one account, our rich experience derives from a correspondingly rich internal representation of the visual world. However, research from a wide variety of sources suggests that our ability to retain and compare visual details across views is quite limited (see Simons and Levin, 1997 for review), and that without actually attending to a stimulus, we may not perceive it at all (Mack and Rock, 1998). Accordingly, a number of authors have made the compelling argument that our understanding of visual experience is hampered by a 'Grand Illusion' whereby we falsely believe that the basis of continuous visual experience lies on a representational founda- tion that actually does not exist (Blackmore *et al.*, 1995; Dennett, 1991; O'Regan, 1992). Here, I describe research that explores this illusion by systemat- ically documenting people's beliefs about vision, and argue that these beliefs do lead people to predict that they would be able to see changes that usually go undetected. This research suggests that this lapse in judgement occurs because a

Journal of Consciousness Studies, **9**, No. 5–6, 2002, pp. 111–30

series of beliefs about attention, centrality and the effects of scene organization converge to produce a radical misprediction of visual capability.

In developing this research, it rapidly became clear that adults' beliefs about vision are almost completely undocumented. The one systematic exception to this is research focussed on understanding why people hold an incorrect extramissionist account of vision. That is, most children and many adults seem to believe that seeing involves extramissions of something from the eye, in stark contrast to the reality that vision arises from reflected and emitted light entering the eye (Winer and Cottrell, 1996; Winer et al., 1996a; 1996b). One interesting fact about this research is that it started as an attempt to understand children's misunderstanding of vision, and ended by concluding that at least some adults share this misunderstanding if only implicitly. A small amount of additional research has explored children's beliefs about visual attention, and this will be reviewed below.

The nearly complete lack of research on visual metacognition is all the more striking when it is contrasted with the large body of research exploring metamemory. An extensive tradition of research over the past 30 years has explored people's understanding of their own memory and their ability to use this understanding in effectively selecting memorization strategies and allocating study time to materials of varying levels of difficulty (see Metcalfe and Shimamura, 1994 for review). Not only has this research been important from a theoretical standpoint, but it has also recently found application in a wide variety of settings.

One of the most recent and dramatic applications of metamemory highlights the importance of understanding not only how beliefs about memory affect strategic memorization, but also of understanding these beliefs in their own right. During civil and criminal trails, juries and judges continually make judgments about other people's experience based on their own beliefs about memory. When an eyewitness identifies a suspect or gives other testimony based on their memory for long past events, jurors must evaluate that testimony in light of their understanding of memory. How accurate is this person likely to be given limited exposure to the suspect, an identification in a simultaneous line-up, and pre-line-up exposure to the suspect? It turns out that jurors (and judges and lawyers) have a rather vague notion about the impact of these variables (Stinson et al., 1996; Devenport et al., 1997), but more important is the one thing that jurors think they do know. That is, a confident witness should be an accurate witness (Wells et al., 1998). In contrast to repeated empirical demonstrations that confidence in memories is not necessarily correlated with accuracy, juries typically find a confident witness a nearly incontrovertible one, and will convict based on eyewitness testimony even when other evidence suggests that the suspect was not responsible for the crime. In a recent review of overturned felony convictions, 90% of false convictions were found to have occurred because of faulty eyewitness testimony (Wells et al., 1998). Most disturbing was the fact that five of these exonerated convicts were on death row. Thus, it appears that faulty metaknowledge has led to a massive number of false convictions, and may even have led to erroneous executions. So, if incorrect beliefs about the confidence–

accuracy correlation have landed innocent people on death row, we should not be sanguine in predicting that the problem begins and ends with long-term memory.

Change Blindness and Change Blindness Blindness: History

In the early 1980s empirical evidence began to suggest that people do not represent and fuse details from one view with another (see for example, Bridgeman and Mayer, 1983; Irwin, 1991; Pollatsek and Rayner, 1992), and more recently research from a variety of labs has shown that subjects frequently miss large between-view visual changes. This phenomenon, referred to as 'change blindness' occurs for visual changes in object arrays, still pictures of natural scenes, motion pictures, and even in the real world (for example, Blackmore *et al.*, 1995; Grimes, 1996; Henderson, 1997; Levin and Simons, 1997; McConkie and Currie, 1996; Pashler, 1988; Phillips, 1974; Rensink , 1997, Simons, 1996; Simons and Levin, 1998; for a review see Simons and Levin, 1997). For example, in several experiments subjects were asked to view an initial array of a dozen or fewer objects that disappeared for a moment, and then reappeared. When the array reappeared, it was identical except that one of the objects that had been in the initial array was replaced with a different object. Whether the objects are letters, numbers or pictures of real-world objects, performance in detecting the change falls off in arrays with more than 4–5 items (Pashler, 1988; Simons, 1996).

Other paradigms demonstrate a similar phenomenon more dramatically. In Grimes (1996), subjects viewed real-world scenes while their eye movements were being monitored. During a subset of saccades, large details were changed. For example, in one case the heads of two people were quickly swapped mid saccade. Despite the salience of the change, many subjects failed to detect it. Researchers quickly discovered that eye tracking was not necessary to produce this striking effect. For example, Blackmore *et al.* (1995) observed similar failures to detect changes between scenes when one was displaced relative to the other, or when a grey field briefly intervened between the two. Rensink *et al.* (1997) extended this paradigm by cyclically alternating between the original and changed scenes (separated for 280 ms by a blank grey field) until the subject detected the change. This technique, referred to as the flicker paradigm, has the advantage of allowing a continuous measure of the difficulty of detecting a change, and once again, subjects often require a considerable number of flickers before detecting changes that are quite striking in retrospect.

Change blindness also occurs if the original and new views are taken from different station points as is the case in the between-shot cuts in motion pictures. Levin and Simons (1997) confirmed filmmakers' long-held intuition that between-view inconsistencies often go unnoticed (Kuleshov, 1920/1974). They created a film in which hand positions, clothing, and object colours changed on every cut. Subjects who were not on the lookout for changes noticed nothing amiss, and even when they were intentionally searching for changes, they still detected only a minority of the inconsistencies.

One straightforward conclusion one could draw from these findings is that change detection is not automatic. Instead, one must focus attention on an object

before and after it changes to see the change (see Rensink, 2000a for elaboration
of this idea). Accordingly, there is no consistency-checking mechanism that represents and compares all objects in the visual field. However, it is possible to
extend this hypothesis a bit further, because attending to an object before and
after the change does not guarantee change detection. Levin and Simons (1997)
found that even changes within the putative centre of attention are often missed,
especially if the subject is not on the lookout for changes. In one experiment subjects viewed short two-shot films in which one actor began an action that was
completed by a different actor in the next shot. For example, one film showed an
initial shot of an actor sitting in her office as she hears the phone outside ring. She
gets up to answer it, and as she walks past the camera, the video cuts to a view of
the hall in which another actor walks into the picture and answers the phone.
Even though the actor(s) were the centre of attention for the entire event we
found that two thirds of subjects still missed the change. In an extension of this
finding, we have observed change blindness for real-world substitutions of conversation partners. In Simons and Levin (1998) an initial experimenter began a
conversation with a pedestrian on a college campus. Mid conversation, two other
experimenters carrying a door walked between the first experimenter and the
subject. While the subject's view was momentarily blocked by the door, one of
the experimenters carrying the door stayed behind and the first experimenter
walked away occluded by the door. Despite the fact that the person standing right
in front of them suddenly changed into another person, approximately half of
subjects fail to detect the change. These experiments, and others like them (see
for example, O'Regan *et al.*, 2000), suggest that attending to an object does not
automatically lead us to track all of its features across views. Instead, in order to
detect a change, attention must be directed efficiently within an object and must
focus on the specific features that change.

The Current Problem

Change blindness is interesting for what it reveals about the relationship between
attention and scene perception, but it is also interesting for what it reveals about
people's intuitions regarding vision. At almost every step of the development of
our research on this topic, intuitive predictions by our ourselves and others were
consistently wrong. When we edited our first films we thought that people would
surely see the glaring inconsistencies we put in them. When they did not, we
made changes to central objects and again suspected that we had gone too far —
surely everyone would see when we substituted one actor for another! Again,
subjects missed the changes and we once again upped the ante by changing
real-world conversation partners. This time, we nervously set up the experiment
and suspected we would spend a few afternoons getting laughed at by our subjects. Once again, however, our prediction (and the confident predictions of others) was strikingly confounded when half of our subjects missed the substitution
and continued the conversation as if nothing had happened. Apparently, we had
rather strong intuitions about seeing that led us astray repeatedly despite the fact
that we understood something about attention, scene perception, visual search,

and even change blindness. Thus, change blindness appears to confirm the metacognitive blind spot implied in the grand illusion — something about people's understanding of their own visual process leads them to falsely believe that they will be aware of visual events of which they are not aware. We refer to this metacognitive error as 'change blindness blindness' (CBB).

Of course, it is possible that we, as psychologists, are unusual. Perhaps we were led to be overoptimistic about change detection based on our knowledge of the icon, high-capacity implicit processes, or even the putative representational requirements of directing eye movements. Indeed, although our subjects were usually incredulous at their omissions, they were occasionally unsurprised. For example, subjects who miss the real-world-person change sometimes mention that they tend to be inattentive and therefore might well miss such a change. In another situation, a colleague of ours was about to give expert testimony on change blindness in court, but was disallowed because the judge asserted that change blindness is consistent with intuition. Therefore, to document the existence of CBB, Levin *et al.* (2000) surveyed naive subjects about their intuitions regarding change detection. In these experiments, a series of scenarios was described in which unexpected visual changes occurred. Each scenario was based on one of our previous CB experiments, allowing us to compare subjects' predictions with actual empirical findings. For example, in an initial experiment we described object changes, an actor change, and a real-world-person change to a large group of general psychology students (on the first day of class). Each change was first described verbally, then illustrated with stills from the stimulus videos used in the actual experiments (see Figure 1, back cover). In the case of the real-world-person change, we used a still of the experimenters standing side by side. The instructions also emphasized that the changes were unexpected.

As illustrated in Table 1, we found that subjects overwhelmingly predicted far more success in change detection than was the case in our actual experiments. In one case, the scarf change, 90.5% of subjects predicted they would see a change that was actually detected by 0% of subjects in Levin and Simons (1997). For the real-world-person change, 97.6% of subjects predicted they would detect a change noticed by only 46% of subjects in Simons and Levin (1998). In addition, subjects were quite confident in their predictions — giving mean confidence estimates ranging from 3.83 (on a 5-point scale with 'very confident' as the anchor point for a response of 5) to 4.43 for the real-world-actor change. These misestimates persist whether subjects make predictions about themselves or

Scenario	% Predicting Success	Confidence (5 = Very Confident)	Actual Success (%)
Plate	76.3	3.88	0
Scarf	90.5	3.98	0
Actor	69.5	3.83	0
Person	97.6	4.43	46

Table 1. Percentage of subjects predicting successful change detection (Levin *et al.*, 2000).

others (Levin *et al.*, 2000), and even when the changes are illustrated dynamically with the actual videos used in the original experiments (Levin *et al.*, in
review). Accordingly, it appears that CBB represents a massive misestimate of
visual performance that extends far beyond the typical overconfidence effects
observed in the decision-making literature. In these cases, subjects typically
overestimate the probability of recognizing a multiple-choice answer by about
20% (see, for example, Fischoff, 1982; 1988).

What Causes CBB?

Given that CBB appears to be a large and robust misestimate of visual experience, we have been exploring its causes. A number of explanations for CBB are
plausible, and some of these have already been suggested by others. For example, one possibility is that people believe that a perceptual transient akin to apparent motion will make the change immediately visible (Rensink, 2000b). Another
alternative is that people mistake the ease with which we can access the visual
world for a rich internal representation of that world (O'Regan, 1992; Rensink,
2000a). On this view, people may believe that they have a powerful short-term
visual memory that can retain visual detail over short periods. Both of these
hypotheses imply that something inherent to the process of vision causes CBB,
and therefore that people should make comparatively broad misestimates about
most kinds of change and most change-detection tasks. In contrast, other hypotheses might be more specific in their focus on beliefs about particular visual
subprocesses and kinds of stimulus. For example, it is possible that people do not
appreciate the degree to which visual attention typically focuses on only a small
subset of the information in a scene. Therefore they might believe that merely
paying attention to some part of a scene allows them to track a fairly large extent
of the scene. Other beliefs about the degree to which scene-like organization supports visual perception might also cause CBB by leading subjects to believe that
they can 'chunk' the entire scene into a single percept and therefore track any
detail change within that chunk. In this section, each of these hypotheses is
explored in turn.

In initial follow-up experiments we asked whether CBB is caused by a
misestimate of the perceptual experience of seeing a change. It is possible that
subjects think that changes would 'jump out' at them because they expect a perceptual experience akin to apparent motion. To test this alternative, Levin *et al.*
(in review) compared predictions for immediate changes with predictions for
changes in which the pre- and post-change views were separated in time. For
example, in one of the delayed-change scenarios, subjects imagined that they
were watching a movie in which two actors were talking, and that on a particular
shot in which one of the actors was wearing a scarf, the phone rang. In response
to the phone subjects imagined that they stopped the VCR, and walked into
another room to answer the phone. Upon completing the call, they imagined
returning to the TV and restarting the VCR which showed the next shot in the
movie in which the same actor was visible, but this time her scarf was not present. Presumably, if subjects believe that a perceptual transient will make the

changes visible, these conditions ought to eliminate CBB because it should be clear that no transient is possible if the pre- and post-change views are separated by time and intervening visual experience.

Across three experiments, inserting the delay did not significantly reduce CBB overall despite imagined delays of up to an hour. In addition, in one experiment, a one-minute delay was illustrated concretely by showing a model stopping the VCR, walking to another room to talk on the phone, and finally returning to restart the VCR. Again, this did not shake subjects' confidence that they would detect these changes.

The second alternative mentioned above is that subjects believe that they have a rich short-term memory for visual details. Although one would think that most people would not hold this view because failures of memory might be more familiar than those of vision, there are some interesting historical examples that might lend credence to this hypothesis. Some initial research exploring the integration of visual information across views suggested that people do have a short-term memory buffer for visual information that could be used to retain and compare (or fuse) information from one fixation to the next (see, for example, Averbach and Sperling, 1968; Breitmeyer, 1984). This buffer, referred to as iconic memory (Neisser, 1967), was explored in a series of clever experiments in which subjects viewed letter arrays for 50 ms, then were asked to report as many of the letters as possible. Normally, subjects can remember between three and five letters under these circumstances, and if there were more than that in the display, the additional letters appeared to be lost. The letters were lost, that is, once subjects got them out of their mouths. In a textbook example of the importance of listening to what subjects say, researchers noted that some of their subjects claimed that for a brief moment after the offset of the display, they would have been able to report any of the letters by 'reading them off' an afterimage they had momentarily retained. To test this intuition, researchers developed the well-known partial report procedure in which subjects reported only a subset of each display. This was achieved by dividing large displays into rows, and asking subjects to report a given row depending on the pitch of a tone played after the offset of the display (or by placing a pointer near a target letter). Using this task it became clear that subjects had access to considerably more than the three to five letters that they had initially reported (see Averbach and Sperling, 1968, for review).

The interesting thing about these experiments is that subjects correctly reported not only the afterimage, but also intuited its potential use as a means of overcoming the limits of the whole report procedure. In fact, James (1892) discusses afterimages and suggested that it might be possible to read information off the image. To determine whether more naive individuals would share this intuition, a group of 20 general psychology students was asked to make predictions about the experience of seeing an array of letters for a brief moment. Students who had not heard about iconic memory (or any experiments involving briefly presented arrays) consistently predicted that they would be able to report only a part of the array (mean of 3.9 out of 12 items), but 100% (of 20) predicted that they would be able 'see' letters during the moment after the array disappeared, and 85% predicted that they would be able to report more letters were it not for the fact that they would 'forget' letters while producing their report. It is important to emphasize that these students were not simply assuming they have unlimited powers. Not only did they correctly estimate that they would be able to report only a few of the letters, but 75% did not believe that the letters, if they formed a word, would affect their behaviour or emotions without awareness (although it is important to note that these students had heard about change blindness).

Thus people seem to understand afterimages and despite the fact that they might be inherently ill-suited to view integration (see Neisser, 1967; Haber, 1983), people may generalize this understanding to include a short-term memory for visual detail that could be useful in detecting changes. Although data showing that CBB persists across delays is problematic for this explanation, it is possible that people simply ignore the temporal limit of this visual memory and assume that it, or a related type of visual memory, would be useful to see even delayed changes. However, another observation from Levin et al. (in review) also suggests that explicit beliefs about memory for visual detail are not central to CBB. After making their estimates, all subjects completed open-ended response justifications for each scenario. When discussing the change scenarios, between 0% and 5.4% of subjects mentioned memory for the immediate changes, and between 2.8% and 19% of subjects mentioned memory in the delayed scenarios. In contrast, for a scenario asking subjects whether they could successfully reproduce ten random digits, they frequently discussed memory in justifying their responses, for both the immediate (78%) and delayed scenarios (81%). This finding suggests that an explicit belief in a detailed visual memory is not central to CBB.

These initial experiments suggest that CBB is a robust phenomenon, and also suggest that expected perceptual transients, and explicit beliefs in memory for visual details do not cause CBB. One might therefore ask how CBB fits in with more specific beliefs about vision. As mentioned above, with the exception of research on extramissionist beliefs and children's beliefs about visual attention, very little research explores visual metacognition. However, both of these lines of research document metacognitive errors, and give important hints about the causes underlying CBB.

Particularly important has been research exploring children's emerging understanding that visual attention is limited in spatial extent by showing that children believe that paying attention to one thing does not preclude seeing another nearby object. Flavell et al. (1995) asked children to imagine looking at a box with tacks in it or a framed picture. They would then be asked if they could see the box while looking at the tacks or if they could see the frame while looking at the painting. It is not until late childhood that children begin to realize that they might not be able to see these peripheral objects. Flavell et al. characterize this incomplete understanding of visual attention using a lamp metaphor. On this view, children believe that visual attention is like a lamp which illuminates an entire environment while adults learn that attention is more like a spotlight, illuminating only a small portion of the environment. Similar research suggests that children also fail to appreciate the degree to which selective looking helps one to remember a subset of target objects (Miller and Weiss, 1982). Interestingly, this research often assumes that adults represent the final developmental milestone of an essentially complete and correct understanding of seeing (for more discussion see Winer and Cottrell, 1996). As suggested by both CBB and extramissionist beliefs, this conclusion might be incorrect in many situations.

Recently completed research confirms that adults' intuitions about visual attention are, indeed, quite diverse. In one series of experiments, Levin (2001) followed up on Flavell *et al.*'s developmental findings by asking adults whether looking at one thing precludes seeing other nearby things. For example, in one scenario adults imagined that they were at a museum looking at a painting, then judged whether they would see the painting's frame while viewing the painting. In another situation, subjects imagined they were looking at a friend across the street from them, then estimated whether they would see a fire hydrant ten feet away from their friend. Typically, there is considerable variation in responses to these questions. In one representative experiment, 29% of adults believed that they would 'definitely not' or 'probably not' see the frame while 50% believed that they definitely or probably would see the frame (the remaining subjects thought that there would be a 50% probability that they would see the frame). In the same experiment, 47% of subjects thought they would probably or definitely not see the fire hydrant while 22% predicted that they would see it.

To further explore the relationship between beliefs about visual attention and CBB, Levin (2001) combined the above scenarios with two others testing the degree to which subjects believe that they typically look at a large proportion of the objects in a scene, and the degree to which subjects believe that they look at objects that are not directly related to the task at hand. The former scenario is based on Schooler's (2001) recent work on meta-awareness as it relates to memory. He argues that people overestimate the proportion of time that they are aware of their mental contents and reflect upon them. Similarly, it is possible that people overestimate the proportion of the visual world they typically look at. The other scenario is based on the idea that people's fixations are almost exclusively related to the task at hand and are very rarely focussed on irrelevant objects (Hayhoe, 2000). Again, if people misunderstand this, it might lead them to believe that they would typically focus attention on peripheral objects and therefore see these changes. As with the spotlight items, subjects' responses on these items vary considerably. For example, 26% subjects in one experiment indicated that 95% or more of their fixations would be task relevant (nominally the correct estimate according to Hayhoe, 2000) while 28% indicated that 50–79% of their fixations would be task relevant. Similarly, 41% indicated that they typically look at 0–25% of the objects, 43% indicated that they look at 26–50% of the objects, and 16% thought they would look at 50% or more of the objects. Combined, we refer to these four items as the attentional breadth and countenance (ABC) questionnaire.

These basic results emphasize the variability in adults' intuitions about visual attention, but more important is the relationship between the ABC scenarios and CBB. Across several experiments we find consistent moderate correlations between these responses. Subjects who believe in a broad attentional countenance tend to predict that they would see more changes (mean r = 0.3033). In addition, it is possible to look more closely at which of the scenarios are most closely related to CBB responses. The strongest and most consistent correlation is between the 'percent looking' scenario and CBB. In addition, the two spotlight items are correlated with CBB. In contrast, there is no correlation between the task-relevant focus item and CBB. These findings confirm the hypothesis that CBB is at least partially dependant on beliefs in that visual attention is broadly focussed, and also the intuition that we typically look at a large proportion of the objects in a scene. However, beliefs about the nature of task focus seem less central. Subjects either do not consider the degree to which visual attention is closely focussed on some specific task, or if they do, they may not believe that this focus is important for change detection.

This latter hypothesis receives some support from experiments showing that subjects tend to under emphasize the role of intention in detecting changes. A few findings confirm the straightforward hypothesis that intentionally searching for changes makes them more likely to be detected (see, for example, Levin and Simons, 1997), and in some cases, change blindness has been assumed to require a limited-capacity location-by-location visual search (Rensink, 2000a). However, when asked about change detection, subjects do not appear to take this into account. Beck and Levin (2001) asked subjects whether they would be able to detect changes to real-world scenes that included varying numbers of objects. Some were told to make their estimate under the assumption that they were actively searching for changes, and some were told to make their estimate assuming that they did not expect the change beforehand and were not actively searching for them. Despite repeated reminders about the nature of their task, there was no difference in estimated change detection between these groups.

In a sense, the two findings reviewed above might be contradictory. If a failure to account for the importance of attention in change detection causes CBB, then why should specific beliefs about attentional focus affect CBB? There are a number of plausible ways of integrating these findings which are not mutually exclusive. First, subjects' reasoning about change detection may vary systematically across stimuli and situations. A related possibility is that these intuitions vary across individuals. Alternatively, it is possible that subjects' responses to the CBB scenarios do not reflect a particularly coherent or organized theory of seeing. Instead, they may use a less systematic series of heuristics, perhaps borrowed from a number of other systems of knowledge. For example, subjects may borrow from a specialized system for reasoning about representations underlying theory of mind (Leslie, 2000). A key feature of this hypothesis is that contradictory intuitions are used to reason about vision, a possibility previously documented in the concept and memory literatures.

It is interesting to note that although CBB may reflect a relatively loose and internally inconsistent collection of heuristics, this doesn't mean that subjects make tentative predictions — they are often highly confident in their incorrect predictions. The theoretical issue to understand is how subjects become so confident in their metacognitive predictions for novel perceptual situations. One might argue that responses about situations that fit within an well-organized theory should be more confident, but perhaps this isn't the case. People may be relatively poor at detecting whether they are using error-prone ad hoc categories and conglomerations of heuristics that may not apply to a given situation. This may be particularly true in domains about which subjects have little explicit knowledge (Kruger and Dunning, 1999)

Some initial findings do reinforce the hypothesis that subjects reason differently about different kinds of changes. As reviewed above, Levin *et al.* (in review) observed similar degrees of optimism for immediate and delayed-change scenarios. However, when responses were collapsed across all three experiments in the report, an interesting interaction appeared between the kind of change scenario and the effects of delay on CBB. Scenarios describing peripheral changes did show small delay effects — subjects were slightly less likely to predict success for the plate- and scarf-change scenarios if they involved a delay (although estimates in the delayed condition still far exceeded performance without a delay). On the other hand, the scenarios describing central-person substitutions either showed no effect of delay, or showed the reverse effect: a paradoxical increase in optimism for the delayed change.[1] One reasonable explanation for this effect is that at least some subjects realize that the delay will reduce the detectability of peripheral changes because the object is a small part of a complex scene. Response justifications give more weight to this possibility: 63% of subjects mentioned centrality (or lack thereof) for the peripheral changes, while only 26% mentioned this for the central changes. It is important to note that this possibility does not necessitate a specific, explicit detail-tracking belief. As discussed above, subjects rarely mention anything about memory in their response justifications for any of the scenarios, least of all those involving peripheral delayed changes (for which 2.8% and 5.6% of subjects mentioned memory in the plate and scarf scenarios). It is more likely that subjects believe that the delay will reduce the perceptibility of the change more directly, perhaps because they expect something akin to a 'pop-out' effect to draw attention to a changing object in the immediate condition. This would be similar to the perceptual transient hypothesis except that it might allow for an exogenous cue in a more broad set of circumstances. Most important, subjects may believe that the delay does not completely foreclose the possibility that the change will call attention to itself. This more broad hypothesis fits peripheral CBB better than a perceptual transient hypothesis primarily because a large percentage (40–65%) of subjects still believed they would detect peripheral changes even across delays.

If beliefs about attentional focus and relative status in the scene underlie CBB for peripheral changes, then how might a different style of reasoning about

---

[1] It is important to note that there are a couple of important differences between the 'central' and 'peripheral' changes described here. The central changes are substitutions of intentional agents and of an attended object, while the peripheral changes occur in inanimate objects, and in objects that are outside the putative focus of attention or in objects that are features of attended objects (for example, the scarf change). Either could be responsible for the observed contrast between these stimuli.

central changes lead subjects to show the paradoxical increase in optimism for delayed central changes over immediate central changes? Based on response justifications in Levin *et al.* (in review), the most likely possibility is that within the focus of attention, subjects abandon their beliefs about attention and instead focus on the similarity of the pre- and post-change objects. First, subjects mention the similarity of pre- and post-change objects in the central-change response justifications far more frequently than for the other scenarios. Even more interesting was the pattern of results when subjects' predictions were conditionalized on whether they mentioned the pre- and post-change similarity of the actors in the actor-change scenario. In the delayed-change condition, 56% of subjects who mentioned the similarity of the actors predicted that they would see the change, a degree of optimism very similar to that expressed by the immediate-change condition (with 61% predicting success). Among subjects in the delayed condition who did not mention similarity, 96% predicted success. One way of interpreting these findings is to assume that the delay caused subjects to forget (or fail to consider) how similar the actors were. In the absence of awareness of this similarity, subjects almost universally predict they would see these central changes.

It appears, then, that subjects will almost universally default to the prediction that they will detect a central change unless they are given some reason to believe otherwise. This default may reflect the broad importance of tracking the identity of individual objects across views. It is critical for a wide variety of conceptual inductions to know that some object that we now see is the same object that we saw previously. (Whether the previous observation was only a moment ago, or many years ago. See, for example, Gutheil and Rosengren, 1996.) A positive change-detection prediction might result if subjects fail to realize that identity tracking is more conceptual than perceptual.

More generally, the contrast between central and peripheral CBB is predicated upon a sense of scene-like organization. Centrality is simply not relevant for object arrays, so perhaps subjects would show less CBB or a different pattern of CBB for object arrays. One possibility is that subjects implicitly believe that scene-like organization helps them to understand a scene, and therefore would also help them detect changes. This is particularly interesting in light of subject responses to open-ended questions asking them whether it is necessary to pay attention to the changing object in order to see it change. For example, one subject wrote 'I think you could see the change without paying direct attention to the objects because the changes often affected the whole scene', and another wrote 'I would often notice the change without paying direct attention to the object, but to the entire scene itself'. Both of these responses imply that scene-like organization allows the scene to be perceived as a single unit, or 'chunk', and therefore that changes will cause a holistic or configural change to the scene that would be easily detected. Although we currently have no data directly testing this hypothesis, data from Beck and Levin (2001) do suggest this possibility indirectly. Recall that subjects showed little CBB for an intentional change-detection task. It is possible that subjects were less optimistic than they would have been otherwise because the scenes were similar to object arrays in that they emphasized varying numbers of objects in stereotypic and oft-repeated contexts. Another interesting possibility is that the actual effects of scene-like organization are to increase central change detection and interfere with peripheral change detection (at least for incidental tasks; for relevant findings see Myles-Worsley *et al.* 1988; Werner and Theis, 2000), whereas subjects believe that organization globally increases CBB. This would lead them to make particularly large errors for peripheral changes in incidental tasks.

In summary, CBB occurs whether subjects make estimates based on still images illustrating the change, motion pictures, or delayed changes. This appears to be related to beliefs about the breadth of visual attention, and the degree to which one typically looks at a large percentage of a scene. In addition, CBB is affected by the centrality of changing objects. Subjects believe that changes to peripheral objects will be readily detected, but that this becomes slightly more difficult across delays. On the other hand, subjects default to assume that central identity changes will always be detected unless some contravening factor such as the similarity of the pre- and post-change stimuli overrides this assumption.

As with any novel line of research, it is reasonable to wonder whether the basic questions being asked are substantive, and can be answered in some compelling, organized way. After all, if there was something interesting to know here, why haven't these questions been explored more systematically before? Perhaps this is because CBB represents the straightforward failure on the part of subjects to understand perceptual inference, a failure that anyone who has attempted to teach perception to undergraduates knows well. Thus, subjects fail to realize that perceptual continuity is based not upon riffling through visual details, comparing them between views, but is rather based upon an inference that views are consistent unless one gets information contradicting this conclusion (Bridgeman *et al.*, 1994; Levin and Simons, 2000; Pani, 2000). Alternatively, perhaps subjects are surprised at CBB because they expect that they will be aware of events that occur in front of them (Noë *et al.*, 2000). On both accounts, perhaps there is no need for a series of experiments exploring the issue — the answer is already fairly clear.

The final section of the paper first asks why, in theory, this kind of explanation is not sufficient to understand CBB or other issues in visual metacognition. Following this we illustrate the need for research on visual metacognition more concretely by reviewing a series of real-world examples that demonstrate the critical need to understand why people think the way they do about vision.

So why is it insufficient to understand visual metacognition by simply referring to a broad failure to understand perceptual inference, or by assuming that subjects simply expect to see what is in front of them? In some sense, both of these explanations are probably correct — CBB clearly does demonstrate that subjects don't understand inference, and that they expect to see what happens in front of them. However, both of these explanations are essentially broad restatements of the problem, not fully articulated theories that can usefully predict behaviour in specific circumstances. This is why they almost have to be true, and why they are insufficient without extensive empirical backup. By analogy, we could assert that things are classified in the same category because they are similar. This is a simple, broad explanation that might encompass all of categorization, and is, at some level, certainly true. However, without unpacking this hypothesis and developing some systematic account of the process by which we decide that two things are similar we haven't explained anything substantive about categorization (Armstrong *et al.*, 1983; Medin, 1989). For example, if one is creative about choosing what features enter into a similarity comparison, then any two objects can be either very similar (in which case they would be placed into the same category) or very dissimilar (in which case they would be placed into different categories; see Goodman, 1972).

For the same reasons, it is critical to explore visual metacognition systematically, unpacking people's failure to understand perceptual inference and their belief that they ought to perceive important visual events. The most basic reason that these hypotheses need elaboration is that people don't always demonstrate CBB with visual stimuli. Recall the experiments mentioned above by Beck and Levin (2001). In these experiments, subjects estimated whether they would detect changes to natural scenes that varied systematically in the number of objects they included (for example, a given scene of a living room might be presented with three, four, or more objects in it) under the assumption that they were intentionally searching for changes or under the assumption that they were not looking for changes. A key finding was that estimates about the intentional task were reasonably accurate when compared with actual intentional performance while estimates about the incidental task far exceeded actual incidental performance. This implies that CBB is not a blanket overestimate of the detectability of changes as might be implied by these broad hypotheses, or an even more general overconfidence effect (Metcalfe, 1998). It is therefore necessary to develop some principled explanation of CBB's limits. The intentional/incidental contrast suggests that this will probably entail some explanation of subjects' beliefs about the interaction between visual attention and mental effort in allowing one to see changes.

The 'seeing-what-is-there' hypothesis suggests an important question. That is, what counts as an event that people think they ought to see? Clearly, there are changes that are small enough or irrelevant enough that people think they will not see them. To answer this question we need to understand a network of beliefs about the role of scene structure as a support for perception and memory. The research we discussed above suggests that subjects take the centrality of the change into account, but that they still show CBB for peripheral changes. This suggests that there are different categories of important events that subjects reason about differently. The notion of centrality is particularly interesting because it, in turn, also needs unpacking. Following a distinction in the concept literature, an object might be central in a scene because it is typical or atypical of a given kind of scene based on the statistical correlation between the category of scene and the object (see, for example, Ahn, 1998). Alternatively, centrality may depend on a deeper analysis of the causal structure of the scene. In this case, subjects may consider the functional relationships among the elements of the scene and assign centrality to objects that receive functional support from many other objects in the scene. For example, imagine a scene in which a mechanic is changing a tire in a garage. A pool of oil on the floor would be typical of such a scene, and a white leather couch would be atypical because they are, and are not, correlated with the category of garage scenes. On the other hand, the tire being changed would not only be typical, but also causally central, because other objects in the scene have functions that support the new tire; the mechanic is there to change the tire, the tire iron is there to take the tire from the rim, the computerized alignment-checking machine is there to make sure the tire is on straight, etc. The question is, when making predictions about change detection, to what degree to subjects do this kind of causal reasoning when they try to decide what will be 'important' enough for them to detect? This is an open question, and it would seem necessary to learn the answer to it via a program of research.

Why is Visual Metacognition Important to Understand?

At the most concrete level, any time people systematically make gross mispredictions about some psychological phenomenon, we would argue that it is critical to understand why they do so, and to determine the limits of their misprediction. More specifically, there are two basic reasons we should be interested in the kind of visual metaknowledge implicated by CBB. The first reason that researchers in cognition and perception would point to is the possibility that visual metaknowledge affects visual performance. If people believe that some task is easy, they may not devote sufficient effort to it. This is particularly important for understanding visual tasks that draw on executive functions and deliberated, strategic processes. However, we have frequently heard the argument that this is the extent of the usefulness of understanding visual metaknowledge, and if it has no strong relationship with visual performance (a distinct possibility given the metamemory literature; see e.g. Herzog and Dixon, 1994; Justice and Weaver-McDougall, 1989), then there is no point in doing science on what is essentially an epiphenomenon. This view is short sighted. As discussed in the metamemory literature, there is more than one reason to understand metaknowledge (Nelson and Narens, 1994). Not only might it be important for guiding actual memory processes, but it also serves as the basis for judgments about our own and other's psychological experience. If these judgments are founded on incorrect understandings of cognition and perception, then the potential for error, and even downright disaster is nearly unlimited. Whatever we eventually discover about the deeper causes and effects of CBB, we hope that a few real-world examples will make clear the importance of understanding this kind of metaknowledge in its own right.

As discussed in the introduction, criminal convictions may arise based on faulty metamemory, and without the benefit of an extensive review, we have already discovered cases where litigation turns on beliefs about perception. Many of these cases involve question of whether someone 'should have seen it'. For example, some law firms specialize in 'underride' accidents in which a driver is killed or seriously injured when they hit a long trailer that has turned sideways, blocking a highway (see, for, example, www.fonhink.com/lawtalk/lt-trucks.html). Often in these situations, there are no skid marks or any other signs of evasive driving attributable to the driver who simply smashed into the trailer at full speed. Litigation based on these accidents usually hinges on *ad hoc* hypotheses about what the typical attentive driver should be able to see under the circumstances (see Badger, 1993 for some interesting examples). Are the reflectors placed on the side of the trailer sufficient stimuli? Will a driver be able to 'see' the reflectors with the truck's headlights shining in their eyes? (Often the jack-knifed trailer's cab is on the highway shoulder facing oncoming traffic with its lights on, sometimes in an attempt to make the trailer more visible). Is gross negligence on the part of the driver the only explanation for these accidents, especially when one considers the fact that the driver's headlights should illuminate the trailer, giving at least some warning about the upcoming danger?

Just as with eyewitness testimony, jurors will try to simulate the victim's putative experience based on metaknowledge. They decide what is perceptible, and what the driver should have seen, so if this metaknowledge is grossly inaccurate we should be concerned. Also, consider the kind of evidence that might be presented in defence of the adequacy the side reflectors. A trucking company might present data from a driving simulator showing that 100% of subjects saw a simulated trailer with reflectors and argue that misses are very rare and therefore must be due to unusually poor attentiveness. So, how are jurors (and lawyers) to evaluate this evidence? What if their beliefs about visual attention lead them to neglect the key issue in evaluating these data? Our findings suggest that this is a very real possibility. As we have shown, people may fail to consider the difference between intentional and incidental visual tasks, responding that they will detect as many changes when they are not looking for them as when they intentionally searching for them. So, it may be a non-obvious necessity to educate people about the difference between a simulator task where the subjects may have been aware that they were looking for obstructions, and the real-world task in which they were not. More generally, this example illustrates the importance of a detailed understanding of visual metacognition because it may uncover a situation where people make confident but incorrect assessments of evidence about others' psychological experience, leaving them blind to critical questions that are necessary to ask in evaluating that evidence.

Another situation that illustrates the importance of visual metaknowledge is the process of designing usable human–machine interfaces. Frequently, these interfaces are developed by programmers who must judge the degree to which they will fit within the cognitive limits of users. The fact that these decisions are less than perfect is well known, and recent reviews have argued that computers have been surprisingly ineffective at increasing productivity, in part because they are poor matches to the people who must run them (Landauer, 1995). Accordingly, a good understanding of programmers' lay beliefs about their users might be a good first step in identifying problems of design early in the process. In addition, current interfaces use a metaphorical visual approach in which well- organized visual information is presumed to help users to recruit existing knowledge and spatial skills in understanding the interface. If visual organization can increase CBB, as suggested above, then these interfaces are particularly prone to the belief that the signals they give will be perceived.

Examples of these failures abound. At the most basic level, despite their confidence, programmers are often quite poor at differentiating easily used interfaces from poor ones. In one experiment (Nelson, 1989 as reported in Landauer, 1995), programmers were given two interfaces for a text-processing program, one of which proved to be very poor, and one of which was very effective. When asked to choose the better interface, half of the programmers chose each. Thus, programmers may believe they understand vision when they actually do not. Related research and anecdotes confirm this image. For example, in the early development of AOL's electronic messaging service, a mailbox was placed in a GUI under the assumption that people would see when its red flag popped up indicating new mail. Not only did many users fail to see the flag pop up, but some used the interface for months before they realized it was there, and complained that their mail service was never started despite the fact that they had boxes with many dozens of unread messages in them! In another situation, a large company designed their employee web page to visually emphasize the availability of web classes by using a large colourful banner only to discover that nobody found the information, and in fact were signing up for the wrong class. This phenomenon was dubbed 'banner blindness' by the human factors researchers who stumbled across it (Benway and Lane, 1998). In both of these situations, programmers overestimated the visibility of visual information and because of this created situations where users were bound to fail.

Not only can these failures hinder productivity, but they can also be dangerous. In the early 1980s, for example, NASA was testing new heads-up displays and found that pilots had the shocking tendency to ignore obvious environmental dangers when using them. These displays project navigation-relevant information in the cockpit windshield and make it appear as if the information is floating out in the environment. In an experiment by Haines (1991), the displays were being tested on a landing simulator. Pilots would be using a display, commenting on how nice it was, while landing their aircraft right on top of another aircraft taxiing onto their runway in plain view. Not only does this illustrate another situation where *a priori* hypotheses about the detectability of visual information fail, but it also demonstrates the importance of metacognition when strategically allocating attention. Pilots and aircraft designers know full well the danger of landing 'heads-down' with one's eyes cast down on the instrument panel because everyone understands that you won't see something outside when you are focussed on something that is inside. So, when your head comes back up, you have to check the scene again for danger. However, this understanding breaks down when the target of attention is one thing (that appears to be outside) and another thing that is in the same line of sight. Accordingly, the belief that this visual information should have been perceptible may have reduced vigilance for an unexpected event.

Summary and Conclusions

In essence, we have argued that the grand illusion is real and should be considered an important topic of research in its own right. People's beliefs about what they will see can depart dramatically from reality, and we have argued that this departure should be considered a metacognitive error akin to the failures (and successes) of metamemory. However, we also believe that this illusion is not necessarily a broad misapprehension that ruins all reasoning about vision, or that it implies that people have no understanding of representation. Clearly, adults know more about representation than children and can successfully reason about mental contents. On one account, this understanding may be overridden by the immediacy of vision, but this hypothesis is incomplete. It cannot tell us whether people will overestimate their capabilities in intentional vs. incidental tasks, in well-organized vs. poorly organized scenes, and even in visual vs. nonvisual perceptual tasks.

We also want to emphasize that these metacognitive errors do not necessarily imply that people are generally deluded about visual experience, or that their ability to reason about vision is poorly suited to visual survival in everyday environments. People's beliefs about vision may actually be well suited to most environments where visual information is stable in many respects across views. Put another way, it is probably true that the visual world can be used as an outside memory (O'Regan, 1992) and in most circumstances, allowing our beliefs to reflect this is not problematic. This kind of assumption may reflect a heuristic approach to reasoning about vision that is necessary for the same reason it is necessary in problem solving and decision making where complexity would otherwise overwhelm our limited capacity to consider a complex tree of alternatives, expected utilities, and consequences. However, the key reason we need to understand the shortcuts inherent to this reasoning is that visual experience does not all occur in 'the natural world'. In many cases, we must also see in circumstances where things can suddenly change, and where an endless variety of unusual novel circumstances can outstrip our understanding of vision. Without understanding exactly how people's understanding of vision breaks down under these circumstances we will not be able to fully understand visually guided behaviour in exactly those challenging circumstances where it is most important.

Given our belief that this is useful research, one might reasonably ask why researchers have discounted visual metacognition for so long. Perhaps it is because the dominant mode for studying perception has been primarily bottom-up. In this tradition, higher-order processes have been peripheral, or been considered to fall within the intractable domain of consciousness (Dennett, 1991; see Fodor, 1983 for an argument of this type). However, if there is one thing that change blindness tells us, it is that basic, automatic perceptual processes do not operate on all of the features we encounter in the real world. We don't track all details automatically, even for attended objects, but we definitely see some of them. So, without some systematic account of why we see the features we do, we shall find ourselves without any means of predicting behaviour in the real world. This account will inevitably require an understanding of how abstract knowledge guides perceptual processes that includes not only concepts, but also metacognitive models of perceptual processes, and the interaction between these models and perception.[2]

---

[2]   I would like to thank Dan Simons and Julia Noland for reading and commenting on previous versions of this manuscript.

References

Ahn, W. (1998), 'Why are different features central for natural kinds and artefacts?: The role of causal status in determining feature centrality', *Cognition*, **69**, pp. 135–78.

Armstrong, S.L., Gleitman, L.R. and Gleitman, H. (1983),'What some concepts might not be', *Cognition*, **13**, pp. 263–308.

Averbach, E. and Sperling, G. (1968), 'Short-term storage of information in vision', in *Contemporary Research and Theory in Visual Perception*, ed. R.N. Haber (New York: Holt, Reinhart, and Weston).

Badger, J.E. (1993), 'Tractor–trailer underride — another look — and another', www.harristechnical.com/ttur1.htm.

Beck, M.R. and Levin, D.T. (2001), 'The role of beliefs about intention in producing change blindness blindness', Poster presented at the Vision Sciences conference, Sarasota, FL.

Benway, J.P. and Lane, D.M. (1998), 'Banner blindness: web searchers often miss "obvious" links', *Internetworking: ITG Newsletter*, **1.3** (Dec. 1998).

Blackmore, S.J., Brelstaff, G., Nelson, K. and Troscianko, T. (1995), 'Is the richness of our visual world an illusion? Trans-saccadic memory for complex scenes', *Perception*, **24**, pp. 1075–81.

Breitmeyer, B. (1984), *Visual Masking: An Integrative Approach* (New York: Oxford University Press).

Bridgeman, B. and Mayer, M. (1983), 'Failure to integrate information from multiple successive fixations', *Bulletin of the Psychonomic Society*, **21**, pp. 285–6.

Bridgeman, B., Van der Heijden, A.H.C. and Velichkovsky, B.M. (1994), 'A theory of visual stability across saccadic eye movements', *Behavioral and Brain Sciences*, **17**, pp. 247–92.

Dennett, D.C. (1991), *Consciousness Explained* (New York: Little, Brown and Company).

Devenport, J.L , Penrod, S.D. and Cutler, B.L. (1997), 'Eyewitness identification evidence: Evaluating commonsense evaluations', *Psychology, Public Policy and Law*, **3**, pp. 338–61

Fischoff, B. (1982), 'For those condemned to study the past: Heuristics and biases in hindsight', in *Judgment under Uncertainty: Heuristics and Biases*, ed. D. Kahneman *et al.* (New York: CUP).

Fischoff, B (1988), 'Judgement and decision making', in *The Psychology of Human Thought*, ed. R.J. Sternberg and E.E. Smith (New York: Cambridge University Press).

Flavell, J.H., Green, F.L. and Flavell, E.R. (1995), 'The development of childrens' knowledge about attentional focus', *Developmental Psychology*, **31** (4), pp. 706–12.

Fodor, J. (1983), *Modularity of Mind: An Essay on Faculty Psychology* (Cambridge, MA: MIT Press).

Goodman, N. (1972), *Problems and Projects* (New York: Bobbs-Merrill).

Grimes, J. (1996), 'On the failure to detect changes in scenes across saccades', in *Perception*, ed. K. Akins (Ed.), (Vancouver Studies in Cognitive Science) (New York: Oxford University Press).

Gutheil, G. and Rosengren, K.S. (1996), 'A rose by any other name: Preschoolers' understanding of individual identity across name and appearance', *British Journal of Psychology*, **14**, pp. 477–98.

Haber, R.N. (1983), 'The impending demise of the icon: A critique of the concept of iconic storage in visual information processing', *Behavioral and Brain Sciences*, **6**, pp. 1–11.

Haines, R.F. (1991) 'A breakdown in simultaneous information processing', in *Presbyopia Research: From Molecular Biology to Visual Adaptation*, ed. G. Obrecht and L.W. Stark (New York: Plenum Press).

Hayhoe, M. (2000), 'Vision using routines: A functional account of vision', *Visual Cognition*, **7**, pp. 43–64.

Henderson, J.M. (1997), 'Trans-saccadic memory and integration during real-world object perception', *Psychological Science*, **8** (1), pp. 51–5.

Herzog, C. and Dixon, R.A. (1994), 'Metacognitive development in adulthood and old age', in *Metacognition: Knowing about Knowing*, ed. J. Metcalfe and A.P. Shimamura (Cambridge, MA: MIT Press).

Irwin, D.E. (1991), 'Information integration across saccadic eye movements', *Cognitive Psychology*, **23**, pp. 420–56.

James, W. (1892), *Psychology: A Briefer Course* (New York: Holt and Company).

Justice, E.M. and Weaver-McDougall, R.G. (1989), 'Adults' knowledge about memory: Awareness and use of memory strategies across tasks', *Journal of Educational Psychology*, **81** (2), pp. 214–19.

Kruger, J. and Dunning, D. (1999), 'Unskilled and unaware of it: How difficulties in recognizing one's own incompetence lead to inflated self-assessments', *Journal of Personality and Social Psychology*, **77** (6), pp. 1121–34.

Kuleshov, L. (1920/1974), *Kuleshov on Film*, tr. R. Levaco (Berkeley, CA: University of California Press).

Landauer, T. (1995), *The Trouble with Computers: Usefulness, Usability, and Productivity* (Cambridge, MA: MIT Press).

Leslie, A.M. (2000), '"Theory of Mind"' as a mechanism of selective attention', in *The New Congitive Neurosciences*, ed. M. Gazzaniga (Cambridge, MA: MIT Press).

Levin, D.T. (2001), 'Visual metacognitions underlying change blindness blindness and estimates of picture memory', Poster presented at the Vision Sciences conference, Sarasota, FL.

Levin, D.T. and Simons, D.J. (1997), 'Failure to detect changes to attended objects in motion pictures', *Psychonomic Bulletin and Review*, **4**, pp. 501–6.

Levin, D.T. and Simons, D.J. (2000), 'Perceiving stability in a changing world: Combining shots and integrating views in motion pictures and the real world', *Media Psychology*, **2**, pp. 357–80.

Levin, D.T., Momen, N., Drivdahl, S.B. and Simons, D.J. (2000), 'Change blindness blindness: The metacognitive error of overestimating change-detection ability', *Visual Cognition*, **7**, pp. 397–412.

Levin, D.T., Drivdahl, S.B., Momen, N. and Beck, M.R. (in review), False predictions about the detectability of visual changes: The role of beliefs about attention, memory, and the continuity of attended objects in causing change blindness blindness.

Mack, A. and Rock, I. (1998), *Inattentional Blindness* (Cambridge, MA: MIT Press).

McConkie, G.W. and Currie, C.B. (1996), 'Visual stability across saccades while viewing complex pictures', *Journal of Experimental Psychology: Human Perception and Performance*, **22**, pp. 563–81.

Medin, D.L. (1989), 'Concepts and conceptual structure', *American Psychologist*, **44**, pp. 1469–81.

Metcalfe, J. and Shimamura, A.P. (1994), *Metacognition* (Cambridge, MA: MIT Press).

Metcalfe, J. (1998), 'Cognitive optimism: Self-deception or memory-based processing heuristics?', *Personality and Social Psychology Review*, **2** (2), pp. 100–10.

Miller, P.H. and Weiss, M.G. (1982), 'Childrens' and adults' knowledge about what variables affect selective attention', *Child Development*, **53**, pp. 543–49.

Myles-Worsley, M., Johnston, W.A. and Simons, M.A. (1988), 'The influence of expertise on x-ray image processing', *Journal of Experimental Psychology: Learning, Memory and Cognition*, **14**, pp. 553–7.

Neisser, U. (1967), *Cognitive Psychology* (New York: Meredith Publishing).

Nelson, T.O. and Narens, L. (1994), 'Why investigate metacognition?', in *Metacognition: Knowing about Knowing*, ed. J. Metcalfe and A.P. Shimamura (Cambridge, MA: MIT Press).

Noë, A., Pessoa, L. and Thompson, E. (2000), 'Beyond the grand illusion: What change blindness really teaches us about vision', *Visual Cognition*, **7**, pp. 93–106.

O'Regan, J.K. (1992), 'Solving the "real" mysteries of visual perception: The world as an outside memory', *Canadian Journal of Psychology*, **46**, pp. 461–88.

O'Regan, J.K., Deubel, H., Clark, J.J. and Rensink, R.A. (2000), 'Picture changes during blinks: Looking without seeing and seeing without looking', *Visual Cognition*, **7**, pp. 191–211.

Pani, J.R. (2000), 'Cognitive description and change blindness', *Visual Cognition*, **7**, pp. 107–26.

Pashler, H. (1988), 'Familiarity and visual change detection', *Perception and Psychophysics*, **44**, pp. 369–78.

Phillips, W.A. (1974), 'On the distinction between sensory storage and short-term visual memory', *Perception and Psychophysics*, **16**, pp. 283–90.

Pollatsek, A. and Rayner, K. (1992), 'What is integrated across fixations?', in *Eye Movements and Visual Cognition: Scene Perception and Reading*, ed. K. Rayner (New York: Springer-Verlag).

Rensink, R.A., O'Regan, J.K. and Clark, J.J. (1997), 'To see or not to see: The need for attention to perceive changes in scenes', *Psychological Science*, **8**, pp. 368–73.

Rensink, R.A. (2000a), 'The dynamic representation of scenes', *Visual Cognition*, **7**, pp. 17–42.

Rensink, R.A. (2000b), 'Seeing, sensing, and scrutinizing', *Vision Research*, **40**, pp. 1469–87.

Schooler, J.W. (2001), 'Discovering memories in light of meta-awareness', *The Journal of Aggression, Maltreatment, and Trauma*, **4**, pp. 105–36

Simons, D.J. (1996), 'In sight, out of mind: When object representations fail', *Psychological Science*, **7** (5), pp. 301–5.

Simons, D.J. and Levin, D.T. (1997) 'Change blindness', *Trends in Cognitive Science*, **1**, pp. 261–7.

Simons, D.J. and Levin, D.T. (1998), 'Failure to detect changes to people in a real-world interaction', *Psychonomic Bulletin and Review*, **5**, pp. 644–9.

Stinson, V., Devenport, J.L., Cutler, B.L. and Kravitz, D.A. (1996), 'How effective is the presence-of-counsel safeguard? Attorney perceptions of biased line-up procedures', *Journal of Applied Psychology*, **81** (1), pp. 64–75.

Wells, G.A., Small, M., Penrod, S., Malpass, R.S., Fulero, S.M. and Brimacombe, C.A.E. (1998), 'Eyewitness identification procedures: Recommendations for line-ups and photo spreads', *Law and Human Behavior*, **22**, pp. 1–39.

Werner, S. and Theis, B. (2000), 'Is "change blindness" attenuated by domain-specific expertise? An Expert-novices comparison of change detection in football images', *Visual Cognition*, **7**, pp. 163–74.

Winer, G.A. and Cottrell (1996), 'Does anything leave the eye when we see? Extramission beliefs of children and adults', *Current Directions in Psychological Science*, **5**, pp. 137–42.

Winer, G.A., Cottrell, J.E., Karefilaki, K.D. and Chronister, M. (1996a), 'Conditions affecting beliefs about visual perception among children and adults', *Journal of Experimental Child Psychology*, **61**, pp. 93–115.

Winer, G.A., Cottrell, J.E., Karefilaki, K.D. and Gregg, V.R. (1996b), 'Images, words, and questions: Variables that influence beliefs about vision in children and adults', *Journal of Experimental Child Psychology*, **63**, pp. 499–525.

Charles Siewert

Is Visual Experience Rich Or Poor?

I

Is our ordinary visual experience of our surroundings rich and detailed, or is it, contrary to appearance, surprisingly 'sparse' and 'gappy'? A number of psychologists and philosophers advocate the latter, 'poverty' answer — provocatively put by saying that the visual world is an 'illusion' (Blackmore *et al.*, 1995; Dennett, 1991; O'Regan, 1992; Rensink, 2000).[1] In support of this perspective, they appeal to experimental studies in which it is found that we are remarkably 'change blind'; that is, unaware of changes occurring right before our eyes. For under appropriate conditions — interruptions, intervening stimuli — rather big changes in the scene with which we are presented can pass entirely unnoticed by us. From our failure to detect these changes it is inferred that our experience of the scenes is dramatically poorer in content than (in some sense) it seems. Studies of so-called 'inattentional blindness' present related results (Mack & Rock, 1998). For example, when subjects focus their attention on some task involving a figure (such as a cross) on a screen presented in their visual fields, they often fail to report the appearance of an unattended stimulus (e.g., a small square) flashed elsewhere on the screen. From such findings it is concluded that our experience extends no further than our focus of attention.

But does psychology really call for some radical revision in our appraisal of experiential wealth? This is controversial. For example, some oppose the 'poverty theorists' by arguing that the change and inattentional blindness research does not banish experiential richness, it just teaches us to locate this rather differently than would traditional approaches to explaining vision (Noë *et al.*, 2000; Noë, 2002). They agree that experimental studies suggest that no *detailed internal representation* lies at the terminus of a visual process, but reject the notion that this implies we do not visually experience a detailed world. They conclude that what makes for the wealth of visual experience is not the intricate detail of an internal model, but rather the fact that we act and can act in many specifically visual ways, subtly responsive to our environment. The lesson they draw then, is

---

[1] The basic idea has been forcefully expressed by Kevin O'Regan: '...[W]e have the subjective impression of great richness and 'presence' of the visual world: But this richness and presence are actually an illusion...' (1992, p. 484).

Journal of Consciousness Studies, **9**, No. 5–6, 2002, pp. 131–40

that the richness of visual detail is not to be found *represented in our heads* — but *out in the world*.

Evidently a lot is at stake here. One interpretation of the evidence purports to massively discredit the kind of first-person awareness we readily take ourselves to have of our experience. An alternative view leads to a radical questioning of the premises that have often guided projects for vision science. But while the stakes appear high, the debate sometimes suffers from a lack of clarity regarding the central claims at issue. Just what does it mean to say that we have a 'subjective impression' of great 'richness' in the 'visual world'?

I will argue that, once certain crucial distinctions are acknowledged, and the issues interpreted in their light, we will have reason to reject 'grand illusion' interpretations of change and inattentional blindness research. Further, as a result of this critique, we are led to question the assumption sometimes made that our visual *experiences* are only as *rich* as our internal visual *representations* (i.e., descriptions or images formed in our heads) are *detailed*. My conclusions thus provide additional support for some important aspects of the Noë–Pessoa– Thompson perspective mentioned earlier.

II

In my view, we need to start by acknowledging distinctions among:

1.   Differences in how some area *looks* to someone — how he or she *visually experiences* it, or how it *visually appears*;
2.   Differences in how someone *believes* this area looks to him or her, on the basis of first-person reflection;[2] and
3.   Differences in what visible spatial characteristics *actually belong* to entities in this area.

---

[2]   I will take it that the 'subjective impression' whose accuracy is here in question must be some sort of *belief* that we hold or *judgment* we make about visual appearances — about how things look to us. The impression at issue cannot be *visual appearance* itself: If *that* were grandly illusory the world itself would have to be substantially poorer in spatial detail than it appears to us — and clearly that is not what is being alleged. (For similar reasons, the illusion cannot consist in our holding a lot of false beliefs about the spatial environment.) And since I do not think that our experiences themselves appear to us some way — as distinct from our believing or judging them to be some way — there seems nowhere left to search for the alleged illusion but in our beliefs or judgment about how it visually appears to us.

Further, I assume not just *any* beliefs about one's experience are at issue, but specifically the 'subjective' ones; those suggested to us by the 'experience of seeing'. I can see no way to make out what this amounts to, other than to say they are those formed *on the basis of first-person reflection*. What do I mean by this? I assume that we take ourselves to have a warrant for first-person judgments about experience that differs in kind from that had for judgments about other people's experience: you think you sometimes know how things look, feel and (generally) appear to you in a way that no one else does. And where we take ourselves to have this first-person sort of warrant, or know in this first-person way, we do not think this requires us to justify the claims in question by inferring their truth from others. Where one takes one's first-person judgments about experience in this way to have warrant, or express knowledge, which is in this sense non-inferential, and distinct in kind from that had in the third-person case through observation, I will say they are made 'on the basis of first-person reflection'. The grand illusion hypothesis then will say that what we *think* we know in this special way (or have a special first-person warrant for believing) regarding the richness of our visual experience is really not so at all.

These are, I assume, distinguishable from one another. Differences in how some region *looks* to you may be other than, fewer than, or greater than you *believe them* to be, and either of these may vary independently of differences in what occupies the area before you eyes. Thus we may distinguish: (1) differences in visual appearances of space; (2) differences in what we believe, on a first-person basis, those differences in visual appearance are; and (3) actual spatial differences and relationships. Once this is granted, two basic points are in order.

First, poverty theorists need to show that the actual sorts and number of differences in (1) — differences in the ways some area ordinarily looks to us — are much fewer or of fewer sorts than we are disposed to believe on the basis of first-person reflection. For if the differences in how our surroundings look to us are pretty much as various as first-person reflection takes them to be, then there is no false impression of richness, and no grand illusion. Thus, the argument for experiential poverty requires both an accurate characterization of what first-person reflection seems to tell us, and sound reasoning from the research data to claims about the true (impoverished) character of ordinary experience.

Second, to counter with the claim that experience is not poor, but rich, one needs to say more than that we experience or see a detailed environment. For that may mean no more than:

a. There are many spatial details — differences of type (3) — that characterize an *area that we see* (or an area *of* which we have visual experience).

And this is distinct from claiming:

b. There are many differences and many kinds of difference in *how that area looks* to us, or is experienced by us — differences of type (1).

Claim (a) says only that a certain region of space is rich in spatial differences (thus very spatially detailed), *and* that region is seen or visually experienced by us. Claim (b) says that such rich differentiation characterizes not only this area of space, but *also* our experience of it. The truth of (a) does not entail that of (b). For region R at t_1 may differ in its spatial characteristics from R at t_2, even though the way R *looks to x* at t_1 does *not* differ from the way R looks to x at t_2. The poverty theorists need not quarrel with (a). However, if they can show that (b) is rarely or never correct, though we believe quite otherwise, they will have gained their point.

Now we face the question of whether one can accurately characterize the 'subjective impression' of richness, so as to show its vulnerability before the experimental evidence. So, just what *do* we think on the basis of first-person reflection about how rich our experience ordinarily is? Some characterizations that have been offered: we have a 'subjective impression' or 'feeling' that we usually form 'in our brains' a 'uniformly detailed', 'complete' and 'coherent' 'picture' or 'representation' or 'image' of what is before our eyes.[3]

Noë *et al.* (2000, pp. 102–3) have argued, persuasively, I think, that such ways of portraying our subjective impression of visual richness are unacceptable. I would add to their case as follows. To begin with, subjective or first-person reflection does not tell us we form *pictures in our brains* — detailed *or* sketchy. For that matter, it does not even tell us we *have brains*. However, quite apart from any study of vision science, such reflection does dispose us to say that detail is *not* equally visually apparent to us throughout the area before our eyes. First-person reflection tells us that we do not attend equally well to all of this, and that we need to look *at* something, to focus attention on it, to perceive much detail in it. Surely most people would regard this as obvious. But this conviction is evidently quite at odds with the notion that we possess a complete and uniformly detailed visual image of what is before us — the notion that, supposedly, we naively endorse on the basis of the subjective experience of seeing.

Now it is sometimes inferred that we must implicitly hold something like the 'detailed picture' view of vision, for otherwise there would be no explaining our surprise when confronted with the experimental demonstrations of how limited our ability to perceive change can be. But this inference is unwarranted. It is true that people are initially surprised by (many of) the change and inattentional blindness demonstrations. And it is also true that we expect to notice large scale changes that happen before our eyes. However, we need to keep in mind the following relevant facts. First, our expectation of being able to detect big changes is rather vague, in that it includes no very definite ideas about what qualifies as a 'big' change. And many who have this expectation would also admit that the claim that they will see big changes before their eyes stands in some need of qualification. For many would agree to this, when reminded of how the stage illusionist's successful sleight of hand depends on our oblivion to rather big changes that happens right in front of us.[4] Finally, our rather vague expectation of being able to detect large changes is *ordinarily correct* — and the studies do not show otherwise.

So, prior to awareness of the change and inattentional blindness studies, we do not know that our capacity to notice change is restricted in the kinds of situations they involve; ordinary experience does not teach us under just what conditions we become oblivious to change through the interruption and direction of attention. And yet we do have the vague expectation of being able to notice big changes. *As a result, we have some tendency to think we can notice more than it turns out we can.* Where one has an expectation of being able to perform a certain

---

[3] Blackmore and her colleagues write, for example, 'We believe that we see a complete dynamic picture of a stable, uniformly detailed, and colourful world...' and they refer to '[t]he illusion that we are simultaneously aware of every aspect of the view in front of us' (Blackmore *et al.*, 1995, p.1075). And Rensink (2000) asks: 'Why do we feel that somewhere in our brain is a complete coherent representation of the entire scene?'
 O'Regan does not assume we think we form 'complete' or 'uniformly detailed' brain pictures, though he does indicate that our subjective beliefs about the richness of experience are to be expressed in terms of the richness of an internal representation: '...[H]umans' internal representation of the visual field is much sparser than the subjective experience of "seeing" suggests' (1999, p. 34). Dennett contrasts the 'apparent continuity' of consciousness with what he considers its actual 'gappiness' (1991, p. 356) and thinks of the apparent richness of conscious experience as an illusion that involves its seeming to us as if we represent in our minds the intricate details of the scene before us (*Ibid*, p. 408).

[4] A point emphasized by Noë *et al.* (2000, p. 103).

task in a very wide (but ill-defined) range of situations, and one is ill-equipped by experience to anticipate the circumstances in which one's competence fails, it is likely that one will overestimate its reach. That is why we are initially surprised and impressed by change and inattentional blindness demonstrations. We need not attribute to ourselves some belief in a complete and uniformly detailed brain picture to explain this.

Of course, some people may start talking about pictures in their heads if asked to speculate about what happens in them to constitute visual experience. Perhaps to modern people like us that will seem a plausible first stab to take at a theory of vision, since our mentality has been so shaped by the Western tradition of pictorial realism and the omnipresence of photographic images in our lives. And some may naively assent to this 'detailed brain picture' notion because they confuse this with the idea that visual appearances are richly varied. However, as we have seen, if change and inattentional blindness studies refute the idea that we form a complete and detailed visual image or brain picture, in this they support the verdict of first-person reflection, they do not overturn it.

III

So, once more: just what is the illusory subjective impression here? Another way to try to confront our first-person belief in an abundance of experience with the reality of its poverty appeals to the concept of *attention*. We normally believe, on the basis of first-person reflection, that we visually experience *more* than we attend to during a given time. But, it is claimed, research shows that this is false. We have absolutely no visual experience of such areas. They look no way to us at all, for we experience nothing in a given time but what we are then attending to. (This way of contrasting visual phenomenology with the outcome of vision science (to the former's detriment) can be found in Churchland *et al.*, 1994; Mack & Rock, 1998; O'Regan *et al.*, 1999; and Rensink, 1997.)[5]

This time we do seem to have a fair statement of the deliverances of first-person reflection. For if I consider what I am disposed to say about my experience, relying on the kind of warrant available to first-person judgment without appeal to observation and theory, I find something like this. Though I am not, at a given time, directing my attention to part of the area before me, often it still looks some way to me, and it looks some way to me before I turn my attention to it. Further, the way it looks is not entirely uniform. There is variation — spatial variation — visually apparent in that area. And it is not just *some sort of spatial*

[5] Rensink writes '. . . [T]he visual perception of change in a scene occurs only when focussed attention is given to the part being changed', 1997, p.368) According to Patricia Churchland *et al.* (1994, pp. 26–7): 'Although unattended objects may be represented in some minimal fashion (sufficient to guide attention shifts and eye movements, for example), they are not literally seen in the sense of being "visually experienced".' Mack & Rock (1998, p. 227) conclude '. . . [t]here is no conscious perception at all in the absence of attention. . . '. And O'Regan *et al.* (1999, p. 34) ask: 'If only attended parts of the environment are represented in the brain, how can we have the impression of such richness and completeness in the visual world outside us?' Clearly he regards the antecedent as true, the problem being how to account for the illusory impression of the consequent.

variation or other. At different times (as I move my eyes or body, as things before me move) the way the unattended background looks varies.

But is *this* 'subjective impression' refuted by experimental results? Perhaps we should say that, in the right circumstances, lack of attention (and change blindness interruptions) keep us from *remembering* our experiences well enough to judge that they are different. Nevertheless, varying experiences of unattended stimuli do occur. So perhaps there is *change* blindness without *inattentional* blindness. The issues raised by this challenge are not trivial, but for present purposes they can be waived — I now want to focus on something else.

Let us grant that in a case of change blindness (where the railing of a fence is raised higher without subjects noticing the change), one's experience of the position of the railing in the first picture does not differ from one's experience of the railing in the second: the position of the fence's railing looks no different. And let us grant that in a case of inattentional blindness, one's experience of the region in which the square is flashed is the same regardless of whether the square is flashed: that area looks no different to the subject in the two cases. Still, it is another thing entirely to say that one has no visual experience of those *areas* in which the changed elements (e.g., the railing), or the flashed figures (e.g., the squares) occur. For that stronger conclusion, one must show more than that there are *some* changes in those areas which occur without our being able to detect them. For, as noted earlier, it is compatible with one's having visual experience of a given area during a certain period that real objective changes occur there, though the way the area *looks* to one does not change.

Now, it *would* furnish a reason to doubt subjects' claims to have visual experience of some unattended or (at least partially) change-blind area if it were found that *no* changes that could be made to that portion of the scene were visually detectable by them. However, that is neither found nor alleged by vision researchers. So it seems that the research fails to support the conclusion that we have no experience of those areas of the visual field on which we are not training our attention.

In response to this objection, one might say that those areas in which changes *are* visually noticeable are never really 'unattended'. We devote at least *some* attention to them, so still there is no visual experience of the (completely) unattended. But, then, just what has become of the supposedly counterintuitive thesis? We are now dealing not with the bare claim that only the attended is experienced but with the more qualified view that *some* attention has to be given to an area presented to subjects if it is to visually appear to them. And the dramatic conflict alleged between the experimental data and 'subjective impressions' slips away. Consider: I believe that, when I hold up my hand eighteen inches or so before my face and focus my attention on the lines in my palm, following them with my gaze, still, not only the hand as a whole, but the area beyond my hand looks some way to me. And I experience enough of the scene beyond what I am most attentively examining at the time to redirect my visual attention as need be and notice at least some kind of change that occurs outside my palm. Does this conflict with the claim that the unattended is not experienced?

Apparently not, because I can simply say that at least some *low-level* of visual attention is given to the world beyond my palm — enough to make it the case that it also appears some way to me. So harmony between first-person reflection and experimental studies is found easily enough. Once more we seem hard pressed to get a strong contrast between the actual differences in visual appearance and those merely subjectively believed to occur.

IV

I will consider one final strategy to set our subjective impression of seeing at odds with psychological reality. Regarding the less attended but still (we believe) visually apparent regions before us, we might ask, just what spatial details do we *think* we experience there? Answering this may give us some hope of identifying specific differences in spatial characteristics (shape, position, size, motion) that we subjectively think visually appear to us but which vision science will then show do not really appear to us after all. However, a key problem arises for this approach. We often do not know precisely *what* to say, through reliance on first-person reflection, to specify just what spatial relationships appear to us or how things look to us spatially in regions to which we are attending less. At least, I would say that I am largely helpless to describe just what shapes, positions, etc., are experienced by me there or how it looks to me as if things are situated in that part of my visual field. If I try to describe this very much by redirecting my attention, then that portion of the field is no longer 'relatively unattended', and so I am not even addressing the question at hand. Also, it seems that, whatever pronouncements I make in ordinary circumstances about how it looks as if things are in the less-attended area, these are often likely to be influenced by some *memory* of what I saw there when I attended more to it. Nevertheless, I am inclined to say that there is some fairly highly variable character to the way relatively unattended regions look to me. And I do not think there is just *some variation or other.* I think I can detect the variations and distinguish them in ways that allow me to direct my attention appropriately. However, when I try to *say* just what those specific differences are by describing the apparent shape, size and position of things in that area, I find I cannot do so without altering the character of the visual experience.

I would sum this up by saying that differences in the way things look to me outstrip my power to identify them relative to verbal reports of shapes, positions, etc., visually experienced. I find I cannot specify differences I believe obtain in how it looks to me by means of differentiating contents of sentences I might plug into the 'content clause' of some 'It looks to me as if . . .' locution. Notice further that it appears not to help if I try to specify the differences in experiential character relative to some *non-sentential* means of representation — like maps or pictures. For I will also be unable to identify the differences in how it looks to me by attributing to my visual experience the contents of varying pictures or maps of the area of which I have visual experience.

This suggests two observations, relevant to assessing the implications of change and inattentional blindness. First, we face a considerable obstacle to using these experimental studies to debunk some 'subjective impression' of visual richness by demonstrating the actual poverty of experience. For again we have a hard time locating the beliefs that will make suitable targets for large-scale debunking. On examination, the 'grand illusion' eludes us.

The second point is this. Suppose *representational* content must be expressible by means of a sentence or image. Suppose further that if experiential differences are specifiable by attributing distinguishing representational contents, such attributions should be available to first-person reflection. Then, first-person reflection (or phenomenology, if you like) yields — not an illusory impression of representational riches — but rather, the idea that the real richness in visual experience is just not specifiable through the richness in detail of a spatial *representation*. That is to say: *the ways in which our environment looks to us are not fully specifiable relative to distinct representational contents.*

Here I seem to be pointing down the road Noë, Pessoa, and Thompson would have us follow — turning the grand illusion controversy into an occasion to challenge the representationalist picture of the visual process. But clearly, we would need to do more to establish the claim that the differences in the way things look to us are not, or not always, to be cashed out in representational (i.e., sentential or pictorial) terms. For one of the above assumptions leading to this conclusion may be fairly questioned — the assumption that if experiential differences are specifiable via representational content differences, they should be thus specifiable through first-person reflection. So we need to inquire whether psychological theory can find a way to fill the gap in representational specification that is left open by first-person reflection. This is not a question to be settled quickly and simply. However, we can get some idea of the nature of the challenge by considering an example that may heighten our awareness of the relevant subtleties.

We can, with first-person reflection, note the contrast between the experience of a figure on which visual attention is focussed and the experience of the relatively unattended background. There is a difference in the way the background looks and the way the more attended figure looks, which makes the one an experience of a *background* and the other an experience of a *focal* figure. Now consider the visual experience one has in redirecting one's attention to something in what had been the background — the experience of losing detail in the way the former focal figures looked as one gains detail in the way the former occupants of the background look. This is a visual experience of gaining (and simultaneously losing) detail but its character is different from that of other experiences that might be similarly described. Compare that case with the experience had in watching a film when a figure in the foreground goes out of focus while one in the background grows sharper. Consider also the experience had in watching a film in which the camera zooms in on a part of the scene to reveal greater detail.[6] Both of these visual experiences of detail simultaneously gained and lost are different in subjective character from that had in directing one's attention in a real setting.

---

[6]   Merleau-Ponty (1962 [1945], p. 68) uses this cinematic example to make a related point.

But how do we identify the difference? In first-person reflection I can identify the experiential character of attention shift in a real setting, and distinguish it from the cinematic cases, only by thinking of it as the experience had in directing my attention in a certain way. ('*This* way', I say to myself as I direct my gaze.) However, perhaps this marks nothing but a limitation of first-person reflection. We need to think about how we might account for the experiential differences here in terms of distinguishing representational contents unavailable to first-person reflection.

It is difficult to see how this is to be done. One is tempted to suppose that the representational content that distinguishes the visual appearance of background from that of the focal figure must lie in some lower level of resolution in the visual representation of the background — some resolution that is heightened or sharpened when attention is shifted. But this seems to wrongly assimilate the experience of attention shift in a real setting to the first of my cinematic examples (where the out-of-focus background suddenly sharpens). Perhaps then we will say that when attention shifts, the extent of the area visually represented (the boundary of the 'visual field') expands or contracts. But then we will have difficulty preserving the experiential contrast between the real-setting visual attention shift and the second of the cinematic examples (the camera-zoom case).

These difficulties suggest that it may be wrong to think of vision as producing something like pictures in our brains (whether high or low resolution, whether detailed or sketchy). And they suggest that the character of visual experience cannot be identified independently of the motor activities involved in experience (e.g., the direction of the gaze). But these are delicate issues that require further thought. I introduce them only to show that it may not be so easy to maintain that our inability to distinguish visual appearances by attributing distinct representational contents to them merely reflects the limits of first-person reflection.

V

Let me close by presenting the challenge here more generally. There are differences, detectable on a first-person basis, in how it looks to us (differences in visual appearance), which, nevertheless we cannot on such a basis distinguish by means of attributing differentiating representational contents to our experiences. To the extent one can capture such experiential differences in first-person reflection, it is by reference to a kind of direction of one's gaze one can identify only in performance using demonstrative concepts. The question, then, is whether we can, by some other, non-phenomenological means, justify a representationalist specification of such differences in the way it looks to subjects. If not, then reflection on questions raised by change and inattentional blindness will have led us to preserve the subjective richness of visual spatial experience, but at the cost of abandoning the idea that this consists in the rich detail of a mental representation. If, on the other hand, theory does supply what first-person reflection cannot, and captures differences in phenomenal experience by attributions of differentiating representational contents, then, again, we will not have revealed our subjective impression of visual wealth to be illusory but only given it an articulation otherwise unavailable to us.

I conclude that once we take care to formulate accurately what we believe, on a first-person basis, about the richness of our ordinary visual experience, efforts to expose this as erroneous on a grand scale collapse. We find the grand illusion hypothesis does not hold up. This saves us from hastily rejecting first-person reflection and needlessly underrating our experiential wealth, but it leads to another issue regarding the foundations of vision science as well. We come to examine more closely the idea that the richness of experience must find reflection in such content as sentences or images express. What change and inattentional blindness studies ultimately bring into question is not our subjective impression of seeing, but mental representation as traditionally conceived.

Acknowledgements

For helpful comments, suggestions and questions, many thanks to Angela Brandt, Barbara Held, Sean Kelly, Amie Thomasson, and audiences for versions of this paper, delivered at a meeting of the International Society for the Study of Phenomenology (Asilomar, California, June 2001), and at the Tucson Conference 2002 'Toward a Science of Consciousness'.

References

Blackmore, S.J., Brelstaff, G., Nelson, K., Troscianko, T. (1995), 'Is the richness of our visual world an illusion? Transsaccadic memory for complex scenes', *Perception*, **24**, pp. 1075–81.

Churchland, P.S., Ramachandran, V.S., Sejnowski, T.J. (1994), 'A critique of pure vision', in *Large-scale Neuronal Theories of the Brain*, ed. C. Koch & J.L. Davies (Cambridge, MA: MIT Press).

Dennett, D.C. (1991), *Consciousness Explained* (Boston, MA: Little, Brown).

Mack, A., Rock, I. (1998), *Inattentional Blindness* (Cambridge, MA: MIT Press).

Merleau-Ponty, M. (1962 [1945]), *The Phenomenology of Perception*, trans. Colin Smith. (London: Routledge Press).

Noë, A., Pessoa, L., Thompson, E. (2000), 'Beyond the grand illusion: what change blindness really teaches us about vision', *Visual Cognition*, **7**, pp. 93–106.

Noë, A. (2002), 'Experience and the active mind', *Synthese*, **29**, pp. 41–60.

O'Regan, J.K. (1992), 'Solving the "real" mysteries of visual perception: the world as an outside memory', *Canadian Journal of Psychology*, **46**, pp. 461–88.

O'Regan, J.K., Rensink, R.A., Clark, J.J. (1999), 'Change-blindness as a result of "mud splashes"', *Nature*, **398**, p. 34.

Rensink, R.A. (1997), 'To see or not to see: the need for attention to perceive changes in scenes', *Psychological Science*, **8** (5), pp. 368–73.

Rensink, R.A. (2000), 'The dynamic representation of scenes', *Visual Cognition*, **7**, p. 17.

Jonathan Cohen

The Grand Grand Illusion Illusion

This paper considers a number of ways of understanding the hypothesis that change blindness and inattentional blindness reveal a grand illusion about visual perception. It argues that the most prominent readings of this hypothesis in the literature are untenable. It concludes that, while these results have much to teach us about perception, the only illusion they can be said to uncover is a modest and familiar one.

In recent years, a pair of intriguing phenomena has caused researchers working on vision and visual attention to reevaluate many of their assumptions. These phenomena, which have come to be called change blindness (CB) and inattentional blindness (IB), have led many to the conclusion that ordinary perceivers labor under a 'grand illusion' concerning perception — an illusion that is exposed by CB and IB.[1]

This paper is about the hypothesis that CB and IB reveal a grand illusion. I find in the literature a number of different ways of understanding this hypothesis. Unfortunately, I shall argue, these understandings are untenable or unmotivated by the empirical data and general considerations about visual perception (Sections II–IV). As far as I can see, there is no grand illusion about visual perception that is uncovered by CB and IB. Of course, these results are interesting and important, and it seems that at least part of their importance is due to their shattering some sort of illusion. However, I believe that the illusion shattered by CB and IB is a rather banal belief of the sort that is shattered by literally thousands of other results (Section V). I shall conclude that, while CB and IB raise a number of interesting empirical questions, the view that they show up a widespread grand illusion concerning perception is itself something of a grand illusion.

I: Which Grand Illusion?

Before we can evaluate the hypothesis that there is a grand illusion, we must come to some understanding of what that hypothesis is supposed to mean. It

---

[1] Since CB and IB have been described in many other places, I won't reiterate the experimental findings here. For good overviews, see Simons (2000) on CB, and Mack & Rock (1998a,b) on IB. In fact, the hypothesis of a grand illusion predates the discovery of CB and IB; I believe these themes first arose in connection with the discussion of perceptual 'filling in' of the visual blind spot (Dennett, 1991; 1992).

Journal of Consciousness Studies, **9**, No. 5–6, 2002, pp. 141–57

seems to me that researchers have had a number of different claims in mind when they talk about CB and IB as revealing a grand illusion about visual perception. To substantiate this claim, here is a representative sampling of claims about the grand illusion:

> . . . despite the poor quality of the visual apparatus, we have the subjective impression of great richness and 'presence' of the visual world. But this richness and presence are actually an illusion, created by the fact that if we so much as faintly ask ourselves some question about the environment, an answer is immediately provided by the sensory information on the retina, possibly rendered available by an eye movement (O'Regan, 1992, p. 484).

> It does not seem to us as if we only see that to which we attend. It seems to us, rather, as if we are perceptually aware of the densely detailed, stable and persistent environment around us. But since we do not attend to all that detail, at least not all at once, then it would seem to follow that perceptual consciousness — that feeling of awareness of all the detail — is misguided (Noë & O'Regan, 2000, p. 2).

> You hold a bottle in your hands and your eyes are shut. You make finger-to-bottle contact at a number of isolated points. It seems to you, however, that you have tactile experience of the whole bottle. On the 'detailed internal model approach' it would be supposed that the brain builds up a model of the bottle as a whole on the basis of information about the bottle contained in the points of contact.... You seem perceptually to experience something about which you do not have complete information (Noë and O'Regan, 2000, p. 5).[2]

> A rather counter-intuitive aspect of the world-as-outside-memory idea, and the associated notion that there is no picture-like internal representation of the outside world, is that, in a certain sense, only what is currently being processed is being 'seen'. How then, if at any moment only a small fragment of the world is actually being seen, could we ever have that strong subjective impression that we continually have of seeing 'everything' (O'Regan and Noë, 2001, Section 4.2)?

> We believe that we see a complete, dynamic picture of a stable, uniformly detailed, and colourful world ... [but] our stable visual world may be constructed out of a brief retinal image and a very sketchy, higher-level representation along with a pop-out mechanism to redirect attention. The richness of our visual world is, to this extent, an illusion (Blackmore et al., 1995, p. 1075).

> ... if we do not have representations that are everywhere detailed and coherent, why do we have such a strong impression that these kinds of representations underlie our visual experience (Rensink, 2000a, p. 18)?

> Only one object in an environment, or scene, can be given a coherent representation at any time. Moreover, this representation is limited in the amount of information it can contain. But if this is so, why do we not notice these limitations? Why do we feel that somewhere in our brain is a complete, detailed representation of all the objects in the scene (Rensink, 2000a, p. 28)?

> . . . despite the fact that the eyes saccade about three times each second and vision is suppressed during saccades, we do not experience the tens of milliseconds that transpire during these movements as blank periods or 'holes' in our visual experience, nor do we experience the world as a series of discrete snapshots from each fixation.

---

[2] Note that Noë and O'Regan offer this tactile example as an analogy for visual perception, and encourage the reader to extend their claims to the visual case.

Instead, when we glance about our visual environment, we have the perceptual experience of a complete, full color, highly detailed, and stable visual world. That is, our perceptual experience suggests to us that the visual system in some sense creates a high-resolution internal copy of the external world, similar to the way a camera creates a detailed color photograph (Henderson and Hollingworth, 2000, p. 1).

I find in the above quotations several different understandings of the hypothesized grand illusion. In each case, the claim is that ordinary perceivers suffer from a grand illusion because they hold a certain belief that, as it turns out, is false. As I read these matters, the illusory beliefs in terms of which the supposed grand illusion is understood generally comes under one of the following three headings:[3]

- World richness: It seems to ordinary perceivers that the world is stable, rich, detailed, subjectively present, etc., but in fact it is not.
- Representational Richness: It seems to ordinary perceivers that the visual representations they form are everywhere detailed, coherent, complete, photograph-like, etc., but in fact they are not.
- Representational Reality: It seems to ordinary perceivers that their visual system makes use of visual representations — real, internal, representational, mental states whose content is generated (at least in part) by the visual system, but in fact it does not.[4]

I want to argue that no understanding of the grand illusion in terms of the beliefs listed above is tenable. I'll do this by urging that none of the beliefs considered meets all of the conditions that it must meet if it is to be used to explain the grand illusion.

To see the sorts of conditions I have in mind, consider how such an explanation would go. Presumably, this sort of explanation would involve these claims: (i) that ordinary perceivers hold the belief in question, (ii) that the belief is, as it turns out, illusory, and (iii) that CB and IB show up the grand illusion because they disconfirm the belief in question. That is, if any one of these beliefs is to serve its intended purpose of explaining the grand illusion, it must meet the following three criteria:

- Falsity: The belief involved in the grand illusion must be illusory — it must be false.
- Ubiquity: The illusory belief imputed by an understanding of the grand illusion must be a belief that is held by ordinary perceivers, since it is claimed that ordinary subjects suffer from a grand illusion.
- Disconfirmation: The illusory belief imputed by an understanding of the grand illusion must be unambiguously disconfirmed by the phenomena of CB and IB, insofar as these results are held to expose the grand illusion as an illusion.

---

[3] I have intentionally characterized these beliefs in a general way so as to cover as many different views as possible, while leaving room for disagreements about the details.

[4] Of the readings I'll consider, this one is the hardest to find endorsed unambiguously in print. More on this in Section IV.

Considering each proposed interpretation of the grand illusion in turn, I'll argue that none of them meets these three criteria. Consequently, I'll suggest, none of them can be enlisted to sustain the claim that CB and IB expose a grand illusion about perception of which ordinary perceivers are victims.

II: An Illusion of World Richness?

Consider the belief concerning world richness first. Do ordinary subjects labor under false impressions about the character of the extramental world they visually perceive? In my view, this proposed understanding of the grand illusion is, fairly obviously, a non-starter.

The first point to make in this connection is that it would be quite surprising if CB and IB could establish that perceivers suffer from this sort of illusion. CB and IB are, of course, psychological results: they tell us something about our perceptual interaction with the world. But it is extremely hard to imagine how they could, by themselves, tell us about the character of the extramental world itself. Or, to put this in terms of the explanatory criteria in Section I, it is extremely hard to imagine how a belief in world richness could possibly be disconfirmed by the phenomena.

However, we needn't tax our imaginations to answer this question, as this reading of the grand illusion hypothesis has another, more serious, defect: an illusion of world richness is a poor aspirant to the title of grand illusion because it is no illusion. Standardly a visual illusion occurs when we represent the world as having some property that, in fact, it lacks (or as lacking a property that, in fact, it has); to take a classic example, I suffer from an illusion when I represent an immersed oar as bent when in fact it is straight. But if CB and IB show that visual perception represents the world as containing rich, continuous, subjectively present detail, this cannot be taken to show that perceivers undergo an illusion — the world *does* contain rich, continuous, subjectively present detail. If understood as an illusion of world richness, then the grand illusion is a grand truth.

Beliefs about world richness, then, are not disconfirmed by the data, and they are not false. For these reasons, I am unsympathetic toward proposed explanations of the grand illusion in terms of a belief in world richness.

III: An Illusion of Representational Richness?

I am not the first to remark on the implausibility of taking perceivers to be victims of an illusion of world richness; several authors, including Rensink (2000a), Churchland *et al.* (1994, pp. 37–9) and Dennett (1992), have made just this point, and consequently have insisted that the grand illusion exposed by CB and IB cannot be an illusion about the extramental world. Rather, according to these authors, the grand illusion is an illusion about visual representations. In particular, and as revealed in some of the quotations above, these authors claim that ordinary perceivers hold the false beliefs that their visual representations are everywhere detailed, coherent, complete, or photograph-like. On this reading, then, the grand illusion under which subjects labor is an illusion of representational richness.

Although this reading of the grand illusion hypothesis seems more promising than that considered in Section II, I find it untenable as well. For in holding that ordinary subjects err in their beliefs about visual representations, this reading presupposes that ordinary subjects hold beliefs about visual representations. But this presupposition is implausible. Visual representations are the stuff of explicit cognitive theorizing. To attribute beliefs about representations to ordinary subjects is to think of them as engaging in theorizing about perception as an everyday matter. Dennett seems to endorse this view when he says (of a related perceptual illusion) that 'It is, if you like, a theorist's illusion, but it turns out we are all theorists' (Dennett, 1998, p. 754). But surely this is an inaccurate picture. Ordinary subjects hold beliefs about trees and train schedules, about shoes and ships and sealing wax. They do not hold beliefs about visual representations unless they are engaged in the kinds of explicit explanatory projects carried out by vision scientists. Since they do not hold beliefs about visual representations, they do not hold false beliefs about visual representations. To say this is to admit that the hypothesized belief is not ubiquitous, and consequently cannot explain the grand illusion.[5]

It should be clear that the argument in this section turns crucially on the the requirement of ubiquity — the requirement that the illusory belief involved in the grand illusion must be the sort of belief held by ordinary perceivers. This requirement seems warranted in that ordinary perceivers are often extremely surprised on finding out about CB and IB.[6] On the other hand, cognitive scientists, too, are typically surprised to hear about CB and IB, which is to say that these phenomena expose some sort of grand illusion for cognitive scientists as well. Of course, cognitive scientists *can be* assumed to hold beliefs about visual representations; could we, therefore, explain the grand illusion in cognitive scientists as an illusion of representational richness? We could, but then (for reasons already adduced) we would need some other explanation for the grand illusion suffered by ordinary subjects. In this case, there would be not one but two different grand illusions, divided between the population, and explained in different terms.

[5] Noë *et al.* (2000) also resist attributing to ordinary subjects beliefs about visual representations (cf. Pessoa *et al.*, 1998, p. 794, and Noë, 2001, pp. 48–9). Thus, even though they agree with Rensink (2000a), Churchland *et al.* (1994) and Dennett (1992), that CB and IB undermine the assumption that the visual system constructs detailed representations of the environment ('The change blindness studies show that we lack certain kinds of internal representations', Noë *et al.*, 2000, p. 102; 'Phenomena such as change blindness demonstrate that the brain does not produce models of the detailed environment to support vision', Noë, 2001, p. 46), these authors deny that the phenomena reveal a grand illusion.

As I've been urging so far in this section, I think these authors are right to reject the reading of the grand illusion hypothesis under consideration on the ground that the belief in representational richness is not ubiquitous. But my objection goes further than theirs: I shall contend below not only that the belief in rich representations is not ubiquitous, but that it is (contrary to what they claim) not disconfirmed by the phenomena, and true rather than false.

[6] Scholl (2000), p. 380, reports that ordinary subjects in CB experiments, upon finally detecting the change that had thus far eluded them, stubbornly insisted that the change must not have been occurring until just before the time they indicated detecting it. Clearly the experiment showed to be illusory some beliefs held by these subjects, or they would not have felt the need to fabricate another (incorrect) explanation of what had happened.

Thus, this divided proposal has two significant disadvantages: (i) it increases, rather than decreases, the number of explananda, and (ii) it makes no progress at all toward the original goal of understanding the grand illusion that ordinary subjects undergo.

Be that as it may, I believe that understanding the grand illusion in terms of a belief about representational richness has a further problem: this belief is not unambiguously disconfirmed by CB and IB. After all, while CB and IB show that subjects are unable to report having seen certain objects/events, it does not follow from this that the representations formed by their visual systems are silent about the relevant objects/events. For all that the experimental results show, it may be that perceivers represent these objects/events, but that the representations are not available to conscious access for purposes of explicit reporting.

Notice that I am not advocating the view that visual representations are like photographs, or that every detail within viewing distance is represented. There is abundant evidence against that view from a range of converging considerations. For example, it is widely accepted that there are variations in visual acuity across the retina, that there is a visual blind spot at the place where the optic nerve connects to the retina, that the eyes saccade to a different view every 200–300 msec, and that the visual signal is suppressed during periods of saccadic motion. These phenomena all raise problems for the view that visual representations are pictures in the head, since we don't visually represent the world outside our heads as being variably fuzzy, as containing empty holes, as bouncing around, or as fading out of existence every 200–300 msec.[7] Rather, I am suggesting only that the sorts of normally salient manipulations that escape subjects' attention in CB and IB conditions may, despite their unavailability for conscious reporting, be visually represented.

To make this point clear, it may be useful to consider other sorts of explanations given in terms of representations. To take an example almost at random from another area of cognitive science, consider the story about the formation of passives told by Chomsky's Extended Standard Theory: according to this account, a transformation rule ('Move NP') takes a deep structure representation to a passive surface structure representation by moving a postverbal NP into subject position, leaving a phonetically unrealized trace in the postverbal position that is co-indexed with the moved NP. Famously, ordinary subjects are unable to report on the presence of the (phonetically unrealized) trace that, according to this theory, is present in their syntactic representations. But this is not taken to show that the element is not present in their syntactic representations, or that their syntactic representations are not as rich as the theory would have led one to suppose. On the contrary, the standard response goes, subjects cannot be expected to have transparent access to all the features of their representations, so their inability to report on some alleged representational feature is harmless to

---

[7] For overviews of these and other phenomena, and the threat they pose to picture-in-the-head conceptions of visual representations, see Pylyshyn (2002), chapter 1, and Churchland *et al.* (1994).

In this connection, notice also that even those who believe in a conception of mental imagery as a geometric, pictorial display (e.g., Kosslyn, 1980; 1994) deny that the representations they posit are snapshots taken from the visual signal, or that they encode every detail of the distal scene.

theories that predict the presence of that feature. So long as the predicted feature is independently well-supported by the available evidence and otherwise earns its explanatory keep, this response continues, we have every reason to take it seriously.[8]

But if linguistics can avail itself of representational features that are below the level of conscious access, it is presumably open to visual science to say the same thing. Once again, so long as the predicted representational features are independently well-supported by the available evidence and otherwise earn their explanatory keep, we should regard subjects' inability to access these features as thoroughly non-dispositive.

So are representations of the details that escape subjects' explicit notice in CB and IB experiments independently well-supported? Do they earn their explanatory keep despite being unavailable for conscious reporting? I believe they do. In several cases, researchers have found implicit effects of the objects/events to which subjects are allegedly blind, even when subjects cannot provide explicit reports about those objects/events. For example, Hollingworth *et al.* (2001b) report that, while subjects are unable to identify explicitly changing regions of the visual scene, fixation durations are significantly longer on those regions than on other areas (cf. Hayhoe *et al.*, 1998; Fernandez-Duque and Thornton, 2000; Williams and Simons, 2000). In related work, Henderson (1994; 1997) and Pollatsek *et al.* (1990) have found that, while subjects exhibit the familiar pattern of change blindness when asked to saccade between two simultaneously presented images, there is evidence of implicit coding of the items/events to which they are allegedly blind (for example, they are quicker to identify these items than unrelated items).

Thus, subjects' failures to report on certain details of the visible scene does not show that these details are unrepresented, and there is independent evidence suggesting that these details in fact *are* represented. This is enough to show that the data do not disconfirm a belief in the richness of visual representations. Moreover, as I have suggested, a more expansive look at the data gives reason for thinking that some such belief is true rather than false.

Beliefs about representational richness, then, are not ubiquitous, they are not unambiguously disconfirmed by the experimental results, and there is evidence that they are true rather than false. For these reasons, explanations of the grand illusion in terms of such beliefs seem unconvincing.

IV: An Illusion of Representational Reality?

A related, but more radical, understanding of the grand illusion holds that CB and IB show that there are no visual representations, or at least that the role of such representations is far less significant than has been supposed — that the grand illusion is an illusion of representational reality (see, for example, Noë and O'Regan, 2000; O'Regan, 1992; Rensink *et al.*, 1997; Rensink, 2000b).[9] This

---

[8] Needless to say, I am not endorsing this account of the production of passives, or any of the apparatus of Extended Standard Theory. I am interested only in availing myself of the theory's pattern of response to the accusation that subjects are unaware of the structure of their representations.

interpretation is similar to that considered in Section III in that it explains the grand illusion as an illusion about the workings of the visual system. But, whereas, on that earlier understanding, the illusion is a mistake concerning the nature of visual representations, the illusion is here understood in terms of a mistaken belief that there are visual representations at all.[10]

Before I turn to objections against thinking ordinary perceivers suffer from an illusion of representational reality, why would anyone be tempted to take CB and IB as exposing the non-existence of visual representations? One not unreasonable conjecture stems from a venerable tradition in psychology (with roots at least as far back as Hume) according to which 'visual representation' means roughly *representation that is visible* rather than *representation maintained by the visual system*. On this view (which is presumably also a motivating force in the understanding of the grand illusion discussed in Section III), visual representations are something like pictures in the head — two-dimensional depictive arrays in the brain that exemplify (not merely represent) geometric and topological properties, that represent distal objects by pictorially resembling those objects, and that can be inspected for content just as a picture outside the head can be visually inspected for content.

If visual representations are pictures in the head, then it is true that CB and IB provide evidence against the existence of visual representations: if there were surveyable pictures in the head, then presumably subjects could inspect these picture in CB and IB experiments, compare these pictures against the real distal layout, and effortlessly report any discrepancies. Of course, subjects in CB and IB experiments cannot report such discrepancies, and the conclusion we are invited to draw is that there are no visual representations.[11] But this form of argument is unconvincing as it stands. What CB and IB can be taken to show is that there are no visual representations *in the picture-in-the-head sense of 'visual representation' considered*. Needless to say, this more modest conclusion is compatible with the existence of visual representations, so long as we are willing to understand visual representations as something other than pictures in the head.

This brings me to my first complaint against supposing that perceivers suffer from an illusion of representational reality: that hypothesis is needlessly revisionary compared with an alternative hypothesis already considered — that perceivers undergo an illusion of representational richness. To see this point, notice that the choice between these two hypotheses is an instance of a very general situation that occurs when, in the course of theory building of any kind,

---

[9] Unfortunately, these texts don't commit to an anti-representational interpretation as unambiguously as one might hope for the purposes of exposition (see also Cohen, 2002, regarding this ambiguity). But that's okay — I'm arguing against the position, not any particular authors or texts.

[10] Of course, anti-representational conclusions are sometimes drawn for reasons unrelated to CB or IB (e.g., in such works as Brooks, 1991, and Gibson, 1979; however, I'll restrict myself here to discussing arguments against the reality of representations based on CB and IB.

[11] An example of this sort of argument occurs in O'Regan (1992). Here O'Regan argues convincingly against the existence of pictures in the head, and concludes from this that the visual system does without internal representations of the world. Hence he asserts that 'The "percept" of the bottle is an *action*, namely the visual or mental exploration of the bottle '(p. 472). Cf. O'Regan and Noë (2001).

beliefs about some term or concept figuring in the theory come under challenge. Whenever this happens, we face a choice between concept revision and concept elimination. On the one hand, we can amend the beliefs associated with (or, on some views, constituting) the old concept, thereby retaining it but amending its role in our thinking; perhaps this is what happened to the concept *fish* when ichthyologists determined that whales did not fall under its extension. On the other, we can hold fast to the old beliefs, with the eliminativist result that the target concept will turn out to have an empty extension; presumably this is what happened to the concept *phlogiston* when chemists proposed later and better confirmed accounts of the constitution and behavior of matter. As noted, choices of this form are routine in the course of theory construction; moreover, if (as I suspect) the analytic/synthetic distinction is vague (or worse), such choices will generally be stipulative and unprincipled.

It seems that the choice between the two understandings of the grand illusion under consideration (the choice between taking the illusion as an illusion of representational richness or as an illusion of representational reality) is just such a choice. On the one hand, results such as CB and IB may induce us to amend our beliefs about the nature of visual representations (for example, we may decide to give up our beliefs that visual representations are rich, detailed, continuous, or photograph-like), but to retain the idea that the visual system makes use of representations that turn out to be less rich, detailed, or photograph-like than we had initially supposed — hence, the illusion of representational richness. On the other, we can hold fast to previously held beliefs about the sorts of things visual representations are in the face of the experimental results, with the eliminativist result that there will turn out not to be any visual representations — hence, the illusion of representational reality.

But if this assessment is correct — if the choice between taking the grand illusion as an illusion of representational richness and an illusion of representational reality is of this familiar form — then it would seem difficult, for very general reasons of rational conservatism, to justify favouring the more radical, eliminativist, interpretation instead of the less revisionary alternative. For here and in other cases where a decision between revision and elimination arise, general canons of epistemic conservatism that guide us in the absence of countervailing considerations favour the more conservative course of revision, so the argumentative onus falls to the eliminativist.[12] In my view, this onus remains unmet.[13]

---

[12] *Objection:* If, as maintained above, the vagueness (or worse) of the analytic/synthetic distinction means that a choice between revision and elimination is generally stipulative and unprincipled, then why take seriously the present appeal to epistemic conservatism (as a way of justifying a choice to revise rather than eliminate)? Isn't it, too, stipulative?

Reply: It is stipulative, and for this reason I do not wish to place too much weight on this point — hence I shall offer below other, less stipulative objections to reading the grand illusion as an illusion of representational reality. On the other hand, in the context of an explicit comparison between alternative theoretical options, and in the absence of countervailing considerations, I think such extremely general epistemic constraints can provide *prima facie*, defeasible, support for one choice over another. Accordingly, I have appealed to this consideration only in the absence of countervailing considerations, and only as a way of apportioning the argumentative onus.

Another reason for resisting understanding the grand illusion as a false belief in representational reality arises from an objection similar to one made (against another proposal) in Section III. Namely, understanding the grand illusion as the result of a false belief in representational reality is implausible because a belief of that sort is not ubiquitous among ordinary perceivers: once again, this understanding of the grand illusion hypothesis goes wrong in projecting the concerns of cognitive scientists onto the man in the street.

Yet another objection against the present proposal, also echoing an earlier point, is that a belief in the reality of representations is not unambiguously falsified by the experimental results under consideration. For one thing, as noted in Section III, the inabilities of subjects to report on what seem to be salient features of their surroundings manifested in CB and IB are compatible with their maintaining rich representations of the visual scene; *a fortiori*, the results are compatible with the existence of visual representations. For another, also as already noted, there are empirical motivations for supposing these representations exist, despite being unavailable for conscious reporting.

Finally, broad theoretical considerations tell against the claim that there are no visual representations — a claim that would have to be true in order to show that a belief in representational reality were false. These considerations revolve around a vast number of more or less standard explanations that crucially involve visual representations. For example, perceptual priming and perceptual learning are typically explained by supposing that the visual system forms representations (automatically in priming experiments, but as a result of deliberate rehearsal in learning experiments), and that these representations can be accessed by later processes in solving experimental recall tasks. To take another example, the standard explanation of Shepard's and Cooper's classic mental rotation results supposes that subjects form representations of stimuli, and then apply to these representations certain mental operations that have characteristic chronometric profiles (Shepard and Cooper, 1982). As another, more quotidian example, the standard account of your ability to recall the colour of the coffee cup you used yesterday morning turns on supposing that your visual system forms a representation of the coffee cup while you are using it (a representation that encodes its colour, *inter alia*), and that this representation remains accessible to later processing. Since denying the existence of representations renders these and a whole

---

[13] There is one possible motivation for making this choice rather than the less revisionary alternative that should be mentioned. Namely, one might suppose that, if the visual system represents occurrent features of the visual world, it could automatically make inferences about changes in the features of the visual world. Of course, CB shows that we can fail to be aware of changes in the features of the visual world, so one might apply *modus tollens* to arrive at the conclusion that the visual system must not represent occurrent features of the visual world. (For example, this line of reasoning is suggested by Rensink *et al.* (1997) when they say that the lesson of CB is that 'an observer does not build up a representation of a scene that allows him or her to perceive change automatically', p. 368.)

Of course, this argument against visual representations is only as good as its conditional premise that if there is awareness of features then there will be awareness of change in features. And, as the phenomenon of motion blindness demonstrates, this conditional premise is false: motion is change of position, but subjects suffering from motion blindness can be aware of position without being aware of motion (Zihl *et al.*, 1983). (Thanks to Mohan Matthen for this example.)

host of similar explanations unavailable, one who claims that ordinary perceivers suffer from an illusion of representational reality owes us alternative explanations for all of these phenomena. Although this possibility cannot be written off, it is hard to imagine that alternative explanations of all these phenomena are forthcoming. Consequently, this very wide class of phenomena gives further reason for thinking that a belief in the reality of visual representations is true.

In summary, understanding the grand illusion in terms of a belief in representational reality suffers seems unpromising. This understanding is not only unmotivated when compared against the more modest proposal considered (but also ultimately rejected) in Section III, but it turns on attributing a belief that is not ubiquitous, not disconfirmed by the data, and, as far as I can see, not false. Since the belief in terms of which a successful understanding of the grand illusion is framed must meet all of these criteria, and since a belief in representational reality meets none of them, it would seem advisable to seek other explanatory options.

V: The Grand Illusion as a Banal Surprise

I have argued against understanding the grand illusion in terms of a belief in world richness, a belief in representational richness, or a belief in representational reality. However, I do not wish to suggest that there is nothing to explain. On the contrary, I believe that CB and IB are extremely interesting and surprising results, and that they have important things to teach us about vision. Indeed, I shall claim that these results do uncover a kind of illusion, although I shall be suggesting that the illusion is a much more ordinary affair than the title 'grand illusion' would lead one to expect. On the interpretation I'll advance, the grand illusion is more aptly regarded as a sort of banal surprise.

Before I come to a positive explanation of the illusion, let me say something about what, in my view, needs explaining. Of course, CB and IB provide several data points that must be accounted for by an adequate model of visual attention. However, as I am not here offering a full-scale model of visual attention, I wish to concentrate on another important property of the results that deserves explanation: they are extremely surprising to ordinary perceivers (and also to cognitive scientists). Indeed, it is presumably because they are so surprising that theorists have claimed that these results uncover some sort of grand illusion. In what follows, I shall offer an explanation of why the phenomena seem surprising.[14]

---

[14] Noë and O'Regan (2000) concur that what demands explanation is (*inter alia*) the surprise provoked by learning about CB and IB. They propose the following explanation: 'On our view, vision is a complicated skill-based activity. We tend to be unaware, when we are engaged in our perceptual lives, of the complicated things we do when we see. . . . The surprise we feel in demonstrations such as these is comparable to the surprise we feel when we discover how difficult it is to perform a manual task such as typing or driving with a splint on one's little finger. We are insensitive to the complexity of the things we do when we do things' (Noë and O'Regan, 2000, p. 6; cf. Noë *et al.*, 2000, pp. 103–4).

I think this explanation is on the right track, but that more needs to be said. In particular, I hope to provide an account of just what difficulty is involved, and what ordinary expectations are compromised by the results. Finally, and unlike these other authors, I want to explain the surprise associated with the phenomena in a way that makes room for a robust role for detailed representations in the visual system, since, as mentioned above, the evidence is overwhelmingly in favour of this position.

At this point I am (finally) in a position to offer an explanation of why CB and IB are surprising. In my view, these phenomena are surprising because they show to be false a belief held by ordinary perceivers. In particular, the belief at issue is this: ordinary perceivers believe that they will notice large-scale, unoccluded objects and events in their immediate visual environments.[15]

Of course, ordinary perceivers will typically hold this belief tacitly, and presumably they would not be in a position to unpack the content of the belief in a precise way (this must be so, if the belief in question has any chance of meeting the criterion of ubiquity). However, we might attempt to explain the content of this belief by saying that ordinary perceivers take themselves to be capable of responding — say, by giving a verbal report if one is solicited, or by pressing a button in an experimental setup — to whatever large-scale and unoccluded objects and events occur in their vicinity. My claim is that the CB and IB disconfirm the belief in question, and that this will be surprising to ordinary perceivers because the belief so disconfirmed is a belief that they hold. This, in my view, is why the phenomena are so surprising to ordinary perceivers.

Of course, the explanation I have proposed presupposes that ordinary perceivers hold the kind of belief under discussion. I believe this presupposition is defensible. For one thing, holding such a belief is surely rational insofar as it is inductively supported by ordinary experience. Outside the laboratory, where the experimental conditions for CB and IB are typically unmet, perceivers surely will have noted a correlation between the occurrence of objects and events in the visual environment, on the one hand, and their noticing these objects and events, on the other.[16] And, of course, when perceivers are subject to CB and IB outside the laboratory, they won't notice that the occurrence of objects and events is unaccompanied by their noticing these objects and events since, *ex hypothesi*, they are suffering from CB or IB, and so are unaware of the relevant occurrences. Consequently, all the inductive evidence available to perceivers supports their belief in their ordinary capacity to notice ambient events.

A second set of reasons for supposing that ordinary perceivers hold this sort of belief is revealed in some of the ways we treat legal testimony. For example, juries typically treat eyewitness testimony as holding great evidentiary weight. Presumably at least part of the explanation for this is that jurors believe that eyewitnesses will notice the large-scale, unoccluded objects and events about which their testimony is sought, and that consequently their testimony about these objects and events is likely to be accurate.[17] Of course, this is just to say that jurors hold the belief I am claiming is ubiquitous among ordinary perceivers.

---

[15] As it happens, the belief in question has received extensive empirical confirmation from work showing that visual attention is captured and redirected by transients in the visual scene (Yantis, 1998; Theeuwes, 1991). However, ordinary perceivers are presumably unaware of these findings, and therefore do not hold the belief under discussion because of them.

[16] In saying that this correlation is typically in place, and that subjects are aware of it, I am not suggesting that such a correlation is (metaphysically or conceptually) necessary; consequently, I am not committing to the sort of KK-thesis that has been a subject of controversy in recent epistemology.

[17] The conclusion that the authority given to eyewitness testimony by jurors is misplaced is supported not only by CB and IB, but a host of other results. See Loftus (1996).

Moreover, my claim about ordinary perceivers is further supported by an exception to the general hearsay exclusion rule (Rule 802) in the U.S. Federal Rules of Evidence. Rule 803 of the Rules of Evidence makes hearsay admissible if it is 'A statement describing or explaining an event or condition made while the declarant [the person who made the statement, as opposed to the witness reporting on the declarant's statement] was perceiving the event or condition or immediately thereafter' (Rule 803). This rule seems to express confidence in the abilities of eyewitnesses to report (*a fortiori*, to notice) what they perceive, and to place trust in even (sufficiently immediate) indirect reports of what eyewitnesses perceive. It is difficult to understand these and other of our ordinary attitudes toward perceivers without taking ourselves to believe that perceivers have an ordinary capacity to notice ambient events.[18]

Finally, there is clear empirical support the ubiquity of the beliefs in question. For example, Levin *et al.* (2000) found that naïve subjects predict whether they would detect the changes in CB experiments (after having heard descriptions of the procedures and viewing static versions of the stimuli with the change pointed out to them) at rates vastly higher than the actual success rates. Similarly, Scholl *et al.* (2002) showed that subjects systematically underestimate the magnitude of their blindness to changes even while acknowledging that they themselves are susceptible to CB. Once again, these results indicate that ordinary subjects hold the belief that they will notice large-scale, unoccluded objects and events in their immediate visual environments.

Thus, it is plausible that a belief in the ordinary capacity to notice ambient events is ubiquitous. It is also clear that such a belief is false, and that it is unambiguously disconfirmed by CB and IB. That is to say, unlike the beliefs examined in Sections II–IV, the belief in terms of which I propose to explain the grand illusion satisfies the criteria it must meet if it is to serve in such an explanation (see Section I). And this is just to say that my proposal provides an explanation of the grand illusion, whereas the other proposals considered do not.

That said, the explanation of the illusion I have proposed is, for all that, a rather deflationary account. According to my proposal, the grand illusion stems from a belief in our ordinary ability to notice things; the phenomena show this belief to be illusory. However, this is not to say that CB and IB show the belief to be wholly unreasonable, ungrounded, or unsupported. They show only that it is not unrestrictedly true. That is, these results show that there are conditions (namely, the experimental conditions employed in CB and IB experiments) under which the visual/psychological mechanisms for noticing large-scale, unoccluded objects and events in the visual scene can be impaired. In showing this, the phenomena disconfirm ordinary perceivers' (unrestricted) belief in their ordinary capacity to notice ambient events. These results show up restrictions on our capacity to notice things. I suppose that learning about such restrictions can be said to shatter some naïve illusions about our visual capacities. But if so, then this is precisely the sort of illusion that is shattered when we learn about

---

[18] As Noë *et al.* (2000) point out, further evidence for attributing this sort of belief to ordinary perceivers comes from their incredulous reactions to the performances of skilled magicians.

restrictions on our ability to compare line lengths (in the conditions of the Muller-Lyer illusion or the Ponzo illusion), on our ability to judge line direction (in the conditions of the Pogendorf illusion), to compare the sizes of circles (in the conditions of the Ebbinghaus illusion), and literally thousands of other cases studied by visual scientists. In all these cases, ordinary perceivers hold a naïve, and essentially correct, belief that their visual systems give them correct information about the extramental world; however, as it happens, the visual system has its limitations, and experimentalists can set up conditions under which the system is no longer reliable. This technique is, to be sure, an important way of learning about the properties of the visual system. However, the claim that its employment in the present case shatters grand illusions about the visual system strikes me as misleadingly extravagant; at the very least, this description seems no more warranted here than it would be if applied to the Muller-Lyer illusion or any of thousands of similar illusions.

One might object, at this point, that the label 'grand illusion' is more justifiably applied to CB and IB than to (say) the Muller-Lyer illusion because (as reactions in subject debriefings show readily) subjects are much more incredulous about the former than the latter. But I do not wish to deny that CB and IB are more surprising to subjects than the Muller-Lyer illusion. The former results are indeed more surprising than the latter, and this fact deserves explanation; in my view, we should explain this fact by supposing that the illusory belief disconfirmed by CB and IB (a belief about our ordinary capacity to notice ambient events) is more deeply seated than the illusory belief that is disconfirmed by, say, the Muller-Lyer illusion (a belief about our ordinary capacity to compare line lengths). Thus, in saying that the illusion revealed by CB and IB is not particularly grand, I do not mean that the phenomena are not more surprising than the other, more widely-discussed phenomena mentioned above. Rather, I mean that the belief disconfirmed by CB and IB is not different in kind from beliefs disconfirmed by the Muller-Lyer illusion, etc. (even if the former belief is more deeply held than the latter). In particular, in all these cases, ordinary perceivers believe that their visual systems give them correct information about the extramental world; and while this belief is true in a restricted range of circumstances, the relevant experimental conditions fall outside that range, thereby showing the belief to be false as a completely general matter.

I believe that CB and IB are interesting and significant in just the way that all these other illusions are interesting: they reveal the workings of the mechanisms underlying our visual capacities — in this case, our capacity for visual attention. And as in these other cases, I believe that the most fruitful empirical work on CB and IB will explore the range of conditions under which the mechanisms in question can be defeated as a way of gaining insight into their nature and operation. Indeed, research of this kind has already uncovered a number of interesting results.[19] For example, we have learned that the mechanisms of visual attention are insensitive to changes in the visual scene that occur during saccades (Grimes,

---

[19] For brevity, I restrict myself in what follows to discussing CB; obviously, similar remarks apply to IB.

1996; this result has predecessors, including Bridgeman's work in mid 1970s; see also McConkie and Currie, 1996, and the sources mentioned in Henderson and Hollingworth, 2000, pp. 2–4). Similarly, CB results obtained using the so-called 'flicker paradigm' show that the mechanisms of visual attention can be defeated by briefly interposing a visual mask between the two stimuli; however, without the interposition of the mask, subjects have no difficulty detecting the change between the two stimuli. Moreover, we have learned that there are methods other than those discussed that defeat the mechanisms of visual attention. For example, CB effects have been reported for changes made during a mud splash (O'Regan *et al.*, 1999), a blink (O'Regan *et al.*, 2000), across film splices (Levin and Simons, 1997), and behind real world occlusions (Simons and Levin, 1998) (see the review in Simons, 2000). In addition to these studies of the sorts of presentations that induce CB, there are a number of results bearing on the ways in which visual attention interacts with other effects. For example, it turns out that changes are better detected in the flicker paradigm at regions of higher interest (Rensink *et al.*, 1997), at unusual objects in the scene (Hollingworth and Henderson, 2000), at regions to which attention has been previously directed (Scholl, 2000), and at locations near fixation (Hollingworth *et al.*, 2001a). All of this research contributes to our understanding of the visual system because it provides constraints on acceptable models of visual attention and on proposals for the implementation of these models. In my view, this is where the real payoff from CB and IB lies.

VI: Conclusion

CB and IB have attracted so much recent attention in part because they are extremely surprising phenomena. That they are surprising to nearly everyone who learns about them is itself an important fact that deserves explanation. I have argued that the phenomena are surprising because ordinary perceivers aren't aware that their capacity to notice ambient objects and events is limited in certain ways — they do not expect that this capacity can be impaired in certain conditions. CB and IB are valuable to vision science because they bring out these limitations dramatically, and thereby provide clues to the nature and operation of the mechanisms underlying visual attention.

If I am right, then the so-called grand illusion exposed by CB and IB is not particularly grand after all. Rather, it is an instance of a very general phenomenon: ordinary subjects are ignorant about the limitations on their cognitive and perceptual capacities, and when controlled experimental conditions make these limitations apparent, they (and we) learn something new. Moreover, there is every indication that systematic study of these limitations will tell us quite a lot about the detailed workings of visual attention. If my proposal results in a deflationary view of the grand illusion, I hope that the prospect of further understanding of the visual system will provide ample compensation.[20]

---

[20] I am indebted to Pat Churchland, Mohan Matthen, Ram Neta, Liza Perkins-Cohen, and Brian Scholl for valuable discussions of these matters.

References

Blackmore, S.J., Brelstaff, G., Nelson, K. and Troscianko, T. (1995), 'Is the richness of our visual world an illusion? Transsaccadic memory for complex scenes', *Perception*, **24**, pp. 1075–81.

Brooks, R. (1991), 'Intelligence without representation', *Artificial Intelligence*, **47**, pp. 139–59.

Churchland, P.S., Ramachandran, V.S., and Sejnowski, T.J. (1994), 'A critique of pure vision', in *Large Scale Neuronal Theories of the Brain*, ed. C. Koch and S. Davis (Cambridge, MA: MIT Press).

Cohen, J. (2002), 'Whither visual representations? Whither qualia?', Open peer commentary on [O'Regan and Noë, 2002], *Behavioral and Brain Sciences*, in press.

Dennett, D.C. (1991), *Consciousness Explained* (Boston, MA: Little, Brown and Company).

Dennett, D.C. (1992), '"Filling in" versus finding out: A ubiquitous confusion in cognitive science', in *Cognition: Conceptual and Methodological Issues*, ed. L. Herbert, J. Pick, P. van den Broek and D.C. Knill (Washington, DC: American Psychological Association).

Dennett, D.C. (1998), 'No bridge over the stream of consciousness', *Behavioral and Brain Sciences*, **21** (6), pp. 753–4.

Fernandez-Duque, D. and Thornton, I. M. (2000), 'Change detection without awareness: Do explicit reports underestimate the representation of change in the visual system?', *Visual Cognition*, **7** (1/2/3), pp. 324–44.

Gibson, J.J. (1979), *The Ecological Approach to Visual Perception* (Boston, MA: Houghton Mifflin).

Grimes, J. (1996), 'On the failure to detect changes in scenes across saccades', in *Perception*, volume 5 of Vancouver Studies in Cognitive Science, ed. K. Akins (New York: Oxford University Press).

Hayhoe, M.M., Bensinger, D.G., and Ballard, D.H. (1998), 'Task constraints in visual working memory', *Vision Research*, **38**, pp. 125–37.

Henderson, J.M. (1994), 'Two representational systems in dynamic visual identification', *Journal of Experimental Psychology: General*, **123**, pp. 410–26.

Henderson, J.M. (1997), 'Transsaccadic memory and integration during real-world object perception', *Psychological Science*, **8**, pp. 51–5.

Henderson, J.M. and Hollingworth, A. (2000), 'Eye movements, visual memory, and scene representation', in *Analytic and Holistic Processes in the Perception of Faces, Objects, and Scenes*, ed. M.A. Peterson and G. Rhodes (New York: JAI/Ablex).

Hollingworth, A. and Henderson, J.M. (2000), 'Semantic informativeness mediates the detection of changes in natural scenes', *Visual Cognition*, **7** (1/2/3), pp. 213–35.

Hollingworth, A., Schrock, G. and Henderson, J.M. (2001a), 'Change detection in the flicker paradigm: The role of fixation position within the scene', *Memory and Cognition*, **29**, pp. 296–304.

Hollingworth, A., Williams, C.C. and Henderson, J.M. (2001b), 'To see and remember: Visually specific information is retained in memory from previously attended objects in natural scenes', *Psychonomic Bulletin & Review*, **8**, pp. 761–8.

Kosslyn, S.M. (1980), *Image and Mind* (Cambridge, MA: Harvard University Press).

Kosslyn, S.M. (1994), *Image and Brain: The Resolution of the Imagery Debate* (Cambridge, MA: MIT Press).

Levin, D.T., Momen, N., Drivdahl, S.B. and Simons, D.J. (2000), 'Change blindness blindness: The metacognitive error of overestimating change-detection ability', *Visual Cognition*, **7** (1/2/3), pp. 1–16.

Levin, D.T. and Simons, D.J. (1997), 'Failure to detect changes to attended objects in motion pictures', *Psychonomic Bulletin & Review*, **4**, pp. 501–6.

Loftus, E.F. (1996), *Eyewitness Testimony* (Cambridge, MA: Harvard University Press).

Mack, A. and Rock, I. (1998a), *Inattentional Blindness* (Cambridge, MA: MIT Press).

Mack, A. and Rock, I. (1998b), 'Inattentional blindness: Perception without attention', in *Visual Attention*, volume 8 of Vancouver Studies in Cognitive Science, ed. R.D. Wright (New York: Oxford University Press).

McConkie, G.W. and Currie, C.B. (1996), 'Visual stability while viewing complex pictures', *Journal of Experimental Psychology: Human Perception and Performance*, **22**, pp. 263–581.

Noë, A. (2001), 'Experience and the active mind', *Synthese*, **129**, pp. 41–60.

Noë, A. and O'Regan, J.K. (2000), 'Perception, attention and the grand illusion', *Psyche*, **6** (15).

Noë, A., Pessoa, L. and Thompson, E. (2000), 'Beyond the grand illusion: What change blindness really teches us about vision', *Visual Cognition*, **7** (1/2/3), pp. 93–106.

O'Regan, J.K. (1992), 'Solving the "real" mysteries of visual perception: The world as an outside memory', *Canadian Journal of Psychology*, **46** (3), pp. 461–88.

O'Regan, J.K., Deubel, H., Clark, J.J. and Rensink, R.A. (2000), 'Picture changes during blinks: Looking without seeing and seeing without looking', *Visual Cognition*, **7** (1/2/3), pp. 191–212.

O'Regan, J.K. and Noë, A. (2001), 'A sensorimotor theory of vision and visual consciousness', *Behavioral and Brain Sciences*, **24** (5).

O'Regan, J.K., Rensink, R.A. and Clark, J.J. (1999), 'Change blindness as a result of "mudsplashes"', *Nature*, **398**, p. 34.

Pessoa, L., Thompson, E. and Noë, A. (1998), 'Finding out about filling in: A guide to perceptual completion for visual science and the philosophy of perception', *Behavioral and Brain Sciences*, **21** (6), pp. 723–802.

Pollatsek, A., Rayner, K. and Henderson, J.M. (1990), 'Role of spatial location in integration of pictorial information across saccades', *Journal of Experimental Psychology: Human Perception and Performance*, **16**, pp. 199–210.

Pylyshyn, Z.W. (2002), *Seeing and Visualising: It's Not What You Think* (Cambridge, MA: MIT Press).

Rensink, R.A. (2000a), 'The dynamic representation of scenes', *Visual Cognition*, **7** (1/2/3), pp. 17–42.

Rensink, R.A. (2000b), 'Seeing, sensing, and scrutinizing', *Vision Research*, **40**, pp. 1469–87.

Rensink, R.A., O'Regan, J.K. and Clark, J.J. (1997), 'To see or not to see: The need for attention to perceive changes in scenes', *Psychological Science*, **8** (5), pp. 368–73.

Scholl, B., Simons, D.J. and Levin, D.T. (2002), '"Change blindness" blindness: An implicit demonstration of a metacognitive error', (Under review).

Scholl, B.J. (2000), 'Attenuated change blindness for exogenously attended items in a flicker paradigm', *Visual Cognition*, **7** (1/2/3), pp. 377–96.

Shepard, R.N. and Cooper, L.A. (1982), *Mental Images and their Transformations* (Cambridge, MA: MIT Press).

Simons, D.J. (2000), 'Current approaches to change blindness', *Visual Cognition*, **7** (1/2/3), pp. 1–16.

Simons, D.J. and Levin, D.T. (1998), 'Failure to detect changes to people during a real-world interaction', *Psychonomic Bulletin & Review*, **5**, pp. 644–9.

Theeuwes, J. (1991), 'Exogenous and endogenous control of attention: The effect of visual onsets and offsets', *Perception & Psychophysics*, **49** (1), pp. 83–90.

Williams, P. and Simons, D.J. (2000), 'Detecting changes in novel, complex three-dimensional objects', *Visual Cognition*, **7** (1/2/3), pp. 297–322.

Yantis, S. (1998), 'Control of visual attention', inAttention, ed. H. Pashler (Hove, England: Psychology Press/Erlbaum Taylor & Francis).

Zihl, J., Cramon, D.V., and Mai, N. (1983), 'Selective disturbance of movement vision after bilateral brain damage', *Brain*, **106**, pp. 313–40.

Mark Rowlands

Two Dogmas of Consciousness

Most recent discussions of phenomenal consciousness are predicated on two deeply entrenched assumptions. The first is objectualism, the claim that what it is like to undergo an experience is something of which we are or can be aware in the having of that experience. The second is internalism, the claim that what it is like to undergo an experience is constituted by states, events and processes that are located inside the skins of experiencing subjects. This paper argues that both assumptions should be rejected. What it is like to undergo an experience is not an object of consciousness but something that exists in the directing of consciousness towards (non-phenomenal) objects. What it is like to undergo an experience is not something of which we are aware, but something in virtue of which we are aware. And there is little reason for supposing that the directing of consciousness towards its objects is something that occurs exclusively inside the skins of experiencing subjects. On the contrary, directing of consciousness towards its objects is often extended, involving acts of worldly probing and exploration.

I: Introduction

It is accepted by most that there is *something that it is like* to have or undergo an experience. Equivalently, experiences have a certain *phenomenal character*, or are essentially constituted by their *phenomenal properties*.[1] This claim is, however, crucially ambiguous. The following two interpretations are distinct and have wildly divergent entailments.

(1) Experiences seem or feel a certain way to the subjects of those experiences.

(2) In the having of experiences the world seems a certain way to the subjects of those experiences.

The former interpretation regards what it is like as a property that attaches to experiences; the latter takes it to be a property that attaches to the world in virtue of a subject having or undergoing various experiences. According to interpretation (1), it seems most natural to regard what it is like as something *of* which we

---

[1] I shall use expressions 'what it is like', 'phenomenal properties', 'phenomenal character' interchangeably, depending on which best satisfies the relevant grammatical/contextual requirements.

Journal of Consciousness Studies, **9**, No. 5–6, 2002, pp. 158–80

are aware in the having of an experience. Interpretation (2), on the other hand, makes what it is like something *with* which we are aware in the having of an experience.[2] One ends up with very different conceptions of consciousness and its relation to the world depending on whether one adheres to (1) or (2). At least, this is one of the lines of thought I want to explore. I'm going to argue that what it is like to undergo an experience is not something *of* which we are aware but something *with* which we are aware in the having of an experience. What it is like is not an object of conscious experience but, rather, something that exists in the directing of a conscious experience towards its (non-phenomenal) objects. The arguments for this claim constitute the first half of the paper.

The idea that the what it is like of conscious experience is something of which we are aware in the having of an experience encourages an *internalist* view of an experience's phenomenal character. For it leads naturally to the view that when we turn our attention inwards — roughly, when we introspect — the phenomenal character of experience is one of the items we can expect to come across. That is, it leads naturally to the view that an experience's phenomenal character is an introspectible feature of that experience. Since this introspectible feature is to be found by looking inwards, its location is also naturally thought of as inner. Suppose now, however, that what it is like is something that exists in the directing of consciousness towards its objects, and is not itself an object of consciousness. Then the internality of phenomenal character would not follow. If phenomenal character attaches to acts of consciousness, and is not among its objects, then phenomenal character would be wherever those acts are. Suppose, further, that acts of consciousness are not located purely inside the head (or skins) of conscious creatures. Suppose, for example, that acts of consciousness involve, partly but essentially, acts of worldly probing and exploration. If this were the case, then the internality of phenomenal character would be hard to sustain. This is the second claim for which I want to argue. Phenomenal character is not, generally, an internally constituted item. On the contrary, it is something constituted, in part, by external activity, by acts of worldly exploration. This is not to say that phenomenal character can *never* be internally constituted; still less is it to say that it is *necessarily* externally constituted. Rather, the claim is that it is often externally constituted — at least in part. What it is like to undergo an experience is often constituted by factors outside the skins of experiencing creatures.

I am under no illusions about the counter-intuitiveness of the view I shall defend. What could be more natural than the idea that when we have or undergo an experience we are aware of the way that experience seems or feels to us — indeed, that we know what it is like to undergo that experience.[3] And the claim

---

[2] Dretske also distinguishes between consciousness as something of which we are aware and consciousness as something with which we are aware. See Dretske (1995), Ch. 4.

[3] Of course, there are dissenting voices. Wittgenstein claimed: 'It can't be said of me at all (except perhaps as a joke) that I *know* I'm in pain. What's it supposed to mean — except perhaps that I am in pain' (Wittgenstein, 1953, p. 246). This is usually glossed as a point about linguistic practice — that the practice of giving reasons justifying one's self-ascription of pain literally makes no sense. Nor does the question, 'How do you know?' in response to such a self-ascription. I concur with the gloss. However, this does not explain *why* such practices make no sense. My answer would be that such practices

that phenomenal character is internally constituted, that the supervenience base of phenomenal properties ends at the skin of experiencing creatures, is one whose acceptance borders on the universal.[4] Nonetheless, I shall argue that both claims should be rejected. The view that what it is like is an object of consciousness I shall label *objectualism*. The view that what it is like is constituted exclusively by states and processes instantiated inside the skin of cognizing organisms I shall label *internalism*. Objectualism and internalism are the two dogmas of consciousness advertised in the title.

II: First Dogma: Objectualism

According to objectualism what it is like to have or undergo a conscious experience is an introspectible feature of that experience, it is one of the things of which we are aware when we have that experience. My suspicion is that this will prove the more stubborn of the dogmas. In any event, my strategy is to undermine objectualism precisely as a way of loosening the grip of internalism; so, much of the hard work must be done here.

Accordingly, the case against objectualism has two strands. The first is a sort of frontal assault. I shall try to show that there is no way of reconciling objectualism with any sort of materialist account of phenomenal character. Second, I shall offer a diagnosis of why objectualism should be so intuitively natural even though false. This section focuses on frontal assault.

A preliminary distinction we require is that between consciousness as *act*, and consciousness as *object* of experience. To say that consciousness is, or can be, an object of experience is to record an extremely mundane idea: *introspection is possible*. We can be, and often are, aware of what we are thinking, feeling and experiencing. There are several different models of introspective access, but these need not concern us.[5] We can work with the general idea that introspection gives us access to mental items: fundamentally, states and properties (or perhaps

---

have purchase only in connection with items that can be genuine objects of consciousness — ordinary physical objects would provide paradigm examples. Such practices are inappropriate for items that are not properly separable from acts of consciousness. A similar point is made by Sartre, who famously puts 'of' in parentheses when talking about consciousness (of) conscious states. See, for example, Sartre (1943).

[4]   The most prominent exception is provided by those who think phenomenal properties reduce to representational ones. See, for example, Michael Tye (1996) and William Lycan (1996). I am not a representationist in this sense, and I think the view sketched here is actually incompatible with representationism. The argument for this is in my *The Nature of Consciousness* (2001).

[5]   Simple object perception models accord introspection essentially the same dyadic act–object structure as perception (or as perception is commonly taken to be), a structure constituted by a content-bearing state whose directedness towards its intentional object is effected by way of some sort of causal relation. Such models regard the objects of introspection as, fundamentally, states and properties. Displaced perception models, for example of the sort defended by Dretske, entail that the objects of intentional access are mental facts, ones to which we have access via displaced perceptual access to (typically) environmental objects, states and properties. For present purposes, there is no need for me to choose between these models. I shall tend to speak of access to mental states and properties, but if this offends, the less-committal 'items' can easily be slipped, *mutatis mutandis*, into the following discussion.

mental facts: see footnote 5). When we think of consciousness in this way — as something to which introspection gives us access — we are adopting what I shall call an *objectualist* conception of it. The objectualist conception of consciousness is a conception of consciousness as a collection of states and properties. It is a conception of consciousness as a collection of conscious items.

To say that consciousness is an act of experience is to say something equally quotidian. When we are conscious of something, that thing does not exhaust our consciousness. In addition to the thing of which we are conscious, there is our consciousness of it. This is immediately obvious when our consciousness is of *environ*mental items. No one would suppose that when I am conscious of, for example, this glass, the glass exhausts my consciousness. Most would say that the glass is not even part of our consciousness. So, why suppose that when our consciousness is of a *mental* item — a thought, desire, feeling, or whatever — these items exhaust our consciousness of them. Pretty clearly, they do not. When we think of consciousness in this way as a directedness towards an object, we are adopting what I shall call an *actualist* conception of it. So, on an actualist conception, consciousness is not a collection of states and properties but, rather, *it is the adopting of a perspective from which consciousness can be seen to comprise a collection of states and properties*. It is not a conception of consciousness as a collection of conscious items but a conception of consciousness as the adopting of a perspective towards, and from which consciousness can be viewed as a collection of, such items.

Given that consciousness has this sort of dual structure, where do we place what it is like to undergo an experience? Is the actualist or objectualist conception most appropriate for understanding what it is like? Does it belong among the objects of consciousness, or is it something that attaches to the act? Or both? I shall try to show that it cannot be among the objects of consciousness. Here's the argument.

P1. What it is like to undergo an experience is either a phenomenal particular, or a phenomenal property, or a representational property.

P2. If what it is like is a phenomenal particular then materialism is false.

P3. Materialism is not false.

P4. If what it is like is a phenomenal property, then it cannot plausibly be regarded as an object of consciousness.

P5. If what it is like is a representational property, then it cannot plausibly be regarded as an object of consciousness.

P6. Therefore, if what it is like is an object of consciousness then it can, consistent with materialism, be neither a phenomenal particular nor a phenomenal property nor a representational property.

C. Therefore, what it is like is not an object of consciousness.

P1 is relatively uncontroversial. As for P3, I am willing to give up on materialism only as a very last resort, and I shall assume throughout this paper that some minimal form of materialism is true.

III: Defence of P2

The work starts with P2: the claim that phenomenal particulars are incompatible with any form of materialism. This does not, in fact, require that much work as the claim is almost universally accepted.

Suppose we are looking at a particular visual scene, one containing, say, a pink polka-dotted dress. Our consciousness can, of course, be directed towards this object; it can be an object of our consciousness. In addition, there is, let us suppose, something that it is like to see a pink polka-dotted dress. And according to the objectualist interpretation of what it is like, this means that we are also consciously acquainted with something distinct from the dress: the what it is like to see a pink polka-dotted dress. It is our acquaintance with this latter object, so it is claimed, which marks the difference between our conscious experience of the dress and, for example, a zombie's unconscious perception of the dress. The zombie is acquainted with the dress but not with the what it is like to see the dress.

Now, if we are asked what it is like to experience a pink polka-dotted dress it seems that, at the very least, we are going to have to say things like 'it seems pinkish', 'it seems polka-dotted', and so on. The objectualist–particularist account of what it is like must explain by claiming that the what it is like of seeing a pink polka-dotted dress actually has the properties of being pink and being polka-dotted. The phenomenological character of our experience of a pink polka-dotted dress is explained in terms of our being consciously acquainted with an object — the what it is like of these experiences — which actually has the properties we experience when we perceive, or seem to perceive, the dress. More generally, on the objectualist construal that regards what it is like as a particular, we explain the phenomenological character of a conscious experience E by claiming that we are consciously acquainted with a particular P which really has the properties we experience (i.e., perceive or seem to perceive) when we have E. And a particular P, which really has the properties we perceive or seem to perceive when we have E, is a phenomenal particular.

That materialism is incompatible with the existence of phenomenal particulars is well known, and has been at least since the time of Hobbes. The problem in the above case, for example, is that there is nothing in the brain that really has the properties of being pink and polka-dotted. So, if a phenomenal particular really has these properties, its distinctness from anything occurring in the brain would follow from Leibniz's Law. A materialist might, arguably, be able to get away with the existence of irreducible phenomenal properties. But commitment to phenomenal particulars is, it is generally accepted, constitutive of dualism. So, if we are to adopt the objectualist interpretation of what it is like we cannot, consistently with materialism, regard what it is like as a phenomenal particular.

IV: Defence of P4

There are various well-known materialist strategies for dealing with the apparent existence of phenomenal particulars. And these strategies can, broadly speaking, be divided into two sorts. The first type of strategy covers a spectrum of distinct positions, but all of these are united by the idea that it is possible to eliminate quantification over such particulars by recasting it as quantification over phenomenal properties. The second type of strategy may allow that quantification over phenomenal particulars can be eliminated in favour of quantification over phenomenal properties, but adds to this the additional claim that quantification over phenomenal properties can itself be eliminated in favour over quantification over intentional or representational properties. The phenomenal, that is, ultimately reduces to the representational. This section considers strategies of the first sort.

Classical adverbialist approaches to experience provide one good example of the attempt to eliminate quantification over phenomenal particulars in favour of quantification over phenomenal properties. According to such approaches, having an experience is not, as a particularist position would have it, a matter of experiencing a particular (immaterial) object, but, rather, experiencing in a certain manner. Statements of the form:

P has an F sensation

are allotted an adverbial reconstruction:

P senses F-ly

or:

P senses in an F manner

Thus, statements that purport to be about phenomenal particulars: pains, afterimages, and the like, are, in fact, statements about the way or mode in which a person is experiencing. And the notion of a way or mode of experiencing is explained in terms of properties of the act of experiencing; i.e., phenomenal properties.

Not all materialist accounts of phenomenality, of course, adopt classical adverbialist lines. And constraints of space do not allow me to survey the various alternatives. For our purposes, however, it is not the details of each particular strategy that are important, but their common reliance, in one form or another, on the notion of a phenomenal property. That is, any account that relies on the notion of a phenomenal property and which seeks to provide an objectualist interpretation of the notion of what it is like using the notion of a phenomenal property will be subject to the arguments to follow.

Given the availability of an appeal to phenomenal properties, then, it might be thought that it is possible to give a materialistically acceptable account of the notion of what it is like, and still understand this as an object of conscious acquaintance. That is, it might be thought that we can render an objectualist interpretation of what it is like compatible with materialism by construing it as a phenomenal property, or complex of such properties, possessed by a process occurring in the brain. In undergoing a conscious experience, we become aware not of a phenomenal particular but of a phenomenal property. I shall argue that the idea that phenomenal properties are objects of awareness is untenable.

Phenomenal properties are properties of appearing a certain way. So, for any property P, the corresponding phenomenal property is the property of appearing to be P. When environmental items are the objects of our consciousness, there is little temptation to suppose that phenomenal properties literally belong to those objects. An ingot of gold feels heavy. But this is not a genuine property of gold. Having an atomic weight of 79, and consequently being heavy (or massy) are genuine properties of gold, but feeling heavy is not (it is not, for example, as if the ingot acquires a new property just because I happen to pick it up and notice its weight). Feeling heavy is a property not of gold, but of the way I experience the gold — that is, it is a property of my *experiencing* of the gold. In general, properties of appearing a certain way are not properties of the objects of consciousness, they are properties of the act.

I shall argue that the same holds true when the objects of consciousness are (conscious) experiences. That is, I shall argue that to say that an experience appears P is not to attribute a genuine property to the experience, it is to attribute a property to my having of the experience. It is to attribute a property to the act rather than the object of consciousness. To see this, it is important to clearly distinguish two interpretations of the notion of a phenomenal property. Let P denote a non-phenomenal property. Ph-P is, then, the phenomenal equivalent. Thus, if P = the property of being polka-dotted, then Ph-P = the property of appearing polka-dotted. According to the first interpretation, the possession by experience E of phenomenal property Ph-P entails that E is P.

One hesitates to call this an *interpretation* of the concept of a phenomenal property. It is almost certainly a misunderstanding rather than an interpretation of that concept. It is fairly clear that on this 'interpretation' the invocation of phenomenal properties is no more materialistically acceptable than the invocation of phenomenal particulars. If the possession by a state or process of the phenomenal property of being polka-dotted means that the state or process really is polka-dotted, this will again preclude its identification with anything occurring in the brain.

Therefore, it is fairly clear that we should avoid this misunderstanding of the notion of a phenomenal property. To say that experience E possesses phenomenal property Ph-P is not to say that E is P. It is to say that S appears to be P; that is, that S has the property of *appearing to be P*. My argument against the claim that phenomenal properties are objects of awareness, then, is that it commits us to the untenable interpretation of the notion of a phenomenal property.

To see this, suppose you are having an experience of a pink-polka-dotted dress. How does it seem or feel to have this experience. Well, on the face of it, it seems somewhat *pinkish*, that there's a certain *polka-dottedness* evident. Suppose we tried to explain this seeming or feeling in terms of a property of the experience *of* which we are aware. This property is, thus, an introspectible property of our experiences, one of the things we encounter when we, so to speak, turn our attention inwards. How could encountering this property explain the pinkish, polka-dotted character of the experience unless it was in some way pinkish or polka-dotted? After all, it is, on the objectualist construal, our *introspection* of this property that is supposed to explain the pinkish, polka-dotted character of our experience. But how could introspection of something neither pink nor polka-dotted explain the pink and polka-dotted way it seems to have the experience? It seems that introspective encountering of an item will explain the pinkish, polka-dotted character of our experience only if that item is in some way pinkish and polka-dotted. But, if this were so, then we would be immediately be committed to the mistaken and materialistically unacceptable interpretation of concept of a phenomenal property.

The correct response, I think, is to deny that the pinkish, polka-dotted character of our experience can be explained in terms of the idea that phenomenal properties are objects of consciousness. Invocation of such properties as objects of consciousness explains nothing unless we are willing to bite the bullet and endorse the mistaken interpretation of phenomenal properties. But that is a big bullet to bite. And it's one that would kill materialism just as surely as would the invocation of phenomenal particulars. Far more plausible, at least for the materialistically inclined, is to claim that phenomenal properties attach to the *apprehending* or *grasping* — broadly speaking to the *experiencing* — of objects of consciousness and are not themselves objects of consciousness. That is, we should abandon an objectualist in favour of an actualist account of phenomenal properties. Moreover, if we adopt this line we do not have to explain any awkward disanalogies with environmental objects — for whom phenomenal properties are clearly not genuine properties.

V: Defence of P5

The defence of P5 is more tortuous. Representational properties are, roughly, properties of representing the world to be a certain way. Those who think what it is like to undergo an experience can be reduced to representational properties are known as *representationists*.[6] I argue that (i) there is nothing in representationism that requires representational properties be objects of consciousness, and (ii) if representationists insist on the claim that representational properties are objects of consciousness, many of the advantages of representationism over competing views are lost.

The argument can be developed in terms of the distinction between three types of experiential content.

---

[6] Actually, they are at least as often called *representationalists* rather than *representationists*. Given the manifold opportunities for confusion in this context, however, I propose to restrict the former to the well known thesis about the mediation of experience by way of representations, and the latter for the thesis that the phenomenal reduces to the representational. Unfortunately, however, things are not as simple as this. First, there is a complex web of conceptual connections between the two views, one that I cannot even begin to untangle in a work of this length. Secondly, and more importantly for our purposes, I am, here, not concerned with representationism as such, but with whether representational properties should be regarded as objects of consciousness. Since both representationists and representationalists can affirm or (I shall argue) deny this claim, this serves further to blur the distinctions between the two. Nevertheless, as long as we are careful, this should not matter. The primary thesis to be discussed here is the claim that representational properties are objects of consciousness. Whether this thesis is pressed into service by the representationist or the representationalist is, in the present context, of comparatively minor importance. Indeed, I think that the arguments developed below concerning why representationists should not claim that representational properties are objects of consciousness apply with equal facility to representationalists.

1. Empiricist: the content of an experience is composed of sense-data. When I look at the glass in front of me, what I really experience are sense-data (roughly *ideas*).
2. Russellian: the content of an experience consists in the environmental objects and properties the experience is of, or as of. The content of my experience of the glass is the glass and its various properties.
3. Representational: the content of the experience consists in properties the experience has of representing things to be a certain way.

The representationist, it is generally accepted, requires the third interpretation of experiential content: the content of an experience is its representational content. In these terms, my argument looks like this: (i) there is little reason to suppose that representational properties are objects of consciousness unless we confuse Representational with Russellian content, and (ii) if we do regard representational properties as objects of consciousness, then any advantages Representational content has over the Empiricist alternative disappear.

To see this, consider one of the fundamental objections to empiricist, or sense-datum, accounts of experiential content, an objection than centres on the notion of (what is called) *experiential transparency*.[7] I have a visual experience of the glass in front of me. My attention is currently on the glass, but I can also, apparently, focus on, or attend to, my *experience* of the glass. When my attention is thus turned inwards, what's noticeable is that the glass and its properties are not replaced by some inner private entities — sense-data or ideas. Rather, I attend to my experience by attending to the glass and thinking about this while I do so. My experience is in this sense *transparent*: it does not stop short of the public object itself.

Experiential transparency is thought to create two problems for sense-datum accounts of experience. When we introspect, we (i) do not find what we are supposed to find — sense-data, and (ii) find what we are not supposed to find — public objects and properties.[8]

My argument, then, is that if representationists adhere to the claim that representational properties are objects of experience, representationism suffers from analogues of these problems.

First, with regard to the claim that introspection does not reveal the existence of sense-data, a sort of *tu quoque* response is available to the empiricist: neither does it reveal the existence of representational properties (in anything other than a Russellian sense).

The second problem for the empiricist derives from the fact that she adopts a *mediational* conception of experience. We are immediately aware only of sense-data, and are mediately aware of the environment in virtue of being immediately aware of sense-data. And this is why it is so difficult for the empiricist to

---

[7] See, for example, Moore (1903).

[8] That the empiricist is faced with two problems of differing degrees of severity and not, as it is commonly thought, one as pointed out by Mike Martin in his 'The transparency of experience' (unpublished ms).

account for experiential transparency. Why is it that our experience does not stop short of public objects and properties, even when we are attending to that experience, if we are immediately aware only of sense-data?

Consider, now, what it means to be aware of representational properties. I see a sign 'Beware of the dog!' What does it mean to say that I am aware of the representational properties of the sign? Well, assuming I can read, I might become aware of the presence of the dog. But this is awareness of representational properties only in a Russellian sense. I might become aware *that* the sign indicates the presence of the dog. But this is awareness *that*, not awareness *of*. And it is generally acknowledged that awareness that and awareness of are quite distinct relations with fundamentally different properties.[9] There is also a history of conventional use connecting the sign with the room, but surely I don't become aware *in the relevant sense* of that. Tacit awareness is certainly not phenomenal awareness. The only way of making sense of the claim that representational properties — in the sense required by the representationist — are objects of consciousness is if we adopt the view that I become aware of what the sign represents in virtue of becoming aware of various intrinsic properties of the sign. That is, to be aware of the representational properties of the sign is to be aware of the intrinsic properties of the sign in virtue of which (partly) it represents. However, if we apply this model to experience then we find ourselves back with the mediational conception of experience according to which we become aware of the way an experience represents the world to be in virtue of our awareness of the intrinsic properties of the experience in virtue of which it so represents it. And this means that if sense-datum accounts have problems with experiential transparency in virtue of their mediational character, so too will representationism. Therefore, representationists not only can but *should* reject the claim that we are aware of the representational properties of experiences.

So, if what it is like to undergo an experience is a phenomenal property or a representational property, it is not an object of experience. We can salvage the view that what it is like is an object of experience only if we accept that it is a phenomenal particular. But this requires sacrificing materialism. A better alternative, I suggest, is to abandon the idea that what it is like is an object of experience. It belongs to consciousness as act rather than consciousness as object. It belongs, that is, to consciousness as the directing of experience rather than to consciousness as that upon which experience is directed.

VI: Phenomenology by Proxy

A frontal assault of the above sort can constitute only part of the case against objectualism. An argument that objectualism is incompatible with materialism, for example, is likely to receive the rejoinder: *so much the worse for materialism!* This is because the idea that what it is like to undergo an experience is an object of consciousness is, even I will accept, an overwhelmingly natural one. Why should this be if the idea is false? What is required in order to more

---

[9] See, for example, Dretske (1993).

convincingly substantiate the case against the objectualist interpretation is a *diagnosis* of why it should be such a natural way of thinking about the phenomenal character of experience even though it is false. Here is the diagnosis. The naturalness of objectualism is an illusion that derives from the nature of introspection: *introspection has no specific phenomenology.*

The claim that introspection has no specific phenomenology is by no means a nonstandard one. For example, without any air of controversy, Colin McGinn writes:

> One thing that seems clear is that introspective awareness is not itself a kind of *experience*: you do not have an experience as of your experience as of the sun setting. This is because the act of inner awareness does not have the phenomenology characteristic of a sense-modality. The only phenomenology attending such awareness comes from the *object* of the awareness (McGinn, 1997, p. 64).

This is not to deny that introspection tokens possess a phenomenological character. They clearly do (if in doubt, just try reading Proust). Rather, the claim is that introspection tokens have no *specific* phenomenology; they have no phenomenology that defines them, or otherwise marks them out, precisely as the individual introspective tokens they are. Rather, the phenomenological features possessed by any token introspective act are essentially connected with those of the experience that is the object of the act. The phenomenological features of any token introspective episode are acquired or inherited from the experience that is its object. Introspective phenomenology is *phenomenology by proxy.*

Why should this be so? That introspection lacks any specific phenomenology is, I think, closely connected to the phenomenon of experiential transparency described earlier. Consider, again, my visual experience of the glass. In order to focus on what it is like to see the glass I must, of course, focus on my visual experience. But I can do this only by attending to the glass and thinking about this while I do so. My introspection stops not at my experience but passes all the way through to the public object itself. This is one entailment of the thesis of transparency. Not only that, my introspective efforts must present the glass in the same way as my original experience. If this were not so then it would be unclear, to say the least, how my introspective act is supposed to reveal to me the phenomenal character of my original experience.[10] Thus, when one attempts to introspectively focus one's attention on the what it is like of one's experience, the what it is like that one attempts to focus on, because of the transparency of experience, slips away and one is left with the worldly objects and properties that one's experience is about presented in the same way as in the original experience. Thus, one ends up with an introspective experience that has precisely the same phenomenology as that of the original experience.

Whether or not this explanation of the phenomenon is correct is not essential to the argument. Suppose we accept that introspective tokens have no specific

---

[10] The suppressed premise here is, I think, a plausible one concerning the relation between phenomenal and representational character. Without wishing to identify the former with the latter, I think a supervenience claim of the following sort is eminently defensible. Representational character supervenes on phenomenal character in that there can be no variation in the representational character of an experience without a corresponding change in the phenomenal character of that experience. I defend this at much greater length in Rowlands (2001).

phenomenology — that they acquire whatever phenomenology they have from the experiences that are their objects — and bracket the question of why this should be so. Then, in any successful case of introspection, the introspective act will have the same (or at least a very similar) phenomenal character as the original experience. But this situation will inevitably entail that the following two situations are difficult to discern. Situation 1 consists in the standard account of the success of an introspective act:

(1) The successful introspective act objectifies (i.e., makes in to an object) the what it is like of the experience towards which it is directed.

Situation (1), I have argued, is incompatible with materialism. Contrast this with situation (2):

(2) The successful introspective act has a phenomenal character that is type-identical (or at least very similar) to the phenomenal character of the original experience.

In situation (2), there is no requirement that the phenomenal character — the what it is like — of the original experience be objectified. Rather, the introspective act can have a phenomenal character that exists in the directing of this act to its object (the original experience), whereas the original experience has a phenomenal character that exists in the directing of this experience towards its object (typically, worldly objects and properties).[11] In neither case is the phenomenal character an object of consciousness. In both cases it exists only in the directing of consciousness towards its objects.

The crucial point is that situation (1) and situation (2) would be phenomenologically indiscernible. If we have an introspective act whose phenomenal character — that exists in the directing of this act towards its object — is identical (or very similar) to the phenomenal character that attaches to the original experience — and which itself exists in the directing of this experience towards its object — then what could be more natural than the idea that in successful cases of introspection we have succeeded in objectifying the phenomenal character of the original experience?

If this is correct, then it immediately defuses the objection based on the overwhelming naturalness of the objectualist interpretation of what it is like. This naturalness is equally compatible with the actualist interpretation as long as we are willing to accept the claim that introspection has no specific phenomenology — that its phenomenology is phenomenology by proxy. And this claim is entirely orthodox.

VII: The Second Dogma and the Extended View of Experiencing

Objectualism is what I have called the first dogma of consciousness. If the above arguments are correct, the phenomenal character of experience is something that exists only in the directing of conscious acts towards their (non-phenomenal)

---

[11] And, as argued above, the thesis of experiential transparency neatly explains the congruence of the phenomenologies by way of the idea that both acts are, ultimately, directed towards the same objects.

objects, and is not and cannot be an object of experience. Thus, if this is correct, the first dogma should be rejected.

The second dogma is what I called *internalism* — the idea that phenomenal character is constituted exclusively by events, states and processes that occur inside the skins of experiencing creatures. The first dogma lends to the second support that is psychologically natural if not logically compelling. If phenomenal character were an introspectible feature of experiences, and if we encounter such character by introspectively turning our attention inwards, then the assumption that this character is internally constituted is a natural corollary. Undermining the first dogma, therefore, undercuts this sort of motivation for the second dogma.

If the arguments developed against the first dogma are correct, phenomenal character attaches to experiential acts — to consciousness as the directing of experience. Suppose now that acts of experience occurred, at least in part, outside the skin of organisms that undergo them. Phenomenal character, seen as attaching to these acts, might then not be something that occurred purely inside the skins of experiencing creatures. The what it is like to undergo an experience might then have an *extended* character, a character that derived from the extended nature of the experiential acts to which it attaches.[12] If this were so, then the second dogma would fall too. This is the line of thought I want to explore, initially with respect to *visual* experience.

In what sense might acts of visual experiencing be extended? First of all, consider a general theoretical framework, as laid out in an earlier work of mine.[13] The framework is constituted by the following claims:

(1) The world is an external store of information relevant to cognitive processes such as perceiving, remembering, reasoning, and so on.

It is such a store because, in all essentials, information is *ubiquitous*. It is in virtue of nomic dependencies between items that one item can carry information about another. But such relations can be externally instantiated just as much as they can be instantiated in the relation between an internal representation and its external correlate. In virtue of this, information exists in the environment and there are certain environmental structures that carry information relevant to cognition.

(2) A process such as perceiving is essentially hybrid — it straddles both internal and external forms of information processing.
(3) The external processes involve manipulation, exploitation and transformation of environmental structures that carry information relevant to the accomplishing of the perceptual task at hand.

---

[12] The locution 'extended' is quite obviously an allusion to the notion of the *extended mind*. This view of the mind has been defended forcefully by and in the following: Donald (1991); Hutchins (1995); Clark (1997; 2001); Clark and Chalmers (1998); Hurley (1998); Rowlands (1999). The idea of the extended mind has hitherto largely been restricted to 'cognitive architecture' (Clark, Rowlands) or 'vehicles of content' (Hurley). The attack on the second dogma is, in essence, an attempt to extend this view of the mind to the phenomenal character of experience.

[13] *The Body in Mind* (1999). My account differs from some other versions of the extended mind idea by according a larger role to the notion of representation. This idiosyncrasy, however, has no bearing on the present discussion.

(4) At least some of the internal processes are ones concerned with supply-
     ing the cognizing organism with the ability to appropriately use relevant
     structures in its environment.

While there is no necessity bound up with the notion of the extended mind as
such to take a stand on the nature of these internal processes, I do suggest that
proper recognition of the nature of the external processes involved allows us to
upgrade the role of *pattern-mapping* operations in particular and nonproposi-
tional forms of *knowing how* in general. And in this, my position is fairly typical.

Suppose this schematic account is correct, at least in broad outline. How
would we apply it to the case of visual experience? A useful place to begin is provided by Mackay (1962; 1967; 1973). Suppose you are a blind person holding a
bottle. You have the feeling of holding a bottle. But what tactile sensations do
you actually have? Without slight rubbing of the skin, tactile information is considerably reduced, information pertaining to temperature will soon disappear
through adaptation of receptors, etc. Nonetheless, despite the poverty of sensory
stimulation you actually have the feeling of having a bottle in your hand. Broadly
speaking, there are two general approaches to explaining how this can be.

According to the first approach, the brain supplements, extends and embel-
lishes the impoverished information contained in sensory stimulation with what
are, essentially, various forms of inferential process. The result is the construction of an internal representation of the bottle. We can call this the *representational* approach.[14]

Mackay's answer, however, is quite different, and provides a useful illustration of the *extended* approach. According to Mackay, information is present in
the environment over and above that contained in sensory stimulation, and this
information is sufficient to specify that you are holding a bottle. In what does this
information consist? According to Mackay, in this: your brain is tuned to certain
potentialities. For example, it is tuned to the fact that if you were to slide your
hand very slightly, a change would come about in the incoming sensory signals
that is typical of the change associated with the smooth, cool surface of glass.
Furthermore, your brain is tuned to the fact that if you were to move your hand
upwards, the size of what you are encompassing with your hand would diminish
(because you are moving to the bottle's neck). And so on.[15]

What does this talk of 'tuning' mean? Basically, your brain has extracted various laws of what O'Regan and Noë call *sensorimotor contingency*.[16] Very
roughly, your brain has extracted, and has now activated, certain laws pertaining
to the way changes in motor action will be accompanied by changes in sensory
input; it has, that is, extracted a certain mapping function from motor activity to

[14] With regard to visual perception, the work of David Marr provides a paradigm example of this type of
approach. See especially his *Vision* (1982).

[15] The affinities between this sort of approach and that championed by Gibson are perhaps too obvious
to mention. Indeed, I might have referred to this as the *ecological* approach but for the fact that this
carries some unfortunate connotations deriving from Gibson's unfortunate proclivity for overstating
his case.

[16] O'Regan and Noë (2001a; b). For a more general development of this idea, see Noë (2002).

sensory input. This provides the additional information lacking in sensory stimulation, information that specifies that you are holding a bottle.

According to Mackay, seeing a bottle is an analogous state of affairs. You have the impression of seeing a bottle if your brain has extracted knowledge concerning a certain web of contingencies. For example, you have knowledge of the fact that that if you move your eyes upwards towards the neck of the bottle, the sensory stimulation will change in a way typical of what happens when a narrower region of the bottle comes into foveal vision. You have knowledge of the fact that if you move your eyes downwards, the sensory stimulation will change in a way typical of what happens when the green label is fixated by foveal vision.

As O'Regan and Noë have shown, visual perception, just like haptic perception, obeys its own laws of sensorimotor contingency. A fairly trivial example is the fact that in the contingency that the eyes close, the stimulation becomes uniform (i.e., blank). Here's a less trivial one. As the eyes rotate, the sensory stimulation on the retina shifts and distorts in a very particular way, determined by the size of the eye movement. In particular, as the eye moves, contours shift, and the curvature of lines change. For example, if you are looking at the midpoint of a horizontal line, the line will trace out an arc on the inside of your eyeball. If you now fixate upwards, the curvature of the line will change — represented on a flattened out retina, the line would now be curved. In general, straight lines on the retina distort dramatically as the eyes move, somewhat like an image in a distorting mirror.

Each form of perception has its own contingency rules, and, according to O'Regan and Noë, what differentiates visual perception from other forms is the structure of the rules governing the sensory changes produced by various motor actions. The sensorimotor contingencies within each sensory modality are subject to different invariance properties, and so the structure of the rules that govern the perception in these modalities will be, in each case, different. To learn to perceive visually is to learn the rules of sensorimotor contingency, understood as a non-propositional form of *knowing how*, governing the relation between changes in the orientation of the visual apparatus and the resulting changes in the character of the perceived world.

If the extended approach is correct, there is little need to explain the haptic perception of the bottle in terms of the production or activation of an internal representation. The work of such a representation can be performed by the bottle itself. The bottle is an external structure that carries information over and above that present in any sensory stimulation the bottle is currently inducing in the hand. How does it carry such information? By providing a stable structure that can be probed or explored at will by the haptic modality. Mackay's suggestion is that the same is true of visual perception. The bottle also provides a stable structure that can be explored at will by the visual modality. Thus we arrive back at the general framework for the extended mind outlined earlier. Visual perception is essentially hybrid, made up of internal processes (extraction and activation of the laws of sensorimotor contingency) plus external processes (the probing or exploration of information-bearing structures in the environment). Visually perceiving is a process whereby the world — understood as an external store of information

— is probed or explored by acts of perception, and the results of this exploration are mediated through the non-propositionally instantiated laws of sensorimotor contingency.

So, we have two quite different general approaches to explaining visual perception, one representational, the other extended. How do we adjudicate between them? The case ultimately rests on empirical considerations, and these, I think, strongly favour the extended approach.

VIII: Against Visual Representations

Consider, for example, the important experiments on *change blindness* performed by O'Regan and collaborators (O'Regan, 1992; O'Regan *et al.*, 1996; 1999; 2000). Observers are shown displays of natural scenes and are asked to detect cyclically repeated changes — a large object shifting, changing colour, or appearing and disappearing. Under normal circumstances, changes of this magnitude would be easily noticed. And this is because such changes would create a transient signal in the visual apparatus that would be detected by low-level visual mechanisms. This transient automatically attracts attention to the location of the change, and the change would therefore be immediately seen.

There are, however, ways of nullifying the role of the visual transient, and this is precisely what is done in the change blindness experiments. One method involves superimposing a very brief global flicker over the whole visual field at the moment of the change. A similar effect can be achieved by making the change coincide with an eye saccade, an eye blink, or a cut in a film sequence. In all these cases, a brief global disturbance swamps the local transient and thus prevents it from playing its normal attention-grabbing role. Another method involves creating a number of simultaneous local disturbances — which appear something like mud splashes on the scene — that act as decoys and so minimize the effect of the local transient.

The experiments showed that under these sorts of conditions, observers have great difficulty seeing changes even though they are very large and occur in full view. Indeed, measurements of the observers eyes indicated that they could be looking directly at the change at the moment it occurs and still not see it (see O'Regan *et al.*, 2000).

The idea that visual perception consists in the activation of an internal representation of a portion of the visual world renders these results mysterious. For, on this representational model, all that would be required to notice a change in such a scene would be to compare one's current visual impressions with the activated representation; when and how the discrepancies between the former and the latter arose would be irrelevant. The change blindness results strongly support the claim that there is at least no complex and detailed internal representation. We do not notice even significant changes in a scene because we have no internal template against which to measure or compare them.[17]

---

[17] For a wealth of further empirical support, see O'Regan and Noë (2001a).

IX: What it is Like to See

These results also provide us with a way of correctly locating the phenomenal character of visual experience (see O'Regan and Noë, 2001a; 2001b; Noë, 2002). As we look at a complex and detailed scene, our visual experience seems to be complex and detailed. Complexity and detail are, as we might say, part of the what it is like to have this visual experience. The change blindness results, however, strongly suggest that the impression we have of seeing a complex, detailed world is not an impression grounded in any complex, detailed, visual representation of that world. External complexity and detail is not internally reproduced.

How should we interpret this? Does this mean that our subjective impression of seeing everything is somehow mistaken? Worse, does it mean we can be mistaken about the way our experiences seem to us? Dennett seems to endorse this sort of interpretation, or did so at one time (Dennett, 1991). The interpretation is misguided. The claim that our subjective impressions are erroneous would follow only if we suppose that the subjective impression has to be grounded in an internal representation — that the accuracy of a subjective impression is to be measured by how closely it mirrors the structure of an internal representation — and this is precisely what the present account denies. We are aware of a complex and detailed world but this means only that we are aware of the world as being complex and detailed.

This mistaken interpretation is reinforced by the confusion with which this paper began. The confusion consisted in the idea that to claim that there is like something that it is like to have or undergo an experience entails that this experience seems or feels a certain way. Once we accept that seeming or feeling are properties of experiences it is but a small step to the claim that the way an experience must seem or feel has to be explained in terms of our awareness of those features of the experience in virtue of which it seems this. All this is erroneous. Experiences do not seem or feel a certain way. Rather, in the *having* of an experience, the *world* seems or feels a certain way.[18] Seeming or feeling, that is, are properties of the world — properties that it has *in virtue of* our having experiences.

So, the question is: 'Why does the world seem this way — complex and detailed — when its seeming this way is not underwritten by an internal representation that represents it as being this way? There are two reasons (see

---

[18] Peter Carruthers is commendably explicit in making the claim that one of the principal motivations — perhaps even *the* principal motivation — for higher-order representation models of consciousness consists in the necessity of accounting for the way experiences seem or feel. And he is quite clear that this is distinct from the way the world seems or feels in the having of an experience. Whereas 'horizontal' accounts of consciousness might be able to account for the latter, he claims, only a higher-order account can account for the latter. See his 'Natural theories of consciousness' (1998). This is an excellent reason — one of many I think — to reject higher-order representation accounts of consciousness. It might be thought that in introspection, experiences — as opposed to the world — can seem or feel a certain way. But given the transparency of experience, what would this mean? When I introspectively focus on a visual experience, for example, my introspective experience passes all the way through to the public objects and properties my experience is of. The phenomenal character of my introspective experience consists in the directing of this experience to these objects. If this is correct, then it is only the world — construed broadly enough to include human bodies — that can feel or seem a certain way. Never experiences. See my *The Nature of Consciousness* (2001).

O'Regan, 1992). First, the impression we have of seeing everything derives from the fact that the slightest flick of the eye allows any part of a visual scene to be processed at will. This gives us the impression that the whole scene is immediately available. Suppose you try to ascertain whether you are in fact seeing everything there is to see in a scene. How could you check this? Only, it seems, by casting your attention on each element of the scene and verifying that you have the impression of constantly seeing it. But, obviously, as soon as you do cast your attention on something, you see it. Therefore, you will always have the impression of constantly seeing everything (O'Regan and Noë, 2001a). Is this impression erroneous? Only if we think of seeing in terms of the production of an internal representation isomorphic with the part of the world seen. If, on the other hand, we accept that seeing consists in combining the results of environmental probing with knowledge of laws of sensorimotor contingency, we are indeed seeing the whole scene, for probing the world, and knowledge of these laws, is precisely what we do and have as we cast our attention from one aspect to the next.

Second, in addition to our ability to direct our attention at will to the visual world, the visual system is particularly sensitive to *visual transients*. When a visual transient occurs, a low-level 'attention-grabbing' mechanism appears to automatically direct processing to the location of the transient. This means that should anything happen in the environment, we will generally consciously see it since processing will be directed towards it. This gives us the impression of having tabs on everything that might change and so of consciously seeing everything. If we regard seeing as consisting in exploratory activity combined with knowledge of sensorimotor contingencies accompanying such exploration, then this impression is not erroneous. We do, indeed, see everything. The suspicion that we do not derives from a residual attachment to the idea that seeing consists in the production of an internal representation that maps onto the outside world.

Complexity and detail are genuine features of the phenomenal character of our experience. But this is not because they attach to an internal representation of the perceived portion of the world. Rather, they exist in and attach to the act of probing or exploring a complex and detailed world as this act is combined with knowledge of the laws of sensorimotor contingency.

This general model can quite easily be extended to other types of visual experience. What it is like to see a uniform expanse of red, for example, arises from (but, I shall argue later, *pace* O'Regan and Noë, does not simply consist in) suitable exploration or probing of the red expanse in front of one combined with knowledge of the sensorimotor contingencies associated with such exploration. Thus, one has the ability to flick one's attention at will to any part of the red expanse in front of one and to have an appropriate sensitivity to any visual transients that may tarnish this expanse. In so doing, the sensory stimulation changes in a way consistent with the presence of a red expanse. We experience a uniform expanse of red not because of features of an activated internal representation but because we can explore, in this sense, a worldly uniform expanse of red.

X: Imagery, Dreams, Hallucinations, Etc.

The fact that there is something that it is like to undergo non-perceptual experiences is going to provide the most obvious source of objections to this view. There is something that it is like, for example, to form a mental image of a scene, there is something that it is like to have dreams, hallucinations, and the like.

The first point that should be made is that the dogma of internalism consists in a universally quantified claim: *all* phenomenal character is internally constituted. Therefore, undermining this dogma requires only an existentially quantified counter-claim: *some* phenomenal character is not internally constituted. It is no part of this paper to argue that the phenomenal character of all experiences is externally constituted, just as it is no part of the idea of the extended mind, sensibly construed, to argue that all cognitive processes are externally constituted. I argue only that the phenomenal character of some experiences is externally constituted. Therefore, to point to the existence of experiences — such as imaginings, dreams, hallucinations, and the like — that have a phenomenal character that is, apparently, internally constituted is to miss the point.

This response, however, might itself be thought to miss the point. What underlies the appeal to imaginings, dreams and hallucinations, it might be argued, is the idea that the quasi-visual phenomenal character of these items is so close to the phenomenal character that exists in visually perceiving the world that both cry out for the same unified explanation or, at least, a fundamentally similar explanation. Therefore, since we cannot give an extended account of quasi-visual phenomenal character, it might be thought, this casts significant doubt on the correctness of the extended account of visual phenomenal character.

This thought, of course, has a long and distinguished philosophical history, and is what underwrites both sense-datum and representationalist accounts of perception. The account of what it is like to see developed here, employing so prominently the idea of exploration of environmental structures, should entail that this differs in fundamental ways from what it is like to visually imagine, dream or hallucinate — that the phenomenal character of the former should diverge in significant ways from that of the latter. Thus, it might be thought, the extended account cannot account for the logical possibility of imaginings, dreams and hallucinations being phenomenally indistinguishable from genuine visual perception.

If this is the basis of the appeal to quasi-visual phenomenal character, then we can turn the sense of dissatisfaction that underlies it on its head. Indeed, the appeal can actually be used to *support* the extended account of what it is like to see. The existence of quasi-visual phenomenal character attaching to acts of imagining, dreaming, and hallucinating would pose a threat to the extended account of visual phenomenal character only if the former were indeed indistinguishable from, or at least very similar to, the latter. But suppose the converse were true. Suppose visual phenomenal character not only differed from its quasi-visual cousin, but did so *in ways predicted or entailed by the extended account* of the former. Then, this would not only undercut the force of the appeal to quasi-visual phenomenal character if this is used as an objection to the extended account of visual phenomenal character, it would mean that the appeal to the former would actually support the extended account of the latter.

One entailment of the extended model of visual phenomenal character is that the stability of the perceived visual field is a function of the stability of the visual world — the world towards which the exploratory perceptual activity is directed.[19] Without the stable world to hold our perceptual activity together, we should predict that any quasi-perceptual activity that is not directed towards a similarly stable world should lack the consistency, coherency and stability of genuine perception. And this, of course, is precisely what we get in the case of dreams and hallucinations.

The extended model of visual phenomenal character accords a central role to our ability to direct our attention at will to any part of the visual world. It is this that underlies the sense of complexity and detail that typically attends genuine visual phenomenology. We can direct our attention in this way only because the world provides a stable and enduring structure that supports such exploratory activity. Thus, another prediction that the extended model makes is that it should be much more difficult, if not impossible, to direct one's attention in mental imaginings, dreams and hallucinations. What empirical work has been done on this issue bears out this prediction.

Consider, for example, Chambers and Reisberg's study of perceptual versus imaginative flipping of ambiguous images (Chambers and Reisberg, 1985). Subjects were asked to observe and recall a drawing. The drawing would be ambiguous, of the duck/rabbit, faces/vase, old lady/young lady sort. The subjects, who did not know the duck/rabbit picture, were trained on related cases to ensure they were familiar with the phenomenon of ambiguity. Having been briefly shown the duck/rabbit picture, they were asked to form a mental image of it, attend to this image, and seek an alternative interpretation of it. Despite the inclusion in the test group of several high-vividness imagers (as measured by the Slee elaboration scale), none of the 15 subjects was able to find an alternative construal of their image. However, when subjects were later asked to draw the imaged duck/rabbit, all 15 were then able to find the alternative interpretation. The significance of this is that the ability to re-interpret the external drawing depends on slight changes in foveation: the external structure is subtly probed by the visual modality. The inability of subjects to discover the alternative construal of their image suggest that this sort of probing cannot be performed in the case of mental images. Directing of attention within mental images is, at the very least, much more difficult than within the perceived visual world. And this is precisely what we should expect if the extended model of visual phenomenal character were true.

Finally, visual phenomenology differs from that which attends acts of imagining, dreaming and hallucinating in one final way. The laws of sensorimotor contingency evident in visual perception simply do not operate in the latter sorts of

---

[19] O'Regan and Noë (2001a) argue, correctly in my view, that this is an entailment of enormous significance. Broadly speaking, it renders superfluous an entire tradition of appeals to mechanisms — extra-retinal signals, saccadic suppression devices, etc. — whose function is to somehow construct stability out of the unstable, disjointed information present in sensory stimulation.

experiential acts. To take just one example, even if it were possible to focus one's attention in, say, particularly vivid dreams or hallucinations — and the evidence for this is far from conclusive — such focusing is not attended by the sensorimotor contingencies that characterize visual perception. For example, in dreams, straight lines do not become curved as they move from the centre of foveation (or whatever passes for foveation in dreams).

In short, the appeal to quasi-visual phenomenal character provides the objector with a two-edged sword. Far from undermining the extended account of visual phenomenal character, the most reasonable construal of the evidence, I think, suggests that it actually supports that account.

XI: What it is Like and the Hard Problem

O'Regan and Noë, who adopt essentially the same model of visual perception as defended here, claim that this model solves, or at least dissolves, the *hard problem* of consciousness: the problem of understanding how a pattern of neural activity, functional organization, or whatever could ever add up to phenomenology. Their argument runs as follows.

1. The phenomenal properties of experience are, supposedly, items that attach to internal representations, and the problem — the *hard problem* — of consciousness is one of seeing how the other features of these representations could ever constitute their phenomenal features.
2. The sensorimotor contingency model of perception obviates the need for representations.
3. But phenomenal properties, if they exist, are features of representations.
4. Therefore, phenomenal properties do not exist.
5. Therefore, there's nothing left to explain.

This, I think, is *not* a good argument. O'Regan and Noë are clear, for the most part, that they are concerned with visual consciousness rather than consciousness is general. However, the hard problem arises for more than just perceptual qualia. And it is far from clear how we could apply the extended model to the case of non-perceptual qualia. But without such application we would not have solved the *generalized* hard problem — at best we would have solved it for the case of perceptual phenomenal character. It would be a strange solution to the hard problem that eschewed representations with attached qualia for visual consciousness but reintroduced them for other forms of consciousness. Even when restricted to the latter category, however, the argument still does not work.

Suppose you start off with a certain problem. Then, you identify a common way this problem is theoretically glossed. You then show that the theoretical gloss is untenable and offer an alternative. You cannot legitimately conclude from this that you have solved the original problem. All you can conclude is that one way of understanding or glossing the original problem is inadequate. The problem is the hard problem. The gloss is that phenomenal properties are properties of internal representations. The alternative is the sensorimotor contingency model. But the hard problem is, I think, a deep problem, one that survives the loss this, or indeed a number of other, theoretical glosses. Far from solving or dissolving the hard problem, O'Regan and Noë have, at best, merely managed to *relocate* it.

To see this, consider their account of what it is like to see colour, specifically a uniform expanse of red in front of one. They write:

> Suppose you look at a red-coloured wall. The redness is on the wall, there to be appreciated. Because we have continuous access to the present redness, it is as if you are continuously in contact with it. This would explain the fact that the redness would seem to be continuously present in experience. This point can be sharpened. The 'feeling of present redness' that would seem to accompany the seeing of something red is to be explained by the fact that we understand (in a practical sense) that at any moment we can direct our attention to the red wall (O'Regan and Noë, 2001b, p. 95).[20]

The way it seems or feels to undergo an experience of red consists, in all essentials, in the fact that we are able to direct our attention at will to the red expanse in front of us (and, presumably, that we exhibit an appropriate sensitivity to any visual transients blemishing this expanse). This ability is accompanied by an understanding of how such exploratory behaviour will be accompanied by changes in the character of sensory stimulation.

In this paragraph, O'Regan and Noë are concerned, primarily, with the sense of phenomenological *presence* of redness. However, in later passages, they also seem to suggest that a suitably extended account might explain the experience of redness itself. I do not think this model will, in fact, work for either. Just what is it towards which we are directing our attention at will, and with respect to which certain predicted changes in sensory stimulation accompany this exploration? To something with a certain molecular structure, hence a certain reflectance capacity. Towards a surface that relates to the spectrum of visible light in a certain way and which 'changes the light when the surface is moved with respect to the observer or the light source' (O'Regan and Noë, 2001a). But what we are not directing our attention towards is something that is red in anything like the phenomenal sense. And even when restricted to the issue of phenomenological presence, the model may explain our experience of an expanse of *something* that is present to us, but it will not explain the experience of an expanse of something that is *red*. Of course, we can always define red simply as a type of reflectance capacity, or as a capacity to change light in various law-like ways. But, in the present context, this would simply be a philosophical sleight of hand. That a surface with a certain reflectance capacity and which changes the ambient light when moved with respect to observer or light source should appear the way it appears to us — as red in the phenomenal sense — is just as much a problem as the original hard problem. Indeed, it is the *same* problem. The extended model of visual perception does not solve the hard problem for visual phenomenal character, it simply relocates it: it *externalizes* the hard problem.

Indeed, I have argued elsewhere that if we take seriously the idea that what it is like to undergo an experience attaches to acts of experiencing, rather than being found among experience's objects, we should abandon the idea that what it is like

---

[20] This account is developed in more sophisticated form in O'Regan and Noë (2001a).

can be reduced to anything else — even if our conceptual repertoire is Godlike (Rowlands, 2001, Ch. 10). Roughly, very roughly, this is because reduction is a process whereby the contribution the act of experience makes to an object is bracketed. What it is like to undergo an experience is, I believe, real and irreducible. It is just that it is not at all the sort of thing we have taken it to be.

Acknowledgement

I would like to thank Andy Clark, Paul Coates, Dan Hutto, Julian Kiverstein, Richard Menary, Alva Noë, Marina Rakova, David Spurrett, Susan Stuart, John Sutton, Steven Torrance and Mike Wheeler for comments on an earlier version of this paper.

References

Carruthers, P. (1998), 'Natural theories of consciousness', *European Journal of Philosophy*, **6**, pp. 53–78.
Chambers, D. and Reisberg, D. (1985), 'Can mental images be ambiguous?', *Journal of Experimental Psychology: Human Perception and Performance*, **2**, pp. 317–28.
Clark, A. (1997), *Being-There* (Cambridge, MA: MIT Press).
Clark, A. (2001), *Mindware* (Oxford: Oxford University Press).
Clark, A. and Chalmers, D.J. (1998), 'The extended mind', *Analysis*, **58**, pp. 7–19.
Dennett, D. (1991), *Consciousness Explained* (Boston, MA: Little Brown).
Donald, M. (1991) *Origins of the Modern Mind* (Cambridge, MA: Harvard University Press).
Dretske, F. (1993), 'Conscious experience', *Mind*, **102**, pp. 263–83.
Dretske, F. (1995), *Naturalizing the Mind* (Cambridge, MA: MIT Press).
Hurley, S. (1998), *Consciousness in Action* (Cambridge, MA: Harvard University Press).
Hutchins, E. (1995), *Cognition in the Wild* (Cambridge, MA: MIT Press).
Lycan, W. (1996), *Consciousness and Experience* (Cambridge, MA: MIT Press).
McGinn, C. (1997), *The Character of Mind* (Oxford: Oxford University Press).
Mackay, D.M. (1962), 'Theoretical models of space perception', in *Aspects of the Theory of Artificial Intelligence*, ed. C.A. Muses (New York: Plenum).
Mackay, D.M. (1967), 'Ways of looking at perception', in *Models for the Perception of Speech and Visual Form*, ed. W. Wathen-Dunn (Cambridge, MA: MIT Press).
Mackay, D.M. (1973), 'Visual stability and voluntary eye movements', in *Handbook of Sensory Physiology* (Vol.7), ed. R. Jung (Berlin: Springer).
Marr, D. (1982), *Vision* (San Francisco: W.H. Freeman).
Moore, G.E. (1903), 'The refutation of idealism', *Mind*, **12**, pp. 433–53.
Noë, A. (2002), 'On what we see', *Pacific Philosophical Quarterly*, **83**, pp. 57–80.
O'Regan, K. (1992), 'Solving the "real" mysteries of visual perception: the world as an outside memory', *Canadian Journal of Psychology*, **46** (3), pp. 461–88.
O'Regan, K., Deubel, H., Clark, J.J. and Rensink, R.A. (2000), 'Picture changes during blinks: looking without seeing and seeing without looking', *Visual Cognition*, **7**, pp. 191–212.
O'Regan, K. and Noë, A. (2001a), 'A sensorimotor account of vision and visual consciousness', *Behavioral and Brain Sciences*, **24** (5).
O'Regan, K. and Noë, A. (2001b), 'What is it like to see: A sensorimotor theory of perceptual experience', *Synthese*, **129**, pp. 79–103.
O'Regan, K., Rensink, R.A. and Clark, J.J. (1996), '"Mud splashes" render picture changes invisible', *Invest. Opthalmol. Vis. Sci.*, **37**, S213.
O'Regan, K., Rensink, R.A. and Clark, J.J. (1999), 'Change blindness as a result of mudsplashes', *Nature*, **398**, p. 34.
Rowlands, M. (1999), *The Body in Mind* (Cambridge: Cambridge University Press).
Rowlands, M. (2001), *The Nature of Consciousness* (Cambridge: Cambridge University Press).
Sartre, J.-P., (1943), *Being and Nothingness* (London: Methuen).
Tye, M. (1996), *Ten Problems of Consciousness* (Cambridge, MA: MIT Press).
Wittgenstein, L. (1953), *Philosophical Investigations* (Oxford: Blackwell).

Andy Clark

Is Seeing All It Seems?

Action, Reason and the Grand Illusion

We seem, or so it seems to some theorists, to experience a rich stream of highly detailed information concerning an extensive part of our current visual surroundings. But this appearance, it has been suggested, is in some way illusory. Our brains do not command richly detailed internal models of the current scene. Our seeings, it seems, are not all that they seem. This, then, is the Grand Illusion. We think we see much more than we actually do. In this paper I shall (briefly) rehearse the empirical evidence for this rather startling claim, and then critically examine a variety of responses. One especially interesting response is a development of the so-called 'skill theory', according to which there is no illusion after all. Instead, so the theory goes, we establish the required visual contact with our world by an ongoing process of active exploration, in which the world acts as a kind of reliable, interrogable, external memory (Noë et al., 2000; Noë, 2001). The most fully worked-out versions of this response (Noë and O'Regan, 2000; O'Regan and Noë, 2001)) tend, however, to tie the contents of conscious visual experience rather too tightly to quite low-level features of this ongoing sensorimotor engagement. This (I shall argue) undervalues the crucial links between perceptual experience, reason and intentional action, and opens the door to a problem that I will call 'sensorimotor chauvinism': the premature welding of experiential contents to very specific details of our embodiment and sensory apparatus. Drawing on the dual visual systems hypothesis of Milner and Goodale (1995), I sketch an alternative version of the skill theory, in which the relation between conscious visual experience and the low-level details of sensorimotor engagement is indirect and non-constitutive. The hope is thus to embrace the genuine insights of the skill theory response, while depicting conscious visual experience as most tightly geared to knowing and reasoning about our world.

I: Amazing Card Tricks

There is an entertaining web site where you can try out the following trick (http://member.tripod.com/~andybauch/magic.html; or just feed 'amazing card trick' to a search engine such as Google). You are shown, on screen, a display of

Journal of Consciousness Studies, **9**, No. 5–6, 2002, pp. 181–202

six playing cards (new ones are generated each time the trick is run). In the time-honoured tradition, you are then asked to mentally select and recall one of those cards. You click on an icon and the cards disappear, to be replaced by a brief 'distracter' display. Click again and a five-card (one less) array appears. As if by magic, the very card that you picked is the one that has been removed. How can it be? Could the computer have somehow monitored your eye movements? I confess that on first showing (and second, and third) I was quite unable to see how the trick was turned. It works equally well, to my surprise, using OHPs or a printout! Here's the secret. The original array will always comprise six cards of a similar broad type, for example, six face cards, or six assorted low-ranking cards (between about two and six), etc. When the new five-card array appears, *none* of these cards will be in the set. But the new five-card array will be of the same type, for example, face cards, low cards, whatever. In this way, the trick capitalises on the visual brain's laziness (or efficiency, if you prefer). It seems to the subject exactly as if all that has happened is that one card (the one they mentally selected!) has gone from an otherwise unchanged array. But the impression that the original array is still present is a mistake, rooted no doubt in the fact that all we had actually encoded was something like 'lots of royal cards including my mentally selected king of hearts'.[1]

Most magic tricks rely on our tendency to overestimate what we actually see in a single glance, and on the manipulation of attention so as to actively inhibit the extraction of crucial information at certain critical moments. Las Vegas and the Grand Illusion go hand in hand.

Daniel Dennett makes a similar point using a different card trick. He invites someone to stand in front of him, and to fixate his (Dennett's) nose. In each out-stretched arm Dennett holds a playing card. He brings his arms in steadily. The question is, at what point will the subject be able to identify the colour of the card? Here, too, we may be surprised. For colour sensitivity, it turns out, is available only in a small and quite central part of the visual field. Yet my conscious experience, clearly, is not as of a small central pool of colour surrounded by a vague and out-of-focus expanse of halftones. Things look coloured all the way out. Once again, it begins to look as if my conscious visual experience is overestimating the amount and quality of information it makes available. Talk of a Grand Illusion is clearly on the cards.[2]

II: Seeing, Seeming and The Space for Error

How should we characterise the kind of visual overestimation highlighted by the card tricks (and by the experimental evidence to be examined in the next section)? The matter is delicate. We cannot, surely, make much sense of the idea that we are wrong about how our visual experience visually *seems*. If it seems to me

---

[1] Recall Dennett's 'many Marilyns' example, as described in Dennett (1991).

[2] To my knowledge, the phrase 'Grand Illusion' was first used in Noë *et al.* (2000), which was a critique of the idea that visual experience involved any such illusion.

as if I see colours 'all the way out' then that simply *is* how it seems to me: there is little space for error in this space of seemings.

About what, then, might I actually be mistaken? Not about the visual seeming itself. And not, of course, about the actual real-world scene. That scene, in the typical case, really is coloured all the way out, and really is rich in detail, etc. The space for genuine error is thus rather small. It must centre on what we *come to believe* as a result of how our visual experience presents the world to us. Perhaps, for example, we come to believe that our brains are constructing, moment-by-moment, a richly detailed, constantly updated internal representation of the full, and fully coloured, visual scene. Noë *et al.* (2000) term this the 'reconstructionist' model of vision. The idea of a rich visual buffer (Feldman, 1985), in which more and more information accumulates over time is also grist to this kind of mill.

On both these counts, science could easily show us to be wrong. But (as Noë *et al.* point out) our error would be a technical one: an error in the theory that our experience leads us (some of us) to construct. This sounds rather less grand than the claim that we are simply mistaken about the nature of our own visual experience, or subject to some kind of experiential illusion.

It is possible, even more radically, to be sceptical about the very idea of a 'way things visually seem to us', at least insofar as such seemings are depicted as objects of conscious awareness. In this vein Mark Rowlands (ms) suggests that 'what it is like to undergo an experience is not something *of* which we are aware but something *with* which we are aware in the having of an experience'. Visual seemings, he suggests, are not objects of normal visual experience, so much as modes of experiencing the world. As such, they do not seem any way at all: instead, via the experiences, the *world* seems this way or that.

There is good reason, then, to be a little cautious of statements such as 'The visual world seems to naive reflection to be uniformly detailed and focussed from the centre out to the boundaries, but . . . this is not so'. (Dennett, 1991, p. 53). Much depends, of course, on just what gets built into the idea of 'naive reflection' (how naive, and by whom?). At the very least it looks likely that the path to Grand Illusion is paved by inferences: inferences that concern the internal machinery of seeing and take us far beyond the simple act of visually knowing the world.

But surely, someone will reply, there is also an illusion within the domain of the experience itself. It does not seem to us as if our colour vision is as restricted as it is. So there is error in the way things visually seem. Rowlands would reject this, for the reasons just examined. But in any case, the response assumes, illegitimately, that whatever is true of our experience must be true of the underlying machinery, and at a kind of instantaneous time-slice at that. Perhaps there need be no such match. Or if there is a match, it may be between visual activity over time and the contents of the experience.

The space for genuine error, I conclude, is not as large as it may initially appear. The kernel of truth in the sweeping talk of a Grand Illusion must be sought in a careful analysis of certain theoretical commitments. With that in mind, let's start by taking a look at the experimental data that fuels much of the debate.

III: What Goes Unnoticed[3]

It is well known that the human visual system supports only a small area of high-resolution processing; an area corresponding to the fraction of the visual field which is currently foveated. When we inspect a visual scene, our brains actively move this small high-resolution window around the scene, alighting first on one location, then another. The whole of my bookcase, for example, cannot possibly fit into this high-resolution window at a glance, at least while I remain seated at my desk. My overall visual field (including the low-resolution peripheries) is, of course, much larger, and a sizeable chunk of my bookshelf falls within my course-grained view. As long ago as 1967 (Yarbus, 1967) it was known that the brain makes intelligent use of the small high-resolution area, moving it around the scene (in a sequence of so-called 'visual saccades') in ways suited to the specific problem at hand. Human subjects confronted with *identical* pictures, but preparing to solve *different* kinds of problem (for example, 'give the sex and ages of the people in the picture', 'describe what is going on' and so on) show very different patterns of visual saccade. These saccades, it is also worth commenting, are fast — perhaps three per second — and often repetitive, in that they may visit and re-visit the very same part of the scene.

One possibility, at this point, was that each saccade is being used to slowly build up a detailed internal representation of the *salient* aspects of the scene. The visual system would thus be selective, but would still be using input to build up an increasingly detailed neural image of (selected aspects of) the scene. Subsequent research, however, suggests that the real story is even stranger than that.

Imagine that you are the subject of this famous experiment (McConkie, 1990; O'Regan, 1990).[4] You are sat in front of a computer screen on which is displayed a page of text. Your eye movements are being automatically tracked and monitored. Your experience, as you report it, is of a solid, stable page of text which you can read in the usual way. The experimenter then reveals the trick. In fact, the text to the left and right of a moving 'window' has been constantly filled with junk characters, not proper English text at all. But because the small window of normal, sensible text has been marching in step with your central perceptual span, you never noticed anything odd or unusual. It is as if my bookshelf only contained (at any one moment) four or five proper, clearly titled books, and the rest was fuzzy, senseless junk. But those four or five proper items were moved about as my eyes saccaded around the scene! In the case of the screen of text, the window of 'good stuff' needed to support the illusion is about 18 characters wide, with the bulk of those falling to the right of the point of fixation (because English is read left to right).

Similar experiments have been performed using pictures of a visual scene, such as a house, with a parked car and a garden (McConkie, 1990; O'Regan, 1992). As before, the subject sits in front of a computer-generated display. Her

---

[3]   Most of the experiments descibed below can be viewed on the web. Try
http://nivea.psycho.univ-paris5.fr, http://coglab.wjh.harvard.edu, http://www.cbr.com/~rensink.

[4]   See also discussion in Churchland *et al.* (1994).

eye movements are monitored and, while she saccades around the display, changes are clandestinely made: the colours of flowers and cars are altered, the structure of the house may be changed. Such changes, likewise, go undetected. We now begin to understand why the patterns of saccade are not cumulative — why we visit and repeatedly re-visit the same locations. It is because our brains just don't bother to create even the kind of selective-but-rich inner models we earlier considered. Why should they? The world itself is still there, a complex and perfect store of all that data, nicely poised for swift retrieval as and when needed by the simple expedient of visual saccade to a selected location. The kind of knowledge that counts, it begins to seem, is not detailed knowledge of what's out there, so much as a broad idea of what's out there: one capable of informing those on-the-spot processes of information retrieval and use.

Finally, lest we suspect that these effects (known as 'change blindness') are somehow caused by the unnaturalness of the experimental situation, consider some recent work by Dan Simons and Dan Levin. Simons and Levin (1997) took the research into the real world. They set up a king of slapstick scenario in which an experimenter would pretend to be lost on the Cornell Campus, and would approach an unsuspecting passer-by to ask for directions. Once the passer-by started to reply, two people carrying a large door would (rudely!) walk right between the enquirer and the passer-by. During the walk through, however, the original enquirer is replaced by a different person. Only 50% of the direction-givers noticed the change. Yet the two experimenters were of different heights, wore different clothes, had very different voices and so on. Moreover, those who did notice the change were students of roughly the same age and demographics as the two experimenters. In a follow-up study, the students failed to spot the change when the experimenters appeared as construction workers, placing them in a different social group. The conclusion that Simons and Levin (1997, p. 266) draw is that our failures to detect change arise because 'we lack a precise representation of our usual world from one view to the next'. We encode only a kind of 'rough gist' of the current scene — just enough to support a broad sense of what's going on *insofar as it matters to us*, and to guide further intelligent information-retrieval as and when needed.

In all these cases, the unnoticed changes are made under cover of some distracting event: they are made during a saccade, a screen flicker, a movie cut and so on. These mask the visual transients (motion cues) that might otherwise draw attention to the fact that something is changing.

The importance of attention is underlined by a different series of experiments due to Mack and Rock (1998). These concern what they call 'inattentional blindness'. The focus here is not on change over time, so much as upon what can be noticed in a static scene (for an excellent discussion of this at times elusive distinction, see Rensink, 2000). The question guiding the experiments was thus simply 'What is consciously perceived in the absence of visual attention?' and more particularly 'Will an object, unexpectedly presented in the visual field, tend to be consciously noticed?'

A typical experiment went like this. Subjects were shown a visually presented cross (on a computer screen) and asked to report which arm of the cross was longer. The difference was small, so the task required some attention and effort. The cross was briefly presented (for about 200 ms)and then a mask (an unrelated, patterned stimulus) shown. Then the subjects made their reports. On the third or fourth trial, however, a 'critical stimulus' was also shown on the screen with the cross. It might be a coloured square, a moving bar, and so on. Subjects were not expecting this. The question was, would it be consciously noticed?

The experiment was run in two main forms. In the first, the cross was presented centrally, at the point of fixation, and the critical stimulus parafoveally (to the side). In the second, subjects fixated a central point, the cross was presented parafoveally and the critical stimulus appeared just beside the fixation point. With the critical stimulus presented parafoveally, 25% of subjects failed to spot it. This is already a surprising result. But when presented near fixation, a full 75% of subjects failed to report the stimulus! Why the difference? Perhaps the need to focus visual attention away from the normal central point demanded increased visual effort and attention. Also, subjects may have had to actively inhibit information from the point of fixation. Interestingly, in both cases, subjects did spot more meaningful stimuli, such as their own names, or a smiley face: a quirk which will turn out to make good sense in the light of our final story.

Our unconscious and inattentive use of visual input may, in addition, be surprisingly extensive. For example, other words which were used as the critical stimulus in some of Mack and Rock's experiments, though unnoticed, were capable of priming subsequent choices. Exposure to the word 'provide' increases the likelihood of the stem completion 'pro' with 'vide', despite the subject's total lack of conscious awareness of the initial stimulus.

From all of this, Mack and Rock draw a strong and unambiguous conclusion. There is, they claim 'no conscious perception at all in the absence of attention' (*op. cit.*, p. 227). This would be trivial if attention itself were defined in terms of, say, our conscious awareness of an object. But what Mack and Rock really mean is that there is no conscious perception in the absence of expectations and intentions directed at an object. They offer no clear definition of attention itself. But *inattention* is quite well characterised:

> For a subject to qualify as inattentive to a particular visual stimulus, the subject must be looking in the general area in which it appears, but must have no expectation that it will appear nor any intention regarding it (Mack and Rock, 1998, p. 243).

The importance of attention and expectation is nowhere more apparent than in another famous experiment in which subjects watch a video of two teams, one in white and one in black, passing basketballs (one ball per team).[5] The viewer must count the number of successful passes made by the white team. Afterwards, subjects are asked whether they saw anything else, anything unusual. In fact, about 45 seconds into the film an intruder walks through the players. The intruder

---

[5] The original experiment was done by Neisser (1979). Recent versions, including the opaque case, are due to Simons and Chabris (1999).

might be a semi-transparent, ghostly figure of a woman holding an umbrella, or a semi-transparent gorilla (without any umbrella). Or even, on some trials, a fully opaque woman or gorilla! In the semi-transparent condition, 73% of subjects failed to see the gorilla, and even in the opaque condition, 35% of subjects failed to spot it (see Simons, 2000, p. 152).

Simons interprets these results as suggesting the possibility:

> That our intuitions about attentional capture reflect a *metacognitive error*: We do not realise the degree to which we are blind to unattended and unexpected stimuli and we mistakenly believe that important events will automatically draw our attention away from our current task or goals (Simons, 2000, p.154, my emphasis).

It is easy to see, given the work on change blindness and inattentional blindness, why talk of a Grand Illusion can seem so compelling. Conscious vision, it can quickly seem, delivers far less than we think.

IV: Diagnoses

There are, as far as I know, four main responses to the bodies of data reviewed in Section II. They are:

1. The Grand Illusion
2. Fleeting Awareness with Rapid Forgetting
3. Projected (memory-based) Richness
4. Skill Theory

Hints of the Grand Illusion response can be seen in many treatments from Dennett 1991 onwards, including Ballard (1991), O'Regan (1992) Churchland *et al.* (1994), Clark (1997) and Simons and Levin (1997). The idea is simple and attractive. We do indeed (it is claimed) seem to experience a continuous stream of richly detailed, wide-angled, fully coloured, new-input-sensitive information in the conscious visual modality. But the seeming is just that: a seeming. It is an illusion caused by our ability to visually visit and re-visit different aspects of the scene according to our projects and as 'captured' (sometimes) by motion transients, etc. We thus think that our at-a-glance visual uptake is much richer than it is due to our active capacity to get more information as and when required. Thus we read that:

> The feeling of the presence and extreme richness of the visual world is . . . a kind of illusion, created by the immediate availability of the information in (an) external store [the real world] (O'Regan, 1992, p. 461).

> The experiential nature of the visual scene is a kind of subjective visual illusion created by the use of rapid scanning and a small window of resolution and attention (Clark, 1997, p. 31).

> The visual system provides the illusion of three-dimensional stability by virtue of being able to execute fast behaviours (Ballard, 1991, p. 60).

The real, non-illusory, knowledge built up by our ongoing visual contact with a scene is, on these models, quite schematic and high-level. We maintain a general sense of the situation, just enough to guide attention and saccades while we actively engage in a scene-related task.

An alternative hypothesis is the so-called 'fleeting awareness' account (also known as 'inattentional amnesia') presented by Wolfe (1999). The suggestion is that our moment-by-moment conscious visual experience may be rich and detailed indeed, but that we simply forget, pretty well immediately, what the details were unless they impact our plans and projects very directly. Since these paradigms always involve questioning at least fractionally after the event, subjects say they did not see the new objects, etc. But this reflects a failure of memory rather than a deficit in ongoing conscious visual experience.

Some element of forgetting may, I accept, be involved in some of these cases. But overall, the hypothesis strikes me as unconvincing. First of all, it is not really clear whether 'seeing-with-immediate-forgetting' is really any different from not seeing at all. (Recall Dennett's 1991 discussion of Stalinesque versus Orwellian accounts). Second, we know that only a very small window of the visual field can afford high-resolution input (Ballard, 1991), and we know that attentional mechanisms probably limit our capacity to about 44 bits (plus or minus 15) per glimpse (see Verghese and Pelli, 1992; Churchland *et al.* ,1994). So how does all that fleeting richness get transduced? And last, as Simons (2000) niccly points out, the inattentional amnesia account seems especially improbable when the stimulus was an opaque gorilla presented for up to nine seconds. Could we really have been consciously aware of that and then had it slip our minds?

A third diagnosis invokes memory in a more active role: in the role of 'filling in' the missing detail. The suggestion is that our conscious visual experience is enriched 'top down' by stored memories and expectations. So we do indeed see a highly detailed scene. It is just that, in a sense, we make most of it up! I suspect that this suggestion contains an important kernel of truth and we shall return to it in Section VI where we display strong links between conscious experience and certain kinds of memory system.

By far the most interesting, deep and challenging response, however, is one which rejects the Grand Illusion diagnosis while nonetheless *accepting* the poverty of the moment-by-moment internal representations that the visual system creates and maintains. According to this response, the Grand Illusion is itself a chimera, caused by the fall-out from a classical, disembodied approach to perception. If we were to *really* embrace the idea of cognition as the active engagement of organism and world, the suggestion goes, we would see that there is no Grand Illusion after all. Hints of this idea were present, right alongside the Grand Illusion diagnosis, in O'Regan (1992), drawing on MacKay (1967). But the most clear-cut, powerful and persuasive versions are those of Noë *et al.* (2000), Noë (2001), Noë and O'Regan (2000), and O'Regan and Noë (2001a).

Before proceeding, I must enter a caveat. Noë *et al.* (2000) argue, convincingly I believe, that the Grand Illusion diagnosis is a mistake, and that it is a mistake caused by failing to appreciate that seeing is a temporally extended process involving active exploration of the environment. My critical concern, in what follows, is not with this general claim but with the specific way it is unpacked, in the context of a more fully worked-out version of the skill theory, in O'Regan and Noë (2001a). For this specific version of the skill theory (I shall argue) ties conscious visual experience too closely to the full gamut of (what one might question-beggingly describe as) the 'implementation detail' of the visual apparatus. My goal will be to develop an account in the spirit both of skill theory and of Noe *et al.*'s critique of the Grand Illusion claim. But it will be an account that leaves room for some details of the visual apparatus to make no difference to the contents or character of conscious visual experience.

A good place to start is with the MacKay-based example given by O'Regan (1992; also mentioned in O'Regan and Noë, 2001a). The reader is invited to consider the tactile experience of holding a bottle in the hand. As you hold the bottle, your fingertips are in touch with just a few small parts of the surface. Yet what you experience is having the whole bottle in your grasp. This, it is argued, is because:

> My tactile perception of the bottle is provided by my exploration of it with my fingers, that is, by the sequence of changes in sensation that are provoked by this exploration and by the relation between the changes that occur and my knowledge of what bottles are like . . . I expect that if I move my hand up . . . I will encounter the cap or cork (O'Regan, 1992, p. 471, following MacKay, 1967).

Our conscious tactile experience as of holding a whole bottle is thus generated by our implicit (not conscious, propositional) knowledge of how those more local fingertip sensations would flow and alter were we to actively explore the surface. The conscious perceptual content is thus based on actual and potential action cycles rather than on the instantaneously transduced information. This kind of implicit knowledge of reliable flows of sensory input during the execution of movements and actions is what O'Regan and Noë (2001a) dub 'mastery of laws of sensorimotor contingency' (Section 3.2).

Consider next the case of conscious seeing. In some ways, this is an even better case for the sensorimotor contingency model, since here we combine the input from the high-resolution moveable fovea with low-resolution peripheral signals capable of further aiding intelligent exploration. Our visual awareness of the scene before is thus grounded in a potent combination of:

(1) Our implicit knowledge of how the foveated input will change as we actively explore the scene.
(2) The ongoing sequence of cues provided by peripheral pick-up.
(3) Quite high-level knowledge of the nature of the scene or event we are witnessing.

Taking all these into account, it does indeed seem churlish to describe our ongoing visual experience as misleading. The impression we have of rich and available detail is correct, as long as we avoid a kind of temporal error. The Grand Illusion diagnosis trades, perhaps illegitimately, upon the idea that the content of conscious visual perceiving is given by some instantaneous, fully internally represented deliverance of the sense organs. It trades upon the idea of simple inner state without past or future trajectory.

It may perhaps be useful to consider an analogy. When you encounter certain web pages, you may have a strong impression of richness. This impression is grounded in your perception of a screen rich in pointers to other sites and your implicit knowledge that you can access those other sites with a simple flick of the mouse. Such a web page leaves us poised to access a wealth of other data pretty much at will.

Following Kirsh (1991) I have argued elsewhere (Clark, 1993) that externally stored information which is poised for swift, easy and intelligent retrieval as-and-when needed should sometimes be regarded as *already represented* within the cognitive system. (It is this general commitment that leads, for example, to the 'extended mind' story found in Clark and Chalmers, 1998). The real-world scene, as O'Regan and others have pointed out, often meets this criterion, and should thus be regarded as a temporary, ever-changing module of external memory. The act of foveation-with-attention effectively moves information out of this module and into a kind of working memory buffer, making it available for the guidance of intentional and deliberate action (see Ballard *et al.*, 1997) on 'deictic pointers' for a worked out, experimentally supported version of this kind of story). Indeed, as long ago as 1972, Newell and Simon commented that:

> From a functional viewpoint, the STM should be defined not as an internal memory but as the combination of (1) the internal STM and (2) the part of the visual display that is in the subject's foveal view (Newell and Simon, 1972).

The feeling of visual richness, I want to suggest, is thus a bit like the feeling of 'knowing a lot about pulp detective novels'. It is not that all that arcane knowledge is there all at once, actively co-present in conscious awareness. Rather, what is present is a kind of meta-knowledge: the knowledge that you can retrieve just about any relevant bit of all that information as and when required, and deploy it in the service of your current conscious goals. Our conscious experience of visual richness, if this is at all on track, is an experience of a kind of *problem-solving poise*.

All this, it seems to me, is correct and important. But the rather specific version of the skill theory presented by O'Regan and Noë (2001a) is more radical in at least two respects. First, because it depicts the skill theory as a direct dissolution of the 'hard problem' of visual qualia. Second, because it endorses (what I suspect to be) an overly motoric view of the wellsprings of conscious visual awareness.

My goal in the remainder of the paper will be to flesh out these worries, and to offer a weakened (regarding the 'hard problem') and amended (regarding the role of motor action) version of a skill-theoretic account.

V: Sensorimotor Chauvinism and The Hard Problem

O'Regan and Noë offer an unusually clear, and refreshingly ambitious story. The 'hard problem' of explaining visual qualia (what it is like to see red, why it is like anything at all to see red, etc.) is, they suggest, simply unable to arise. And the explanatory gap thus feared between scientific accounts and the understanding of qualitative consciousness is no gap at all. The trouble arises, they suggest, only if we falsely believe that visual qualia are properties of experiential states. And this is (it is claimed) a theoretical mis-step since:

> Experiences . . . are not states. They are ways of acting. They are things we do . . . there are, in this sense at least, no (visual) qualia. Qualia are an illusion and the explanatory gap is no real gap at all (O'Regan and Noë, 2001a, Section 6.3).

Dispelling the Grand Illusion illusion, it now seems, requires us to embrace an even greater oddity: the idea that qualia, properly speaking, do not exist! To sweeten the medicine the authors use the familiar (ok, so mine's a Ford) example of driving a Porsche. There is, they admit, 'something that it is like to drive a Porsche' but this 'something it is like' does not consist in the occurrence of a special kind of internal representation (the kind supposedly accompanied by qualia). Rather it consists in 'one's comfortable exercise of one's knowledge of sensorimotor contingencies governing the behavior of the car' (Section 6.4). The driver knows, that is to say, how the car will corner, accelerate, and respond to braking, and much more besides. Most of this knowledge is non-propositional, more in the realm of skilled know-how than reflective awareness. But knowing what it is like to drive a Porsche just is, the authors argue, having a bunch of such know-how. Similarly, knowing what it is like to see a red cube is simply knowing how the image of the cube will distort and alter as you move your eyes, how uneven illumination will affect the inputs, etc. In all these cases it is the fact that our knowledge is implicit, knowing-how not knowing-that, that makes it seem as if there is something 'ineffable' going on (Section 6.7).

But this is not convincing. Consider a fairly simple ping-pong-playing robot: a descendent, perhaps, of the fairly successful prototype described in Andersson (1988).[6] The robot uses multiple cameras, and it has an arm and a paddle. A modest on-line planning system plots initial paddle-to-ball trajectories, but this is soon improved during play and practice as the system learns to use simpler visual cues to streamline and tune its behaviour. The robot, let us suppose, develops (courtesy of a neural network controller) a body of implicit knowledge of the relevant sensorimotor contingencies. Finally, it is able to deploy this knowledge in the service of some simple goals, such as the goal of winning, but not by more than three points. At this moment, as far as I can tell, all of O'Regan and Noë's conditions have been met:

> For a creature (or a machine for that matter) to possess visual awareness, what is required is that, in addition to exercising the mastery of the sensorimotor contingencies, it must make use of this exercise for the purposes of thought and planning (O'Regan and Noë, 2001a, Section 2.6).

Assuming, then, that the term 'thought' is not here begging the question (by meaning something like 'experience-accompanied reasoning'), the ping-pong robot is a locus of qualitative visual experience. But while a few philosophers

---

[6]   This example is from Clark and Toribio (in press, 2001).

might take a deep breath and agree, I suggest that the attribution of qualitative consciousness is fairly obviously out of place here. O'Regan and Noë (2001a) appeared to bite the bullet by endorsing a kind of continuum view of qualitative consciousness and allowing that this kind of robot would indeed have some of it . In a footnote to the paper they write that:

> Because we admit that awareness comes in degrees, we are willing to say that to the extent that machines can plan and have rational behaviour, precisely to that same extent they are also aware (O'Regan and Noë, 2001a, Section 2.6, footnote 10).

The question, I think, is whether we should *at this very early stage in the investigation of qualitative consciousness* simply give up on the main intuitions that currently demarcate the very target of our theorising (intuitions such as: we have it, the ping-pong robot doesn't, and we aren't sure about a lot of animals). In my view, the price of giving up these intuitions so soon is that we will never know when (or if) we have explained what we set out to. The pay-off (a very neat theory) is surely not worth this cost. Moreover, we know from our own experience that visual information can guide apparently goal-based activity while we are quite unaware of it doing so. Back in the Porsche, we may make a successful turn to head for home while fully engaged in some other task. Knowing just how much we ourselves can achieve with non-conscious sub-systems at the wheel, we are rightly suspicious of attributing too much too soon to the ping-pong robots of this world.

In response to the ping-pong-playing robot counter-example, O'Regan and Noë suggest that the robot described is ' far too simple to be a plausible candidate for perceptual consciousness of the kind usually attributed to animals or humans' (O'Regan and Noë, 2001b). This simplicity is said to consist both in a lack of advanced sensorimotor skills and in the absence of a thick background of intentions, thoughts, concepts and language (*ibid.*). Nonetheless, it still seems to me that the robot described meets the letter of the requirements laid out and should (on their official account) be granted some small degree of conscious visual awareness — even if not 'of the kind' (though this is a somewhat vague and elusive notion) attributed to more complex beings

In addition, as Mark Rowlands has argued in this volume (2002), even the general form of the attempted dissolution of the hard problem is suspect. First, since the hard problem arises for all varieties of phenomenal experience, it seems fair to ask how well the skill-based account will fare with the others? And for cases such as the feeling of depression, elation, pain, etc., it is not at all clear how it will work. Second, from the fact that a certain theoretical gloss on the hard problem is rejected, we cannot conclude that the problem itself has gone away. Thus, we may agree that it is misleading to think of the hard problem as the problem of how certain internal representations come to generate qualitative experience. But it would not follow that the question, How is such experience possible?, is somehow mis-posed. Taking the full skill-based story on board, the question can still be asked: Why is it like *anything at all* to see red, to drive a Porsche, etc.?

The hard problem really has two components which need to be kept distinct. The first is: Why is such-and-such an experience like this rather than like that (why does Marmite taste like this and not like something else?). The second is: Why is it like anything at all? Many theories that get a purchase on the former fail to illuminate the latter, and the skill theory belongs in this camp. The pattern of sensorimotor contingencies may help to explain why experiences have the contents they do but not why it is like anything at all to have them. (Conversely, accounts such as Clark (2000), which try to address the latter question, often fail to say anything about the former. We learn why it seems like something, but not why it seems the way it does!).

From here on, I shall understand the skill theory as an attempt to shed light on why certain experiences seem the way they do rather than why they seem like anything at all. Even thus understood, the O'Regan and Noë proposal faces a rather important challenge. For the way the story is developed, it runs the risk (or so it seems to me) of a certain kind of *over-sensitivity to low-level motoric variation*. This kind of over-sensitivity I shall label 'sensorimotor chauvinism'. Here's what I have in mind.

It is an implication of the way O'Regan and Noë develop the skill theory that my conscious visual experience depends very sensitively upon my implicit knowledge of a very specific set of sensorimotor contingencies, including those that they term 'apparatus-related', i.e., relating to the body and sensory apparatus itself. Now certainly, they want to allow that what is broadly speaking *visual* experience could indeed be supported by many different kinds of sensing device, including TVSS arrays, etc. It is the structure of the rules of sensorimotor contingency that matters, not the stuff. Nonetheless, it is equally clear that very small differences in the body and sensory apparatus will make a substantial difference to the precise set of sensorimotor contingencies that are implicitly known. And, indeed, the authors are at pains to stress the importance of, for example, the precise way the sensory stimulation on the retina shifts and changes as we move our eyes (O'Regan and Noë, 2001b), as helping to fix the pattern of sensorimotor contingencies. But of course it is (on their account) this very pattern that in turn determines the nature and content of our conscious visual experience.

The suspicion I want to voice, then, is that this may make the contents of my visual experience *too* sensitive to the very precise, low-level details of sensory pick-up and apparatus. Suppose, for example, that my eyes saccade fractionally faster than yours. This will change the pattern of sensorimotor contingencies. But why should we believe that *every* such change in this pattern will yield a change, however minute, in the nature and contents of my conscious visual awareness? If we don't believe this, then we will want to know what makes it the case that *some* changes in patterns of sensorimotor contingency impact conscious visual experience and some don't. In sum, O'Regan and Noë must either accept that *every difference makes a difference* or they owe us an account of which ones matter and why.

In response to this charge, O'Regan and Noë embrace the idea that every difference makes a difference. Indeed, they embrace the strongest form of this idea, saying that their view:

Allows for the judgement that creatures with radically different kinds of physical make-up can enjoy experience which is, to an important degree, the same in content and quality. But it also allows for the possibility *(indeed the necessity) that where there are physical differences, there are also qualitative differences* (O'Regan and Noë, 2001b; my emphasis).

It is this latter consequence which I shall reject. The question of what differences make a difference should, I believe, be an open empirical question. It should not be foreclosed by an overly enthusiastic development of the skill–theory. For skill theory, as I have argued elsewhere (Clark, 1999; in press), has the resources to allow for many different kinds of way in which cognition may be 'action-oriented' and some of these leave plenty of room for loosening the ties between the full gamut of physical apparatus and the contents and character of conscious experience.

Indeed, the resolution of this conundrum is hinted at by O'Regan and Noë's own (very proper) insistence on the importance, for conscious vision, of linking currently exercised mastery of sensorimotor contingencies to planning, deliberation and intentional action. Mastery of the laws of sensorimotor contingency, O'Regan and Noë insist, must be exercised 'for the purposes of thought and planning' (2001a, Section 2.6). But this very role, I shall next suggest, may act as a kind of filter on the type and level of detail (of mastery of sensorimotor contingencies) that matters for the determination of the contents of conscious visual experience.

VI: Reason, Action and Experience

Here's where we seem to be. We began with the idea that our visual experience may not be all it seems: that we may be misled into thinking we see more, and are sensitive to more changes, than we actually are. Careful examination suggests, however, that what is really at fault is a certain theoretical model of that in which conscious seeing consists. If conscious seeing were forced to consist in the internal tokening, moment-by-moment, of a constantly updated model of the scene then we would indeed be wildly misled by our experiences of visual richness. For our persisting internal representations, such as they are, appear to be sparse and high-level, supplemented by more detailed information retrieved at the last possible moment and kept only for the duration of the appropriate element of the task.

The skill-theoretic approach offers an alternative theoretical model, relative to which our error is much less dramatic. By highlighting the way temporally extended information-seeking activity actually *constitutes* successful contact with a rich and detailed external scene, skill theory dispels the miasma of Grand Illusion. Our visual experience reflects our successful engagement with the richness of the scene. O'Regan and Noë's marvellously detailed development of the skill-theoretic line threatens, however, to tie conscious visual experience too closely to the precise details of the low-level sensorimotor routines by means of which this engagement proceeds. Yet the resources are all there to support a slightly different kind of skill-theoretic story. For O'Regan and Noë also insist, importantly, on the profound connection between conscious visual experience and intentional action: the kinds of action we would describe as 'deliberate' and as emanating from the conscious endorsement of reasons and plans. Proper attention to this dimension suggests a slightly different way to develop and deploy the skill-theoretic intuitions.

We can creep up on this by highlighting a second way in which we might perhaps be accused of misunderstanding the nature and role of our own conscious visual experience. This is by making what I call (Clark, in press) the Assumption of Experience-Based Control:

Assumption of Experience-Based Control (EBC)
The details of our conscious visual experience are what guide fine-tuned motor activity in the here-and-now.

We often relax this assumption when reflecting upon, for example, our experiences of playing sports, etc. At such moments we realise that there is really no way our conscious visual experience is fine-tuning our actions. But we seem to believe, for the most part, that our conscious seeings are usually guiding and controlling our visually based activities. To see ourselves aright, then, it is important to be very clear about the precise sense of control and guidance that is most likely actually at work.

Taken at face value, the assumption of experience-based control is increasingly suspect. Thus, consider Milner and Goodale's provocative claim that 'what we think we "see" is not what guides our actions' (Milner and Goodale, 1995, p. 177). The idea, which will be familiar to many readers, is that online visually guided action is supported by neural resources that are fundamentally distinct from, and at least quasi-independent of, those that support conscious visual experience, off-line imagistic reasoning, and visual categorisation and planning. More specifically, the claim is that the human cognitive architecture includes two fairly distinct 'visual brains'. One, the more ancient, is specialised for the visually based control of here-and-now fine motor action. The other, more recent, is dedicated to the explicit-knowledge-and-memory-based selection of deliberate and planned actions (what Milner and Goodale (1998, p. 4) nicely describe as 'insight, hindsight and foresight about the visual world'). The former is then identified with the dorsal visual-processing stream leading to the posterior parietal lobule, and the latter with the ventral stream projecting to inferotemporal cortex.

Computationally, some such division of labour makes good sense. The fine-grained control of action (the precise details of the visually guided reach for the coffee cup etc) requires rapidly processed, constantly updated, egocentrically specified information about form, orientation, distance, etc. Conceptual thought (the identification of objects and the selection of deliberate actions) requires the identification of objects and situations according to category and significance, quite irrespective of the precise details of retinal image size, etc. Achieving a computationally efficient coding for either of these pretty much precludes the use of that very same coding for the other. In each case, as Milner and Goodale note, we need to extract, filter, and throw away different aspects of the signal and to perform very different kinds of operation and transformation.

Concrete evidence in support of the dual visual systems view comes in three main forms. First, single-cell recordings that show the different response characteristics of cells in the two streams. For example, PP (posterior parietal) neurons that respond maximally to combinations of visual cues and motor actions, and IT (inferotemporal) neurons that prefer complex object-centred features independently of location in egocentric space (see, for example, Milner and Goodale, 1995, p. 63). Second, there are the various pathologies. The most famous example is DF, a ventrally compromised patient who claims she has no conscious visual experience of the shape and orientation of objects but who can nonetheless perform quite fluent motor actions (such as pre-orienting and posting a letter through a visually presented slot). Importantly, DF fails to perform well if a time delay is introduced between presentation of the slot and selection (with the slot now out of sight) of an orientation. This presumably shifts the burden from the intact, putatively non-conscious dorsal stream to the impaired ventral resource dedicated to memory, planning and deliberate action selection. Optic ataxics, conversely, are dorsally impaired and claim to see the objects perfectly well despite being unable to engage them by fluent behaviours. These patients are actually helped by the introduction of a short time delay. Third, there is some (controversial) evidence from normal subjects. Certain visual illusions, for example, seem to affect our conscious perceptions without impairing our ongoing visuomotor motions.[7] In these cases, Milner and Goodale suggest, the non-conscious dorsal stream controls the fine-tuned motions and is immune to the illusion, which arises due to processing idiosyncrasies in the ventral stream. (And in these cases, likewise, introduction of a time delay blocks the accurate performance).

Milner and Goodale end their account with a model of how the two visual brains interact. The interaction, they suggest, occurs precisely at the level of intentional agency. Conscious visual experience can select the targets of actions and the types of action to be performed. For example, conscious vision is used to select the red cup on the left and to decide on a grip appropriate to throwing rather than drinking. But it is then left to the non-conscious dorsal stream to work out how to implement these plans and ideas.

Milner and Goodale, it is reasonable to suspect (and see Clark, 1999; in press, for some details), overplay the extent to which the two streams work in near isolation. For example, Pascual-Leone and Walsh (2001), in an elegant application of TMS (transcranial magnetic stimulation) show that feedback from high to low-level visual areas (from V5/MT to V1 and V2) is necessary for certain kinds of conscious visual perception. This opens up the intriguing possibility that upstream activity of many kinds could directly modify conscious visual awareness by altering activity at the common gateway to both streams. And there are, without doubt, many complex and iterated interactions which compromise the

---

[7]   For example, the Tichener Circles illusion discussed in Milner and Goodale (1995, Ch. 6 — see Clark [in press] for an extended discussion of this case.

isolationist integrity of the two streams. Moreover, there is a convincing case to be made that the degree of stream independence, and (conversely) the nature and extent of stream interaction, is both task and attention dependent (see Brenner and Smeets, 1996; Jeannerod, 1997; Decety and Grezes, 1999; Rensink, 2000; Carey, 2001; and discussion in Clark, in press).

A weakened version of the dual visual systems hypothesis, however, enjoys widespread support (for example, Jeannerod (1997), Decety and Grezes (1999)). Such accounts accept the task-variability of the inter-stream relationship and leave room for complex feedback-modulated interactions but they preserve the essential insight, which is that substantial amounts of fine-action-guiding visual processing are often carried out independently of the processing underlying conscious visual awareness. Such accounts accept that when we keep looking while performing a task, we are indeed feeding two sets of (partially interacting) processes: one more ancient, concerned with fine visuomotor action in the here-and-now, the other more recent, and geared towards reasoning and conscious awareness. It is the latter system, geared towards spotting the meaningful in a way fit for reasoned action-selection, that is also most closely associated with semantic and episodic memory systems.

Consider, to take just one more example, a series of experiments in which subjects were required to both visually track and manually point out a visually presented target. This target, however, was sometimes suddenly (unexpectedly) slightly displaced after the original presentation. Bridgeman *et al.* (1979) showed that subjects would accommodate this displacement (as evidenced by accurate saccades and pointing) whilst remaining quite unaware that the target had moved. Moreover, in those cases where the displacement was large enough to attract attention and hence to enter conscious awareness, the on-line adjustments were much less fluid and less successful (for a rehearsal, see Milner and Goodale, 1995, p. 161).

To round this story off, Wong and Mack (1981) showed that subjects who automatically and unconsciously accommodate the smaller displacements will, if subsequently asked to point to the remembered location of the (now-removed) target, actually point to the original (non-displaced) location. Similar results have been obtained for grasping motions directed at present versus remembered visually displayed objects (see Milner and Goodale, 1995, pp. 170–3). Memory-driven responses thus seem to be tied to the contents of conscious visual experience, while on-line object-engaging performance is driven by a distinct and more sensitive resource.

The Assumption of Experience-based Control thus needs to handled with extreme care. Our conscious visual experiences certainly impact our choices of actions. But they do not do so by virtue of providing the visual information that is itself used for the fine-tuned control of movement. Clark (in press) suggests that the EBC should thus be replaced by something like this:

Hypothesis of Experience-based Selection (EBS)
Conscious visual experience presents the world to a subject in a form appropriate for the reason-and-memory-based selection of actions.

In all the cases we have discussed, the alignment of certain memory systems with conscious visual experience looks robust and significant. This simple fact leads to the final idea that I want to consider. It is the idea that, contrary to the most radical versions of the skill theory:

> The key to connecting consciousness with action might involve memory systems rather than motor systems (Prinz, 2000, p. 252).

Prinz's speculation is that the evolution of new episodic and working memory systems fundamentally altered — for certain organisms — the relation between perception and action. Phylogenetically more ancient structures could already support the rapid, input-driven selection of innate and learnt motor responses and could initiate whole cycles of environmental probing in which sensing and acting are deeply inter-animated. But in some animals, new working memory systems began to support the retention and off-line manipulation of perceptual information. Episodic memory systems allowed them 'to encode particular perceptual events in a long-term store and to access those events on future occasions' (*op. cit.*, p. 253). These explicit memories could be called up even when the circumstances to which they were initially keyed were no longer present and put into contact with systems for planning (real planning, in which multiple stages of action are considered, chained together, and assessed) and reasoned action selection. The emergence of these new reason-and-memory-based systems marked, Prinz speculates, the emergence of consciousness itself. In a similar vein Hardcastle (1995), following an extensive review of the neuroscientific and psychological literature, suggests that:[8]

> Conscious perceptions and thoughts just are activations in SE [semantic, 'explicit controlled access'] memory (Hardcastle, 1995, p. 101).

One way or another, then, the links between special kinds of memory systems and conscious experience seem strong. Conscious experience is, above all, the base for reasoned, deliberate action selection. And this requires deep and abiding links with the special memory systems that mediate between sensory input and action.

I should add one important caveat. In speaking of the importance of explicit memory structures, I make no commitment to any specific story about encoding or storage. In particular, it seems highly unlikely that such encodings are in any interesting sense propositional. Instead, the stored information is most likely geared quite tightly to the kinds of action we may need to select, and to the environmental resources upon which we may reasonably rely.

With this in mind, let us finally revisit the rather strong form of the skill theory as advanced in O'Regan and Noë (2001a). Here, knowledge of a specific set of potential movements and their results is said to constitute a given visual perception (O'Regan and Noë, 2001a, Section 5.2). The general idea is that knowledge of the laws of sensorimotor contingency actually constitutes the way the brain codes for visual features and attributes. This idea is economical, elegant and

---

[8] The accounts are by no means identical. Prinz emphasizes a kind of informational poise at the gateways to the memory systems, whereas Hardcastle emphasizes activity in the memory systems themselves. See especially Prinz (2000) p. 255.

attractive. But in the specific case of *conscious* visual perception, the work on the dual visual systems hypothesis suggests an alternative unpacking. For what matters, as far as conscious seeing is concerned, is that the object/event is 'one of those' (i.e., falls into such-and-such a class or category) and that a certain range of actions (not movements but actions such as grasping-to-throw, grasping-to-drink, etc.) is potentially available. Both 'visual brains', I am suggesting, represent by activating implicit knowledge of some set of possible actions and results. In the case of the 'visuomotor brain' these are indeed pitched at the kind of level O'Regan and Noë seem to favour: they will concern, for example, the anticipated distortions of the retinal image in response to certain head and eye motions, etc. But in the case of the 'conscious visual brain' they are more likely to concern types of action and their effects as applied to types of objects, for example, the way 'throwing the cup at the wall' gives way to 'smashed cup on the floor' and so on. These kinds of sparse, high-level understanding are, of course, precisely the kinds of understanding that do seem to underpin our conscious visual experience, as the various change blindness results (and the card tricks) help to show.

One way to dramatise this idea is to exploit the idea (Goodale, 1998) that conscious seeing acts in a way somewhat reminiscent of the interaction between a human operator and a smart tele-assistance device. The operator decides on the target and action type (for example 'pick up the blue rock on the far left') and the robot uses its own sensing and acting routines to do the rest. Knowledge of our capacity to *engage* such routines may, on the present account, be essential to the content of the experience even if the routines themselves employ sensory inputs in a very different, and largely independent, way.

O'Regan and Noë claimed, recall, that

> For a creature to possess visual awareness, what is required is that, in addition to exercising the mastery of the relevant sensorimotor contingencies, it must *make use of this exercise for the purposes of thought and planning* (O'Regan and Noë, 2001a, Section 2.6; my emphasis).

But what exactly does this mean? Imagine again a tele-assistance setup in which the distant robot has implicit mastery of the SMC for, say, reaching and grabbing. This will only *matter*, as far as the conscious controller is concerned, in a functional way: the controller needs to know what the robot can and can't do (it can't fly, it can reach, it can grab gently or harder, etc.). *The SMC knowledge that the robot depends upon could be quite different, in detail, as long as the broad functionality was the same.*

What matters for conscious vision, in this alternative model, is that the visually seen object is recognised as belonging to some class, and as affording certain types of action. The bodies of know-how that count here concern objects and events at this level of description. Insofar as the lower-level SMCs matter here, they do so non-constitutively. Sameness of visual experience thus depends on sameness of what might be called 'intentional role' rather than sameness of all the SMCs.

At best, then, there is an unclarity hereabouts in O'Regan and Noë's account. The skill-theoretic response to the Grand Illusion story is, I think, the right one. But it needs to take two forms to deal with the full gamut of ways the brain uses visual information. One of those ways is geared to the fine control of here-and-now visuomotor action, and the relevant laws of sensorimotor contingency here do indeed concern the very precise and fully apparatus-dependent ways that the eyes are stimulated in response to various kinds of motion and probing. The other is geared to the selection of actions (not motions) and to planning and reasoning, and the relevant implicit knowledge here takes a different and more 'meaningful' form: it is knowledge of what we can do and achieve on the basis of current visual input, knowledge of a space of actions and results, rather than of a space of movements and subsequent inputs.[9]

I would be the last to downplay the significance, in human cognition, of tightly coupled, embodied, embedded sensorimotor loops (see Clark, 1997). But these loops, in the case of humans and (I expect) other higher animals are now themselves intertwined with new circuitry geared towards knowing, recall and reasoning. Understanding both the intimacies *and the estrangements* that obtain between these recently coiled cognitive serpents is, I suggest, one of the most important tasks facing contemporary cognitive science.

VII: Conclusions: Seeing a World Fit to Think In

The skill theory, as developed by O'Regan and Noë, ties conscious visual experience rather too closely (I have argued) to the precise details of our sensory engagements with the world. If (say) my eyes saccade just a little faster than yours, this may have no impact upon the qualitative nature of my visual experience, for conscious vision is geared to presenting the world for reason and for quite high-level action selection. This requires converging on-the-spot visual input (gathered just in time, and as dictated by the task and the allocation of attention) with stored memories and expectations. What matters for visual consciousness is thus (I suggest) at best a select subset of the information O'Regan and Noë highlight. The full detail of the sensorimotor contingencies that characterise my visual contact with specific objects and events is unlikely to matter. What will matter are whatever (perhaps quite high-level) aspects of those sensorimotor contingencies prove most useful for reason, recognition and planning. If this is correct, it is a mistake to tie visual experience too tightly to the invariants that guide and characterise visuomotor action.

Where the skill theory scores, however, is in recognising that conscious perceptual experience need not (and should not) be identified with a single time-slice of an environmentally isolated system. Instead, we need to consider the way temporally extended sequences of exploratory actions and our knowledge of the availability and likely deliverances of such exploratory routines may actually help constitute the contents of my perceptual experience. And this, in turn, requires recognising the way the external scene may itself feature as a kind

---

[9] For a little more on this, see Clark (1999), Section 3: 'Two ways to be action-oriented'.

of temporary memory resource, able to be accessed and deployed as and when the task requires.

As for the Grand Illusion, that really was a trick of the light. For, once we take all this into account, our visual experience is not itself misleading. The scene before us is indeed rich in colour, depth and detail, just as we take it to be. And we have access to this depth and detail as easily as we have access to facts stored in biological long-term memory. It is just that in the case of the visual scene, retrieval is via visual saccade and exploratory action. Our daily experience only becomes misleading in the context of a host of unwise theoretical moves and commitments: commitments concerning the precise role of internal representations in supporting visual experience, as well as our pervasive neglect of the cognitive role of temporally extended processes and active exploration.

A full account of conscious seeing cannot, however, stop there. For the world is seen via these exploratory engagements in a way that continuously converges selective input sampling with stored knowledge, memories and expectations. The contents of conscious visual experience emerge at this complex intersection. What we consciously see is a world tailor-made for thought, reason and planning. That's why we can intentionally act in the very world we experience.

Acknowledgments
With thanks to Alva Noë, Mark Rowlands and Jesse Prinz.

References

Andersson, R.L (1988), *A Robot Ping-pong Player* (Cambridge, MA: MIT Press).
Ballard, D. (1991), 'Animate vision', *Artificial Intelligence*, **48**, pp. 57–86.
Ballard, D., Hayhoe, M., Pook, P. and Rao, R. (1997), 'Deictic codes for the embodiment of cognition', *Behavioral and Brain Sciences,* **20**, p. 4.
Brenner, E. and Smeets, J. (1996), 'Size illusions influence how we read but not how we grasp an object', *Experimental Brain Research*, **111**, pp. 473–6.
Bridgeman, B., Lewis, S., Heit,G. and Nagle, M. (1979), 'Relation between cognitive and motor-oriented systems of visual position perception', *Journal of Experimental Psychology (Human Perception)*, **5**, pp. 692–700.
Carey, D. (2001), 'Do action systems resist visual illusions?', *Trends in Cognitive Sciences*, **5** (3), pp. 109–13.
Churchland, P.S., Ramachandran, V. and Sejnowski, T. (1994), 'A critique of pure vision', in *Large-Scale Neuronal Theories of the Brain*, ed. C. Koch and J. Davis (Cambridge, MA: MIT Press).
Clark, A. (1993), *Associative Engines: Connectionism, Concepts and Representational Change* (Cambridge, MA: MIT Press).
Clark, A. (1997), *Being There: Putting Brain, Body and World Together Again* (Cambridge, MA: MIT Press).
Clark, A. (1999), 'Visual awareness and visuomotor action', *Journal of Consciousness Studies*, **6** (11–12), pp. 1–18.
Clark, A. (2000), 'A case where access implies qualia?', *Analysis*, **60** (1), pp. 30–38.
Clark, A. (in press), 'Visual experience and motor action: are the bonds too tight?', *Philosophical Review*.
Clark, A. and Chalmers, D. (1998), 'The extended mind', *Analysis,* **58**, pp. 7–19.
Clark, A. and Toribio, J. (in press, 2001) 'Sensorimotor chauvinism? Commentary on O'Regan and Noë "A sensorimotor account of vision and visual consciousness"', *Behavioral and Brain Sciences*, **24** (5).
Decety, J. and Grezes, J. (1999), 'Neural mechanisms subserving the perception of human actions', *Trends in Cognitive Sciences,* **3** (5), pp. 172–8.
Dennett, D. (1991), *Consciousness Explained* (New York, Little Brown).
Feldman, J.A. (1985), 'Four frames suffice: a provisional model of vision and space', *Behavioral and Brain Sciences*, **8**, pp. 265–89.
Goodale, M. (1998), 'Where does vision end and action begin?', *Current Biology,* **489**, p. R491.
Hardcastle, V. (1995), *Locating Consciousness* (Amsterdam: John Benjamins).
Jeannerod, M. (1997), *The Cognitive Neuroscience of Action* (Oxford: Blackwell).

Kirsh, D. (1991), 'When is information explicitly represented?', in *Information, Thought and Content*, ed. P. Hanson (Vancouver: UBC Press).

Mack, A. and Rock, I. (1998). *Inattentional Blindness* (Cambridge, MA: MIT Press).

MacKay, D. (1967), 'Ways of looking at perception', in *Models for the Perception of Speech and Visual Form*, ed. W. Wathen-Dunn (Cambridge, MA: MIT Press).

McConkie, G.W. (1990), 'Where vision and cognition meet', Paper presented at the HFSP Workshop on Object and Scene Perception, Leuven, Belgium.

Milner, D. and Goodale, M. (1995), *The Visual Brain in Action* (Oxford: Oxford University Press).

Milner, D. and Goodale, M. (1998), 'The visual brain in action (precis)', *Psyche*, **4** (12), October 1998.

Neisser, U. (1979), 'The control of information pickup in selective looking', in *Perception and its Development*, ed. A. Pick (Hillfield, NJ: Erlbaum).

Newell, A. and Simon, H. (1972), *Human Problem Solving* (Upper Saddle River, NJ: Prentice Hall).

Noë, A., Pessoa, L. and Thompson, E. (2000), 'Beyond the grand illusion: what change blindness really teaches us about vision', *Visual Cognition*, 7, pp. 93–106.

Noë, A. (2001), 'Experience and the active mind', *Synthese*, **129**, pp. 41–60.

Noë, A. and O'Regan, J.K. (2000), 'Perception, attention and the grand illusion', *Psyche*, **6** (15).

O'Regan, J.K. (1990), 'Eye movements and reading', in *Eye Movements and Their Role in Visual and Cognitive Processes*, ed. E. Kowler (Amsterdam: Elsevier).

O'Regan, J.K. (1992), 'Solving the "real" mysteries of visual perception: the world as an outside memory', *Canadian Journal of Psychology*, **46** (3), pp. 461–88.

O'Regan, J.K. and Noë, A. (2001a), 'A sensorimotor account of vision and visual consciousness', *Behavioral and Brain Sciences*, **24** (5).

O'Regan, J.K. and Noë, A. (2001b), 'Authors' response: acting out our sensory experience', *Behavioral and Brain Sciences*, **24** (5).

Pascual-Leone, A. and Walsh, V. (2001), 'Fast backprojections from the motion to the primary visual area necessary for visual awareness', *Science*, **292**, pp. 510–12.

Prinz, J. (2000), 'The ins and outs of consciousness', *Brain and Mind*, **1** (2), pp. 245–56.

Rensink, R. (2000), 'Seeing, sensing and scrutinizing', *Vision Research*, **40**, pp. 1469–87.

Rowlands, M. (2002), 'Two dogmas of consciousness', *Journal of Consciousness Studies*, **9** (5–6), pp. 158–80.

Simons, D. (2000), 'Attentional capture and inattentional blindness', *Trends in Cognitive Sciences*, **4**, pp. 147–55.

Simons, D. and Levin, D. (1997), 'Change blindness', *Trends in Cognitive Sciences,* **1** (7), pp. 261–7.

Simons, D. and Chabris, C. (1999), 'Gorillas in our midst: Sustained inattentional blindness for dynamic events', *Perception*, **28**, pp. 1059–74.

Verghese, P. and Pelli, D. (1992), 'The information capacity of visual attention', *Vision Research*, **32**, pp. 983–95.

Wolfe, J. (1999), 'Inattentional amnesia', in *Fleeting Memories*, ed. V. Coltheart (Cambridge, MA: MIT Press).

Wong, E. and Mack, A. (1981), 'Saccadic programming and perceived location', *Acta Psychology*, **48**, pp. 123–31.

Yarbus, A. (1967), *Eye Movements and Vision* (New York: Plenum Press).